LEARN TO GROW OLD

LEARN TO GROW OLD

Paul Tournier

1817

Harper & Row, Publishers, San Francisco
Cambridge, Hagerstown, New York, Philadelphia
London, Mexico City, São Paulo, Sydney

Learn to Grow Old is published in England under the title *Learning to Grow Old*.

Translated by Edwin Hudson from the French
Apprendre à vieillir
Editions Delachaux et Niestlé,
Neuchâtel and Paris, 1971

First Harper & Row paperback edition published in 1983.

LC   83-10770
ISBN   0-06-068361-9

83 84 85 86 87 10 9 8 7 6 5 4 3 2 1

CONTENTS

I *Work and Leisure*

II *Towards a More Humane Society*

III   *The Condition of the Old*

IV   *A Second Career*

V *Acceptance*

VI *Faith*

I

WORK AND LEISURE

What the sociologists say

I am writing this book at the invitation of two of my publishers. The Revd John Bowden, of SCM Press, London, and Dr Tadashi Akaishi, of Harper and Row, New York, both suggested that I should write a book on the subject of retirement. My immediate reaction was that publishers ought to know what are the problems that are exercising people's minds, what are the difficulties they are trying to cope with, and what sort of books may be of assistance to them.

And yet I hesitated. In the past I have always dealt with subjects which, over the years and almost without my being aware of the fact, have been conceived in my own mind. Then, the period of gestation over, they have forced themselves upon me like the child that comes to birth. The idea of writing to order was too reminiscent of school exercises, and I felt that the harder I tried to do it well, the more artificial it would seem. And then, would I manage to do more than compile a collection of 'hints for those about to retire'? I am not very fond of proffering advice; it is humiliating, even irritating, rather than effective. Active people do not need our advice in order to profit intelligently from retirement – and the others would not be aroused out of their passivity by our advice. As for those who overwork, they will say that they cannot really cut down on anything without betraying their responsibilities.

Retirement and old age must, of course, be accepted. We have to give up all sorts of things, and accept with serenity the prospect of death, while remaining as active, as sociable and friendly as we can, despite an unavoidable measure of loneliness. We must learn to use leisure profitably, take up new interests, interest ourselves in young people and new ideas. We must learn how to pray, how to meditate, how to acquire wisdom, how to be grateful. For its part society must restore to the old their sense of their own value as human beings, and make them feel they are really accepted. It must also safeguard their dignity by means of adequate financial resources and personal attention. But everybody knows all this already.

Furthermore, I am not a specialist in geriatrics. Many people confide in me, people who have made a wonderful success of their retirement and enjoy it, and others for whom it has been a complete calamity; people who look forward to it eagerly and others who are afraid of it; people who grow old happily, and others who are discontented. But of what importance is this trickle of individual testimony, compared with the great flood of sociological evidence?

So I started reading sociology, books on old age, on the condition of retired people, on leisure, on the effect on the mind of the approach of death – so many that my wife asked me one day if I couldn't at least leave the books face down on the table, because their rather funereal titles were so depressing. But I became more and more interested.

I may not have any original material to bring to my readers, but I can at least share with them my reactions, my enthusiasm and my conviction that old age and retirement are major problems today. It is not merely a matter of improving the lot of the old, whom one sociologist has called the 'new proletariat'. It is up to us all, whether or not we are specialists, to give serious thought to the evidence that has been accumulated in recent years, because it raises grave questions about the way our civilization is going, and about the meaning of life.

I have, of course, learned a lot from my reading of the sociologists. I shall spare you the statistical details which you may find in their work, but in general they confirm our feeling that the world population is ageing. In the West at the present time approximately one person in six is over sixty years old,[1] and this proportion is constantly increasing. Sweden holds the record for the longest average life-span. One encouraging fact for us old people is that the older one gets, the longer one is likely to go on living.[2]

I used to think, naïvely, that this great number of old people was a flattering proof of the progress of medicine, which today saves so many patients who only a few years ago would inevitably have died. Not at all! According to Alfred Sauvy,[3] it is the falling birth-rate which up to now has been the specific cause of the ageing of populations. Paul Paillat is even more categorical. He quotes the work of Bourgeois-Pichat, who was, as he says, 'the first to demonstrate that the sole cause of the ageing of our society is the fall in the birth-rate'. In support of this thesis one may point to the instance of Japan, where, since the introduction of family planning, the birth-rate has gone down by 50%, while during the same period the proportion of old people has risen from 3% to 13%. So much for my vanity as a doctor!

On the other hand, I have discovered that sociologists are closer to us psychologists than I thought. I used to harbour unjust prejudices. I had imagined that in the sociologist's eyes a man was no more than a number to be incorporated with others in the anonymous mass of statistics. Not so! I find a sociologist spending hours with each aged person whom he interrogates, chatting familiarly with him in order to win his confidence, and carefully explaining to him that the questions he is being asked will help him to clarify his own opinions.

One sociologist[4] even asserts that one of the most important results of his inquiry has been to give lonely and introverted old people a chance of expressing themselves. That is understandable, of course. The old person who has felt himself to be a reject of society, of no interest to anyone, feels he has been rehabilitated, that his human dignity has been restored, because of this unusual visitor who listens to him so attentively and attaches such importance to all he says. The same thing happens when a television reporter brings his camera and his microphone to bear on a lonely old man. Suddenly he becomes someone again. His lined face, of which he has been ashamed, is really photogenic on the little screen. The great problem with the old is how to integrate them into society.

Another thing that reassures me is that sociology has retained its humility, despite all the public attention given to opinion polls, which might well have intoxicated it. It is conscious of its limitations. J. Dumazedier and A. Ripert note[5] judiciously that statistics about the leisure activities of retired people tell us nothing about how much satisfaction these occupations afford. They quote Kaplan, who says that it is not possible to discover 'what old people are capable of doing merely by compiling statistics about what they are in fact doing now'. And they conclude that research must 'ally creative imagination with scientific vigour'.

Leisure – a 'frightening prospect'?

How to achieve this combination of imagination and science is an ever-present problem. In my own case, I am always afraid that the scientist will kill the poet, or that the poet will compromise my scientific objectivity. As Dumazedier says, 'Essayists and poets may be sorely tempted to imagine ... a new golden age, when all social problems will vanish as if by magic.'[6] The poet in question here is Denis de Rougemont, the Director of the European Cultural Centre. The remark which gave rise to this warning was doubtless the following: 'In twenty or thirty years' time, according to some experts, it will only be necessary for one-third of the (greatly increased) population of the earth to work for four hours a week, in order to satisfy all our "material" needs (and much more adequately than is the case today).'[7]

Note that Denis de Rougemont, like me, had to draw upon acknowledged authorities for his information – so if there is any error in his prognostications it is to be imputed to the 'experts' rather than to him. Sociology can also escape into the realm of science fiction, although the latter, even if it is wrong in the matter of timing, has an element of truth in it. It is a very real problem that is raised by the gradual increase in leisure time. Everyone is aware of this, in the face of trades-union demands for a reduction in the working week, increased annual holidays, and the lowering of the age of retirement.

It is easy to point to what has already been achieved in this respect: 'From 1890 to 1954, the working week in the textile industry has gone down from 65 to 40 hours, and the total of hours worked by railwaymen from 3,900 to 2,000 per annum.'[8] In the United States, 'the average length of the working week in 1870 was 66 hours; in 1956 it was 41 hours'.[9]

In Switzerland, the right of every worker to three weeks paid annual holiday and Federal old age pensions has been in existence for only twenty years. No one doubts that this process is going to continue, and it could well be speeded up owing to the rapid progress of technology and automation.

Thus, De Rougemont calls leisure a 'frightening prospect'. 'What will the masses do,' he wonders, 'if technology really does suddenly liberate them to this extent? I do not know.' Further on, he writes: 'Liberated from physical labour, the Westerner turns at once to travel, sport, gambling, and eroticism.' This may be all right for brief and intermittent periods of leisure. But if leisure-time increases? Inquiries among retired people clearly indicate what that may lead to: regression, boredom, and even anxiety-neurosis.

These same inquiries, as well as our everyday experience, show that consequences depend essentially on the cultural level of those involved. Only culture can ensure the profitable, durable and satisfying use of leisure. 'We are on the threshold of an age in which culture is to become the serious content of the life of each person,' writes Denis de Rougemont, 'where it once was no more than a luxury reserved for the few.'

And so we have come to a theme which will force itself upon our attention throughout our study. What each of us needs is a 'reconversion' from earning our living to cultural activity. So long as we talk only of the use of leisure, we seem to be suggesting that all that matters is to find the means of killing time without getting too bored. To acquire culture, however, is something quite different – it is to develop oneself, to progress, to contribute to the progress of the human race, to find a meaning in life which can survive the cessation of professional activity.

I have a friend, an aged foreign colleague, who built a fine villa for his retirement in Italian-speaking Switzerland, a district which, as he says, is to a certain extent a vast refuge for wealthy old men, as are Florida and California for the Americans; or like the island of Madeira, where I spent last winter reading my books on sociology, and where I observed that I was the only one engaged in an interesting job of work amidst a crowd of people of my own age who were all idle and morose.

Last summer, at a conference on the medicine of the person, my old colleague gathered the oldest of us doctors together to talk about our experiences of old age and retirement. 'I see all these people around me,' he said to us, 'looking for something to do to pass the time. I myself am a lucky man, because ever since childhood I have been in the habit of asking myself philosophical questions. I used to wonder about the nature of man, and the meaning of life, and whether the science we studied at university had any answer to these problems. During my medical career I hardly had time to read philosophy, but I am doing so now and finding it fascinating.'

I hope that these remarks by the aged doctor will not lead to misunderstanding. Not everyone wants to read philosophy. Bridge or golf may very well be as valid activities as philosophical meditation. The real problem is not whether to do this rather than that, but what is the significance for us of what we are doing: whether it is merely in order to pass the time, or whether it is the expression of a vital need to keep on growing and developing our personality right to the end. Many people carefully avoid ever putting the question to themselves.

We must not at this point take too narrowly intellectual a view of culture. Culture is also art, personal relationships, communion with nature, and the understanding of life. So I come back to Denis de Rougemont, who once wrote a book called *Thinking with One's Hands*.[10] He makes reference, of course, to the extraordinary diffusion of culture made possible by modern techniques of sound and pictorial reproduction. In this way, he says, 'we are increasing our opportunities of a better understanding of our lives, and also our chances of misunderstanding the masterpieces of art and literature. As for the quality, the creativity, or the relative harmfulness of this invasion of culture, no one is yet in a position to judge: I merely wish to point out that for better or worse the phenomenon is with us.'[11]

It seems to me, however, that in this statement De Rougemont tends to underestimate the effect of this prodigious diffusion of culture. Discriminating scholar as he is, he quite properly looks for higher standards in both radio and television programmes. But even as they are, by the very fact of their existence they are adding a new mental dimension to our society, and one that is full of promise for the future.

Just recently, in a meeting of the Geneva Committee for Preparation for Retirement, Mlle Comte, a young Red Cross nurse, rightly put forward this view. In twenty years' time, she maintained, retired people will be quite different from those whom we visit today. They will be the men now in the full vigour of life, who, owing to the development of facilities for travel, the increase in leisure-time, the daily session in front of the television set, adult education, and many other innovations, have been wakened to all kinds of interests, which will preserve them from sinking into the passivity which we deplore in retired people of the present day.

It behoves each one of us now to see that this evolution proceeds in depth and quality. I agree with De Rougemont that this implies a careful analysis of the fundamental meaning of culture. Here is the conclusion he reaches: 'That is to say that everything is carrying us towards a religious era. For in the end of the day culture is only a prism which diffracts the religious sentiment in our so-called creative activities, from pure mathematics to pottery, and from metaphysics to furniture-carving. Thus technology, in practical terms, like science, will in the end bring us back to religious choices.' The fact is that in order to make a success of old age, we must raise our culture-level; and this must be done well before we are old. But that necessarily implies a value judgement about culture, about the meaning of culture, and lastly about the meaning of our lives – a religious question *par excellence*.

A difficult reconversion

A friend and a former patient comes to see me. To my surprise he has come on foot.

'Well,' he explains, 'my car has broken down and it was a good opportunity for a bit of a walk. This Geneva coutryside you have retired to really is lovely. There are magnificent trees, fine mansions, and charming old farmhouses. There are little modern villas as well, with well-kept lawns round them. I said to myself as I came along that perhaps one day, when I'm retired, I shall be able to live in a peaceful villa like that, and get back to what life is essentially about.'

'Mind you,' he added, 'I sometimes think that when I was ill I was much nearer the essential reality of life than I am now, up to my eyes in work, and with never a moment to stop and think.'

This 'essential reality' he spoke of is in fact the problem of the meaning of life, which he kept coming back to, and which he had often discussed in the past, without being in too great a hurry to resolve it. He looks back with a certain nostalgia to those days. And now here he is, cured. He has made for himself a brilliant career, which absorbs all his energies. He clearly feels that there is a certain incompatibility between professional life and profound reflection. The thing that used to strike me most about him was his aesthetic sense. In my eyes he was the incarnation of the culture that he had had to repress. The fact that he had come on foot, and given himself up to contemplation on the way, made us talk once more about the 'reality of life'.

'You know,' I said to him, 'if you wait until you are retired before coming back to the problems you used to be concerned about, you'll find it's too late!'

He stared at me in astonishment.

'Yes,' I went on, 'I am very much afraid that when you have been moulded for several decades of life by the great machine of society, you will probably have neither the inclination nor the ability to return to the essential reality of life.' I might have gone on to quote Professor Adolf Portmann, of Basle, who writes: 'The man who has not already learnt to look for the meaning of his life is unlikely to be able to organize his old age in a way that will enable him to find it then.'[12]

Our conversation turned to the subject of the hippies. We agreed in seeing in them a sign of the times, an instinctive protest against the standardization which society tries to force upon its members. But we also saw that the hippies live on the margin of society, and have no real influence upon it. There is no intermingling and no commerce between them. It is not easy to carry on an active life and a contemplative life at the same time, to blend science and poetry. And it is also particularly difficult at the moment of retirement to pass suddenly from the one to the other. All at once a man is cut off from active life, without having been prepared to lead any other sort.

Some manage by going on for as long as their strength and their social situation permit with a life of action very similar to the one they have been living up to then. In a café I met an old comrade from my army days. We get on well together, and are always pleased to see each other. We have so many fine memories in common!

'How are you?' I asked.

'Oh, it's awful,' he replied. 'I've been retired for three months. I'd never have thought it was so tough.' And he added a thought which particularly struck me, since I was writing this book: 'Nothing is worse for a man than to lose his panache!' And we talked for a little about our human condition.

A few weeks later I met him again, in the same place.

'Well, are things going any better?'

He answered me brightly, his eyes shining: 'Everything's fine! Do you know, at the bank where I used to work they had a little job to do classifying documents. So they asked me to come back just for a few hours a day. It's wonderful!'

I congratulated him, of course, and rejoiced with him. I wondered at the capacity a man has for recovering his enthusiasm so cheaply. It was doubtless a pretty uninteresting job, which he would have left to someone younger only a few months before. He is content with a very modest panache indeed! It did not require much to transfigure him. But for how long? The problem had been postponed, but not solved.

I met another man in a society reception. He was a businessman; not an employee this time, but an employer. We talked about this book that I am writing.

'Retirement!' he exclaimed. 'I've never been so busy as I am now that I've retired.' He, too, adds a reflection: 'The essential thing is to go on getting up at the same time in the morning as when you had to go to the office.'

That is marvellous. But here, too, a postponement has taken place, albeit a more valid one. This active, happy man is only administratively retired. He has not really retired yet. He has left his directorial office, but he is taking on other responsibilities. Some day, perhaps, the hour of true retirement will strike for him.

Moreover, I think that he will be more ready to face it than my old army friend. He is a wise and cultured person, and I imagine that for the present, during this respite that has been granted him, he will know how to make the necessary small adjustments in his life. To prepare, that is, for the 'reconversion' I mentioned just now, gradually to curtail the time spent on his professional work, in order to devote more time to what I have called culture, to poetry, meditation, and everything that can go on developing after retirement. The fact is that if this reconversion is to be accomplished at the time of retirement, it must begin much sooner – when we are in our fifties, or even our forties. As Montaigne remarked: 'To retire successfully is no easy matter.'

The two turning-points of life

There are, in fact, two great turning-points in life: the passage from childhood to adulthood and that from adulthood to old age.

Freud has told us of the laws that govern the first. An acute observer of the instinct of sex and of the aggressiveness necessary to
social success, he has provided a masterly description of the evolution of man from childhood to adulthood – both the normal,
successful development and the problems of failure. The Freudians
excel in helping a young person to become, in the full sense, a man
or a woman, to resolve an Oedipus complex, to get rid of an infantile false sense of guilt and achieve independence and the ability to
face life, love and society. But with an older person, the Freudians
are in greater difficulty. They get over the difficulty by saying that
psychoanalysis is not indicated after the age of forty.

Actually, Freud himself had to negotiate the second turning-
point. It is most moving to see the ageing Freud experiencing the
need to go beyond his own theories, concerning himself more and
more with culture and then writing *Beyond the Pleasure-principle*,[13] speaking of a death-instinct and placing man between Eros
and Thanatos. But these later writings, with their mythological and
philosophical tendency, did not have on Freud's disciples an influence comparable with that exercised by his earlier works. Freudians occasionally refer to them as interesting hypotheses of uncertain value. I do not think, however, that they have used them as
the basis for any effective therapeutic technique to help people
negotiate the second turning-point in their lives.

As Cahen has pointed out,[14] it was Jung who formulated the laws
of this second movement, and in this he was not so much contradicting Freud, as has so often been said – though he always denied
it – as complementing him. He, too, like Denis de Rougemont,
speaks of culture: 'Man has two aims in life,' he writes, 'the first
is the natural aim of the procreation of descendants and the care
required for the preservation of his young, involving the acquisition
of wealth and social status. When this aim has been satisfied, another phase begins, the goal of which is culture.' He wonders why
this 'passage from the natural phase of existence to the cultural
phase is such a difficult and bitter process for so many people.
They cling to the illusions of youth, or else to their children, in the
hope that they will thus preserve some vestige of youth.'[15]

This second turning-point, therefore, is in no sense a step backwards. Like the first, it is an advance. The first is an advance to
maturity, the second is an advance into a new fulfilment. It is a law
of life that it must always move forward. Not to take this forward

step, writes Jung, is to fail 'to see that to refuse to grow old is as foolish as to refuse to leave behind one's childhood'. 'It is impossible to live through the evening of life in accordance with the programmes appropriate to the morning, since what had great importance then will have very little now, and the truth of the morning will be the error of the evening.'[16]

But what does Jung mean by this cultural phase of life, and in what way is it distinguishable from the first phase? Do we not already spend most of our youth in school in order to acquire culture? Let Jung himself enlighten us on his meaning: 'In our time the man of mature years is likely to experience a pressing need for a somewhat deeper individual culture, since he has been trained in an exclusively collective culture in childhood and later at the university, so that his whole mentality is a collective one.'[17] So Jung differentiates between two forms of culture. The first is a culture that is learnt from society, from tradition, from school – a standard equipment of knowledge. The other is more personal, more disinterested, more original, and more fully evolved. The first is oriented towards production, the second is more meditative.

In order to make a success of the first phase, which Jung calls the natural life, it is necessary to specialize, to attain a high degree of culture in a restricted field, inevitably at the expense of the broad cultural horizon. The active person allows many of his talents to lie fallow in order to develop a few which are indispensable to his professional and social success. The integration to which Jung calls him in the second half of his life, this new advance towards a more complete human fulfilment, involves the reawakening of everything that he has for a long time had to sacrifice to his career. In the same way, active life demands a measure of conformity: a man must play society's game if he is not to be rejected by society; he must act the conventional part that society imposes upon him. But later on, the time comes to break free from this social conditioning, when a man can rediscover his spontaneity and his originality in order to become himself once more.

Jung asserts that it is a matter of 'discovering the values of the personality',[18] of 'grasping intelligently the meaning of individual life'.[19] Thus, the cultural phase is the one in which we are called to become more personal, to become persons, to face old age with all our personal resources. We measure our success in negotiating the first, Freudian, turning-point – 'becoming adult' – in terms of our success in love and in our career. Later on, the success we make of retirement will be the test of our success in negotiating the second, Jungian, turning-point – the 'maturity of the person'.

It is also a matter of interiorization: 'What youth found, and needed to find, outside,' Jung writes, 'man in the afternoon of life must seek within himself.'[20] He will be able further to enrich this inner store when retirement suddenly gives him the time he needs. Such riches will also save him from boredom and give retirement its true meaning, namely, that it is not a withdrawal but an advance towards personal fulfilment.

For all that, it is necessary that this movement should already have been begun earlier. Jung does not locate the second turning-point at the moment of retirement, in the evening of life, but in its high noon. 'The noon of life,' he writes, 'is the moment of greatest deployment, when a man is devoted entirely to his work, with all his ability and all his will. But it is also the moment when the twilight is born: the second half of life is beginning. . . At midday the descent begins, determining a reversal of all the values and all the ideals of the morning.'[21]

I am not, therefore, addressing only the retired, but also – and more importantly – those who are still in the full flood of life, and I think that this was what my publishers intended when they asked me to write this book. In order to make a success of old age, one must begin it earlier, and not try to postpone it as long as possible. In the middle of life we must stop to think, to organize our existence with an eye to a still distant future, instead of allowing ourselves to be entirely sucked into the professional and social whirl. It is then that it is important to give place little by little to less external activities, less technical and more cultural, which will survive the moment of retirement.

Preparing for retirement

You, men and women in your forties and fifties who read this book, will not mind if I speak to you frankly and with great affection. You are in the full flood of life, and your life absorbs you to such an extent that you live it as if it must last for ever. You know well that that is not the case. Under present-day rules you even known perhaps the exact date when you will be retired. But you do not care to think too much about it, unless it is to work out what resources you will still be able to count on.

'Retirement?' one of you said to me, curtly. 'Don't talk to me about that! Plenty of time to think about that later on!'

The remark reminds me of the reply of a girl to a sociologist who was questioning her about old age.

'Old age?' she exclaimed. 'Oh! I hope I'll die before then!'

A natural enough sentiment in the mouth of an adolescent who is still thinking only of the adult life for which she is preparing. You are now in that adult life, and no doubt you no longer say, 'I hope to die before I'm old.' But if you want to be spared some cruel surprises, you will allow me to open your eyes now to reality.

You know what the sociologist calls the 'expectation of life'. It is the average number of years that men and women have still to live at any given age. You know that a few years ago the expectation of life on retirement was already almost thirteen years for men and sixteen years for women. No doubt it will be still greater in fifteen, twenty or twenty-five years' time, when you yourselves reach retiring age. Fifteen years or more is a long time. They need to be good years, as good years as possible, those last years of your life. No Utopias! You know very well that there will be trying times, bereavements no doubt, possibly infirmities to darken them. But avoid at least those evils that are avoidable!

Your manner of life now is already determining your life in those years of old age and retirement, without your realizing it even, and perhaps without your giving enough thought to it. One must therefore prepare oneself for retirement. But how? The first experiments in preparatory courses were made in America. One of the most successful, in Europe, is that in Grenoble,[22] which owes its inspiration to a doctor, Professor Robert Hugonot,[23] and a philosopher, Professor Michel Philibert.[24] A course of six weekly sessions is organized, several times a year, for some twenty participants, lectures being given by experts in the medical, juridical, economic, social and spiritual problems of retirement.

The results so far are most encouraging. In a way it is as yet a very restricted laboratory experiment, in relation to the enormous task that awaits us. A few hundred people respond to the invitation of the organizers of the courses, out of the many thousands of working men and women who are approaching the age of retirement. And they are perhaps the ones who least need help, since

they are already thinking about these problems. I recognize that
the idea of a 'course' is not a very attractive one. But those who
attend realize that these are more in the nature of seminars or group
discussions, in which everyone has an opportunity of putting forward his own ideas and getting to know the other members. It
is, in fact, one of the most important features of the courses that
they create a fellowship which preserves the retired person from
loneliness.

This is particularly important in the Grenoble sessions, where
almost half the participants are already retired. It is a great advantage to them to have this opportunity for social integration. But it
is obvious that the opportunity ought to be given, several years
before their retirement, to many more of those who have not yet
begun to give sufficient thought to the problems they will meet.
This is why we in Geneva are preparing seminars in co-operation
with several big firms, in banking, industry, and public works. The
personnel managers of the firms taking part know which employees are due to retire during the next five years, and can give
them personal invitations to the seminars, especially if these are
being held during working hours.

You will understand also, however, all those of you who are still
in the midst of your active lives, that it is not enough to be better
informed about the problems you will meet when you retire. You
must take a long, hard look at your way of life now. That is not
easy to do. On all sides you are beset by immediate and pressing
tasks – in your work, in your family, in your social life. They are
what Jung, referring to people of your age, calls the 'natural motors
of existence'. But are you really in control of your life? Doctors'
wives, for instance, have often confided to me that their husbands
are so burdened with work that they no longer have time for a quiet
chat with their wives.

In his book on failure,[25] Jean Lacroix talks of 'men of action
who, around the age of fifty, lose all interest in the work they have
been involved in', obsessed by a feeling of '"What is the point?",
and finding no answer to the question'. From time to time men
have confided feelings of this kind to me. I remember a man who,
in the middle of a successful career, still a long way off retirement,
had been overcome by a strange malaise. All at once his busy life,
which others envied or admired, had struck him as pointless. He had
a feeling of being caught up in a machine which he could neither

escape from nor control. The more responsibilities he took on, the less time and liberty he had. It is the same with all the leaders of society: a wheel turns ceaselessly round and round. Men are born, work, love, suffer, and die; and they are followed by others, and so on and on. Whenever humanity takes a step forward, fresh problems are created, and men labour to solve them, only to find that still more problems have been raised in the process.

You are privileged, because you have an interest in your lives – in both senses of the word: the material interest which will ensure that you are comfortable in your old age, and the passionate interest that you have in your work. And perhaps that is the very reason why you will miss that second turning-point in your lives, of which Jung speaks. You are running the risk of prolonging too far the straight line of your absorbing lives, so that when the moment of retirement comes the turn will be sharp and dangerous. Do not imagine that the problems of retirement concern only other people. Those who are less privileged may for that very reason be better able than you to cope with the emptiness of retirement.

It is not that I am deceived by the resignation of the poor. I have treated too many poor, infirm or lonely old people not to know the distress that can be hidden beneath their apparent acceptance. I have been the confidant of many of them. But their fate is unlikely to have been in their own hands. In future it will also depend in large part on the reforms which will have to be introduced to improve the conditions of the most under-privileged among the retired. It is not really my intention to exert influence upon the political and social authorities whose duty it is to bring about these reforms, and who know as much about the problems involved as I do. As for their protégés, they will not read what I write. Sociological investigations show that the majority of them read only a few newspapers, and never books.

Surprises

It is for you that I write, you who are privileged. For among the problems that will face you when you retire are some which have nothing to do with the law or with pension-fund regulations. They have to do with you yourselves, with your life as you live it now. The privilege of your privileges, if I may be permitted the expression, is that you are a little freer than others to do as you wish with your lives; you can lead your lives instead of being led by them; you can organize your lives intelligently, so that they remain as beautiful, happy and fruitful as possible, right to the end.

For the moment your immediate and natural tasks suffice to give meaning to your life. But you know that they will not last for ever. I am not referring only to professional work. I have just been looking at my morning newspaper, and in it I have read an interview, one of a series in which the author Jacqueline Baron[26] questions the wives of famous men on how they help their husbands. Today it is the turn of the wife of a well-known French press, radio and television reporter, Léon Zitrone.

His wife speaks engagingly of him, of his good qualities and his failings, of his tireless activity outside and his untidiness at home. 'When he is there,' she says, 'he monopolizes one's attention. He always needs something. He's such a baby.' Yes! Helping a famous husband, serving him, making good what he lacks, supplying his needs and coddling him like a baby – that is what gives meaning to a woman's life, and all the more so when the husband is exacting and when, by her eagerness to serve him, the wife cultivates his dependence.

She is happy. She continues: 'He makes us really live. If he went out of my life, everything would collapse.' I have seen many such collapses. Widowhood is a kind of retirement, the retirement of the woman from her job as a wife. Many a wife willingly sacrifices her personal life to a husband's whims. He does not like music, so she gives it up; he does not like her friends, so she drops them. And all at once, on her husband's death, the wife finds herself in a desert. Her life has lost its meaning. She no longer has any power to react, because she has long since stopped her own development. Much the same is true of other cases where it is the husband who has been spoiling his wife; or again, in cases where the whole meaning of life has been in mutual spoiling of each by the other, rather than in each helping the other to evolve.

I am not suggesting that crises of this sort in widowhood are always due to some previous psychological error in married life. That would be quite unjust. Alas! Widowhood is always a terrible trial, and in addition to the emotional shock of separation there is always considerable disturbance in the social and personal life of the surviving partner.

I have been the recipient of moving confidences in this connection. There was a woman who had shared fully in her husband's life, so much so that any social success they had was due as much to her as to him. And then suddenly after her husband's death she finds herself in a void that she must have been quite unprepared for. Good friends whom they used to visit together show her a lot of sympathy, it is true, especially in the early days, but they do not invite her to their houses as they used to, and no longer come to see her. A whole stream of life has dried up, and she depended on it as much as her husband did. She is no longer up to date with what is happening in the political, social and cultural world in which they took such an interest. Her widowhood is indeed a painful retirement for her.

There is another kind of retirement that many women find hard to bear, which comes when their children reach maturity – and it comes at a much earlier age than that of retirement from work, though the date is less precise. And so the woman often tries to satisfy her maternal instinct by continuing to mother her now adult children. This is especially true in the case of an only son. Making him happy and protecting him from the difficulties and obstacles of life is for such a mother the whole meaning of life. Sometimes the son delays getting married, either for fear of his mother's reactions, or because all young women seem to him to be so selfish in comparison with his devoted mother.

Almost always the marriage and departure of the children, especially of the last child, cause in the mother an emotional crisis much more serious than she expected. Beforehand, she may well have thought herself detached, may even have looked forward to the event with sincere pleasure. Afterwards, she is astonished at finding it so hard to overcome the feeling of emptiness. In the same way many men never stop complaining about their work, and the way it gives them more worry and difficulty than satisfaction. They say they are overworked, and look forward to being retired. They, too, may be quite astonished, after they have retired, at finding themselves so unhappy.

There are great surprises of this sort, but you will understand that they are not the result of chance. They have been prepared over a long period by mistakes in the way of life which it would have been better to recognize and correct earlier. As Paul Ricoeur says,[27] analytical psychology is an archaeological science, that is to say that it seeks in the past the origin of the difficulties of the present. Just as Freud goes right back to childhood and even earliest infancy, plumbing the depths of the mind to uncover the distant origins of the crisis which a person may experience on the threshold of adulthood, so Jung teaches us to see in the errors made in the noon of life the origin of a crisis which may blow up when the time for retirement arrives, becoming progressively worse as the deprivations of old age advance.

You, my forty- and fifty-year-old readers, you have had to specialize narrowly in order to build up the fruitful life you lead today. You have had to give up many things which might have interested you. You have worked hard. You have used your time off only for pleasure and relaxation, and you have been disciplined enough not to spend too much time on such things. You have had to direct your energies and to train for success, but in rather too narrow a field. And success has even further enslaved you to your career. It is not enough for you to complain that you no longer have time for anything else. Consider, therefore, what is at stake: it is to make sure that your life will be able to expand once more. It is already time for you to begin a movement in a reverse direction, away from specialization, and to reopen your mind to a wider horizon.

The fear of liberty

There is a certain necessary continuity in life. This is shown by sociological research among retired people. Those among them who used to indulge in do-it-yourself, angling, gardening or reading, continue to do so and enjoy their retirement. On the other hand, it is rare for a retired person who has had no other occupation than his work to take up a new activity. If his friends persuade him to do so, he soon becomes discouraged and gives it up. At the Grenoble study-conference someone quoted a retired person who had always been in the habit of saying: 'After I am retired I shall take up book-binding!' But he never began. How many more are there?

Success in any undertaking always demands some training, the establishment of reflexes and habits, and some ability, if not a proper apprenticeship, and these things do not come easily at a more advanced age if they have not been started earlier. This, then, is the evidence that is going to force itself upon us throughout our study, namely that success in retirement depends in great measure on the way we have lived beforehand. This is why the importance of hobbies or spare-time occupations has often been stressed. But it seems to me that the time has come for us to give more serious attention to rethinking this problem in the light of what Jung and De Rougemont have said.

There is no certainty that do-it-yourself or gardening can suffice to make a happy retirement. The fact is that they have been indulged in only as a hobby, a pleasant pastime, a change from an interesting career. It is true that for some people they may have that character of inner culture, of personal self-realization, spoken of by the two authors I have mentioned. But in that case, it is because they have been much more than a mere hobby, much more than a passing distraction; they have been a choice, a profound inclination, still susceptible of giving a meaning to life after the cessation of a person's working life.

We must therefore look at the problem of the utilization of free time as a whole, from the intermittent leisure-hours of active life to the total and definitive leisure which retirement brings. One cannot dissociate the latter from the former. And the more economic progress increases the worker's free time, the less will be the quantitative difference between that free time and the leisure of the retired person. The worker will find his leisure activities need to be something more than mere hobbies or aimless diversions; they will have to be of a quality that will give meaning to his life.

A hobby may give us great pleasure when we practise it for a few hours, as a change from our work; but after retirement it may lose much of its attraction, when it is the only thing left with which to fill our lives. It is a remarkable fact that this phenomenon, which is so common among retired people, can be observed even before retirement if working hours become sufficiently reduced. Here is an example. The chief industry of Akron, Ohio, is rubber-processing. I know the town, I have lectured there, and have good friends there. Now, no doubt thanks to all of us who put tyres on our cars, and thanks in particular to progress in automation, the rubber industry has flourished to such an extent that it became possible more than ten years ago, without reduction in wages, to reduce 'the working week . . . to thirty-two hours over the whole of the undertakings in the town'.[28]

An enquiry undertaken on behalf of the Chicago Centre for

Leisure Studies by Dr Riesman revealed the following: 'One person in five employed in the rubber industry in Akron works full-time in two firms, and 40% of the population has a second, part-time, employment.' A most interesting revelation! One further intriguing detail: American experts think that it is often the wives who persuade their husbands to take up a second job, because they are afraid that they will go astray if they are at a loose end. Perhaps, too, it is irritating to wives to have idle husbands at home. One often sees the same reaction among the wives of retired men. They have been enjoying a well-regulated existence, and do not like having it disturbed by the unaccustomed presence of the husband.

However that may be, whether the suggestion stems from the worker or from his wife, one question came into my mind as I read the story of Akron: 'Are people afraid, then, of liberty?' Put this way the question is too brutal. It does not have a pleasant sound in the ears of a Swiss, brought up in a positive cult of liberty, symbolized in the legend of William Tell!

Nevertheless, upon reflection, it did seem to me that the question was not entirely without foundation. I thought of many of my own daily observations. A mother toils all day long to polish her floors and serve her little family. She is the first up in the morning to make coffee for her big daughter – who could very well get her own breakfast ready. In the evenings she puts out her husband's slippers, as if he were incapable of going to the cupboard for them himself. She sighs and complains: no rest for the weary! Her children have days off, her husband has his bridge-parties with his friends – but she herself has always so much to do!

And it is true. How often in my family-doctor days did I vainly urge a wife to take a little rest. When I spoke about it to the husband, he would explain: 'Oh, doctor! If you could get her to do it, I'd be very grateful. She gets upset if we do anything at all to lighten her burden. She could easily go and stay for a few days with her sister in the country; we'd manage without her.' – 'What do you think I'd do all day at my sister's, doctor,' she would reply; 'I'd be bored.'

That is it – lots of retired people are bored because they do not know what to do with their enforced liberty! For lack of imagination, lack of habit, lack of training, they let themselves go, and take no interest in anything. They retire into a shell of boredom, and in the end any renewal becomes impossible, and they become a burden to others. But the germ of this passivity has been there within them for years. They have not realized it, because the routine of work and social life has covered up the void in their personal lives. So many people – including young people – claim liberty, and they have little idea of what to do with it when they get it, because they have not been prepared for it.

We have been trained for work and not for leisure. Think of the routine of intensive study we have had to follow in order to fit ourselves for our work. Nothing similar is done to fit us for leisure and liberty. 'It is startling to observe,' write Jores and Puchta, 'how few people are capable of enjoying leisure.'[29] The same is true of their capacity to organize their leisure on any personal basis. The commercial exploitation of leisure, the spirit of gregariousness and the power of fashion have led to mass leisure-time occupations which are hardly less monotonous than work on a conveyor-belt in a factory.

Personal development and spontaneity

There is, however, a delicate question which I must raise here. We have seen that preparation for retirement must be to some extent a school for leisure. But it is not possible to teach people leisure-activities in the way one teaches them to work. If one tries too hard it is no longer a matter of leisure, but of work. There is no doubt why so few people take the courses that are organized in preparation for retirement. The idea of a 'course' suggests study and work. Many people also stay away from recreational clubs for fear of having to apply themselves to the practice of some skill under the too-severe eye of an instructor. I am reminded of a great friend of mine. Having been brought up in a strict puritan atmosphere, he is a very scrupulous person. Everything he does is done to perfection and most carefully. When we talked it over, he realized that he had turned even his pleasures into duties. He took up skiing, rather late in life, in order to take part in it with his children. In our mountains there are first-class ski instructors, and he was their most diligent pupil. His desire to make not a single mistake never left him for a moment, and in his mind he used to go over all the lessons he had learnt. While his children went skiing in order to enjoy themselves, he turned it into an exemplary duty.

For many others sport becomes a profession, and one which

demands unremitting toil. In the Olympic Games, which are restricted to amateurs, we see how difficult it is to draw the line between amateur and professional. Almost all sporting careers entail much earlier retirement than other professions. If you take up chess, there is a good chance that on your retirement, provided you find a worthy opponent, you will be able to spend many enjoyable hours at the game. But if your sport is football or athletics, you will have had to give it up long ago. The King of Sweden, it is true, played tennis until he was well advanced in years. But in his case he had not retired from his royal career.

We must be careful, however, not to take too simplistic a view of preparation for retirement. For example, you will very soon have to give up your cycling or your rowing. But that does not mean that for the time being these activities are not a useful training for retirement, in so far as they help to keep you young in heart, vigorous, active, keen to learn, and enterprising. Success in retirement depends essentially on how well you have developed your personality beforehand. The things that count are the things we do freely, all those things that widen our social relationships, everything that diversifies our lives and counter-balances an over-specialized professional occupation. What matters in leisure is that it should be leisure, recreation in the true sense of the word, an exciting pleasure.

I am reminded also of a woman of aristocratic family who had been brought up in her château like a bird in a cage. I did not know that it was still possible today. As a child she had never even been allowed to talk to the village children through the park gates. She did not go to school; she had a governess instead. But the governess organized and controlled all her games as well as teaching her lessons. She was not allowed to play on her own, as she wished, as her fancy took her. And so for her there was no difference between work and leisure. Everything was regulated in the same way by the governess. It can easily be imagined that, later on, liberty frightened her.

I once gave a lecture in a small industrial town where there was an important factory. Everything in the town either belonged to the firm or depended on it for funds: the neat little houses in which the work-people lived, the gardens they cultivated, the football stadium, the ice-hockey skating-rink, the cinema, and the cultural committee which had invited me to speak. Even if it all worked well, it did not quite have the genuine tang of freedom about it. 'Leisure in our society,' wrote Jean-Marie Domenach in the magazine *Esprit*, 'must always have something "sacred" about it. It is the part of our lives which must not be spoilt by work; it allows us to have a contact with nature which is friendly and poetic, rather than utilitarian exploitation.'[30]

You see? Poetry is being referred to again, and in a sense which contrasts it with utilitarianism. There is indeed a certain contrast between leisure and work: the former symbolizes liberty, the latter constraint. It is because of this contrast that they both have a part to play in the growth of the personality, in its development into a new dimension. Leisure alone, without work, is as soul-destroying as work without leisure. They are complementary, and so lead us towards a more harmonious balance. But the point is that both are equally important in our development, whereas we have always been led to believe that work is much more important than leisure.

When I was a boy I used to loiter on my way home from school, visiting the village blacksmith in Troinex. What poetry was there! I said not a word, and neither did the blacksmith, but there was a mysterious sympathy between us. I was never tired of watching the sheaves of sparks that sprang from the great hammer-beats. Nevertheless I was scolded when I got home: 'Why are you so late? You ought to get your homework done first. You can amuse yourself afterwards.' But afterwards, the blacksmith did not cast the same spell!

Or else I used to spend hours reading Molière and Racine, which I bought in little popular penny editions, badly printed on cheap paper. There were, of course, volumes of Molière and Racine on my uncle's bookshelves, but my little paper-backs, bought with the coppers I was given for buying buns, had something secret about them that turned the reading of them into a true leisure occupation. Furthermore, they were thin enough for me to put them on top of my Latin grammar, and to hide them quickly underneath should someone happen to come into my room. This was to avoid the only too frequent reprimand: 'Work first, play later.'

Who has not heard this notorious maxim? It has made our Western world what it is. Work is above everything: poetry is a luxury! It is the very foundation of our civilization. Throughout the West, in the communist world and in Japan, we have all been thoroughly conditioned by this attitude of worship for work which raises it to a pre-eminent place in our scale of values. If it were only a matter of verbal exhortations such as the reprimands that awaited me at home when I had been lingering in the smithy, it would not be very serious. Such reproofs had little effect on me. But we are subjected to a much more thorough training, a social suggestion which goes deep into our unconscious minds.

The morality of duty

In the West almost everyone agrees in proclaiming in words, in theory, the supreme value of the human person. People everywhere want to defend man, and in the West that means the individual, personal liberty and freedom of thought in particular. In the communist world, 'man' means the proletariat, which must be liberated from all exploitation; it means the advent of a new type of man. We quote the sayings of the ancients: 'Man is the measure of all things.' It is man, we say, who gives work its dignity, and not work which gives man his value.

But in reality things are quite different. The general social atmosphere in which we are immersed from childhood and which influences us without even our thinking clearly about it, teaches us the superior importance of work. It has taught us to look upon work as a duty, unlike the pleasurable activities of leisure. Work, as a duty, is seen to be full of dignity, even if it is tedious or inhuman; in fact it is considered especially meritorious in this latter case. Whereas leisure is constantly undervalued, despite its attractiveness and its ability to develop the personality. It is thought of merely as a concession to man's guilty passions, to his lust for pleasure and his idleness. What confers dignity upon man is the fulfilment of his duty – his work, his productivity, his function in society, his professional occupation. If your work is interesting, you are lucky, but its only true value lies in its being a duty, not in its being a pleasure.

Weber has demonstrated the role played by the puritan mystique in the growth of modern capitalism.[31] It is the fruit of the 'Protestant ethic', which is defined in the following terms: 'frugality, temperance, self-denial, and thrift'. How well I know that Protestant ascetic ideal in which I was brought up in Geneva! I have treated patients who bore its marks firmly imprinted upon them. It is not confined to believers or church members. It is, in fact, much more serious among those who have become detached from the church,

since then all that is left is a moral strait-jacket without any connection with the spiritual origins which gave it its greatness. All
that is left is the half-conscious formula: 'Everything that gives
pleasure is forbidden, everything that gives pleasure is sinful.'

The fact is that in the 'Protestant ethic', all enjoyment is suspect.
In practice it permits only two pleasures: the pleasure of earning
and saving money, and the pleasure of marital sexual relations.
Hence, capitalism and large families. But of course, since the pur-
suit of pleasure is frowned upon, these are only unconscious
pleasures: the pleasure of earning and saving, and even that of thereafter putting one's thrift to good use by gambling on the Stock
Exchange, is looked upon as a duty. Thus, when Freud saw in the
search for pleasure the motive of human behaviour, and formulated
his 'pleasure principle', indignation ran high among all these
people, persuaded as they were that they were following only the
call of duty.

This austere morality, the Christian replica of the Spartan ideal,
produced some powerful and admirable personalities. The architects
of capitalism never became its beneficiaries. They did not live
privileged lives of ease, but were men who worked hard to assure
their descendants' future, as exacting towards themselves as they
were to others, allowing themselves none of those worldly pleasures
which might have turned them away from God, their only joy. But
it is easy to see how in the course of time, when the great families
became enriched, and especially with the decline in religious belief,
all this tended towards a glorification of work, which was made
into an absolute value. Really, one might have expected something
different in the way of a scale of values from a religious tradition
so solidly founded on the gospel – the primacy of man over work,
and not of work over man.

As for communism, opposed as it is in many ways to both
capitalism and religion, it joins them at one point: 'Marx considers
labour to be the basis of wealth,' writes Pizzorno. And he continues:
'Communism also calls for sacrifice for the benefit of future generations.' Thus the two great ideological currents of our time agree in
asserting the primacy of 'doing' over 'being' – at the very moment
when philosophers are wrestling with the problem of being, rejecting the concept of 'being *per se*', and seeing it only in its manifesta-
tions, in its action, in its 'doing'. One can understand the confusion
of young people, who want to win recognition for themselves as

persons, and not merely for their function as cogs in the great pro-
duction-consumption machine.

One can understand also that Dr Gros should write in connection
with the status of the old in our society, that what matters most is
'to rediscover the notion of the indefeasible dignity of the human
being'.[32] That, I believe, is the core of the problem of retirement,
since retirement is by definition the end of occupational work; and
modern man does not feel that anyone is interested in him as a
person. He is considered merely as an instrument of production.
We shall return to this in Part II. For the moment, I shall confine
myself to the way our society asserts the morality of duty, which is
obviously a related idea, and which is itself a serious danger.

I hope therefore that there will be no misunderstanding about
what I am writing here. I am not speaking against work, nor
against technical progress, nor yet against the improved society in
which – and on which – I live. What matters is to know whether we
are playing society's game for the benefit of people, or for things. I
am not writing in praise of laziness, nor advocating outright opposition to the demands of society. What must be questioned is the scale
of values which we have inherited from our parents, and which
glorifies work as the most important thing in life. Nevertheless,
none of us escapes the power of social suggestion; it is still written
deep on my heart. I may protest, I may disobey the call of duty and
deny its primacy; nevertheless, the idea is basic to me.

Duty and pleasure are complementary

Future generations will succeed better than I have in freeing themselves from the worship of work. Already young people are making
us realize the inhumanity of a life exclusively dedicated to it. Indeed the public attitude has already changed a great deal. I imagine
that some of those young people will smile as they read what I
write about the principles of work and duty in which I was brought
up. They think as much of their rights as of their duties. They think
of their pleasures and enjoy them with a clearer conscience than I
do. And I imagine their fathers frowning, fearing that these remarks
will encourage their sons in their opposition to our society and its
demands. But all my working life I have had to attend to the
victims of this justification of work. I still do – young people among
them. Their race is by no means extinct. The most notable cases

have been those where parents have exercised excessive authority, demanding blind obedience from their children as their prime duty in life.

I am not, of course, writing for the benefit of the young, who do not need me to help them to enjoy life. I write for men and women in the full vigour of life, who willingly shut their eyes to what awaits them in ten or twenty years' time, when retirement will suddenly deprive them of the work which assures their position in society today. They are more conditioned than they think by our consumer society, even though they criticize it. Its dogma is inscribed in their hearts: productivity. They bend themselves to it as if it were the whole meaning of life. They size up their contemporaries according to the place they occupy in this great modern machine. With me they are the heirs of 'a system of values which rests essentially upon labour, production, and productivity'.[38]

My ecstasies in the blacksmith's forge and my clandestine reading were instinctive protests against the excessive value accorded to utilitarian work in my upbringing. Most young boys secretly take liberties in face of the demands of work. This is the case, at least, with normal children. Those who apply themselves too docilely to their work are to be suspected of nursing a neurosis. All my life, I am glad to say, I have often put other activities before conventional duty because I found them more interesting.

In our society everything points to the primacy of utilitarian work over other activities which are chosen not out of duty, but from inclination. Our modern outlook is dominated by this idea. The expression which I have already used about it, that of a 'scale of values', is not a happy one, since it suggests a free and deliberate choice, whereas the truth is that it is an attitude dictated by society, and we passively submit to it.

There is no question of turning man away from action. Action is his very nature. Quite, but what action? The utilitarian toil imposed by authority? Or the action that is freely chosen for pleasure? That is where the great social prejudice comes in. 'It is activity, not work, which is fundamental to living,' writes Joffre Dumazedier. The notorious advice to 'work first, play later', which we meet in various forms, suggests a false distinction between work-activity and leisure-activity. In particular it suggests that work is more important than leisure.

There is a certain association of ideas between leisure, idleness, laziness, pleasure, depravity and sin. We find it very strongly in the minds of many of our patients who suffer from an 'enjoyment forbidden' complex. But it floats vaguely at the back of the minds of many others as well. Hence the 'guilt that lies heavy on leisure', to which Jean-Marie Domenach refers. 'Leisure still has something solitary and shameful about it,' he says. The time one devotes to it is stolen from work-time, as a result of weakness, selfishness, or an unholy desire for pleasure. Retired people still retain something of this feeling of guilt about leisure, even though they no longer have a duty to work at their jobs.

To prize leisure to the detriment of work would be to fall into the opposite error. In reality the value is in the man, not in the activity. Everything that contributes towards the lifelong harmonious development of the person derives its value from the performance of that function. Viewed in this light, work and leisure are two complementary factors. Work brings development in depth because of the specialization it requires. Leisure counterbalances it with development in breadth because of the diversity of the interests it cultivates.

Nevertheless, as we have seen, the ratio between these two factors must vary from one period of our lives to another. In youth, it seems to me that they are of equal importance. All that I did outside my studies prepared me for life quite as much as my studies themselves. Then, in the first half of my active life, the 'biological task', as Jung calls it, imposes a preponderance (but not the preeminence!) in the work one does for a living. In the second half, as we have seen, the balance must be gradually altered, leisure taking up more space in order to widen the personal cultural horizon in preparation for the later stage of life, that of retirement, in which leisure will take the first place, though this does not mean that the retired person is excused all duties.

The child who goes out to play before doing his homework is readily dismissed as lazy, whereas the energy and interest he shows in his leisure activities is anything but laziness. What is happening is that he is being judged by the law of adulthood, which gives priority to productive work. Fortunately, less is heard about the 'lazy child' than was the case at the beginning of the century. Then it was the greatest censure, and the maxims of the Book of Proverbs (Prov. 6. 6–11) served to stigmatize idleness. It is no accident that this book is attributed to Solomon, whose prosperity was legendary.

Social success is the secret goal of the morality of duty. Psychologists nowadays have studied the so-called lazy child, and have shown that his behaviour in general is the result of emotional factors. The child goes on strike against duty when his relationship with the person who imposes it is not a happy one.

But if he abandons his exercises for other activities which adults consider to be a waste of time, it may also have something to do with the powerful attraction those activities have for him, and one day they will be the glory of his life. We know that the future Marshal Lyauthey, when he was a child, used to draw in the sand plans of cities with wide avenues, and that this game foreshadowed the work of town-planning that he was to do later on in Morocco.[34] I have a nephew who is now a professor of astronomy. When he was still quite small, instead of being good and going to sleep as all parents make it their children's duty to do, he used to get quietly out of bed and go to the window to gaze up at the sky. And Einstein was refused admission to the Zurich Polytechnic because his maths was not good enough. No doubt his mind was already too much given to creative thought for him to be able to apply himself to the study of arithmetic.

'*Idleness is the mother of all the vices*'

Education for duty and work was also education for activism. One always had to be doing something, and something useful, something valuable in adult eyes. I have just been discussing this with one of my former patients.

'Oh, yes, of course!' she explained. 'You never had to let yourself be caught doing nothing! I always used to keep some knitting beside me so as to be able to justify myself.'

I, too, could quote examples from my own experience. Even on Sundays I could never get out of the obligatory walk. Wrapped up in my dreams, I used to lag behind, and often had to be told to 'keep up'.

The uncle who brought me up did in fact practise what he preached. It could truly be said of him that 'work was his life'. His leisure activities were shooting, picking flowers according to the seasons, gardening, bridge, and billiards. But all these pastimes were regulated with such precision that they were like ritual duties. The important thing was to do only serious, intelligent, rational things, even for pleasure, and to waste no time on trivialities. I still bear within me the marks of this training. My psychoanalyst friends tell me that I have too strict a super-ego. Probably. But I prefer it that way, rather than that it should be too easy-going. It does not stop me from frequently wasting my time over stupidities, but I always do it with a bad conscience.

Many years ago, on the eve of one of the International Weeks devoted to the medicine of the person, I spent a couple of days in preparation for it with my friend Dr Théo Bovet, who later became well known for his books on marriage. We were at Begnins, in the foothills of the Jura. From morning until evening we tramped along footpaths through the fields and woodlands. We sat in the grass or on a low wall, and opened our hearts to each other. We talked about the great problems of the development of medicine, of psychology, of society and of religion. We talked earnestly, but I do not remember what we said.

We also talked more intimately about our experiences in our work, and in our personal lives. Of that, too, I have forgotten the details. But there was one thing that I remember as vividly as if it were only yesterday. It was a trivial confession, but I had thought it over to myself for several hours before deciding to talk about it. It concerned the amount of time I devote to games of patience with playing-cards, and the pleasure I derive from them. Would my friend laugh at me? If it had been chess, or tennis, or bridge, it would have been all right – those are serious games, worthy of intelligent men. But playing patience is only suitable for children or old people who are pretty far gone!

Naturally I also told my friend about this stupid reticence that had held me back, and we had a good laugh about it. Shortly afterwards my friend wrote to tell me that he had taken up playing patience, and that he got a lot of pleasure out of it. Later on, in a magazine, I saw a photograph of Paul Claudel, the great poet. In his beautiful house on the banks of the Rhone, he was sitting at a table in a bay window overlooking the large park, with a game of patience spread out in front of him. I was reassured.

But surely, you ask, haven't we a right to do what we want, what we like, in our leisure time, even if it is stupid? Even if other people think it silly? Haven't we a right, even, to do nothing at all, to think about nothing, to waste our time?

Nevertheless, even where our hobbies are concerned, we are

afraid of what people will think. Lots of people have little fads which they are ashamed to talk about, but to which they are greatly attached. And lots of people poke fun good-humouredly – or wickedly – at other people's useless hobbies. A wife laughs at her husband for collecting stamps, and at the time and interest he puts into it. And who has not felt ashamed of doing nothing while others work? Jean-Marie Domenach describes the sarcastic remarks directed at those who walk about with nothing to do.

A woman is reading a book. But she realizes that she is finding it difficult to concentrate because her daily help is making a lot of noise in the next room. It is not the noise that disturbs her; it is a kind of false guilt because she is peacefully reading while the other woman is working. From time to time the latter comes into the room as if to rebuke her. It could be a trivial book she is reading, merely for pleasure; but the same thing may happen if she is reading a serious book which in her case is as much work as doing the housework is, though less obviously so. To be doing nothing useful, or to seem to be doing nothing useful, it to transgress against the doctrine of productivity.

Several authors have expressed surprise that up to now so little study has been done on the subject of leisure. Domenach, whom I have just quoted, notes also that systems of thought either ignore or disregard leisure, as if it had nothing to say in the understanding of man. This is curious indeed, when one considers the place that leisure has in the life of every one of us. I know something of its importance from what my patients tell me. A businessman, for instance, is fond of talking about the important work he is doing. That is the official side of his life. But in my consulting-room he tells me how much he enjoys his Sunday fishing-trips and how his mind strays to the thought of them, even in the midst of his most important negotiations. No doubt the reason for the scant attention paid to leisure activities is that they are not looked upon as serious, they have a certain air of selfishness about them. To point to the selfishness of others is, to some extent, to confess our own.

Just as I write these lines I have received a letter from one of my patients. She was brought up in this atmosphere of activity and dedication. She is already a little more liberated, and she herself says that she is 'beginning to live'. But she still bears the marks of her childhood deeply imprinted on her life. She is a slave to her work, and only her work gives her the feeling of really living. She is discovering how poverty-stricken her life is outside her work. Much more – she tells me that she is experiencing an immense need for relaxation and for time to think. But when she does get time for some respite, she cannot enjoy it because of the strange feeling of guilt that besets her. This good and sensible woman concludes: 'I have been told so often that idleness is the mother of all the vices.'

In the ethic of duty, writes Pizzorno,[35] leisure is looked upon as the reward of industry. The trouble is that this reward is never forthcoming, because there are always more duties to fulfil if one is not to be accused of idleness. Retirement, similarly, is often spoken of as a recompense for a life of toil. A sociologist is questioning a pensioner, and asks him why he does not choose to occupy some of his time in some kind of work. 'Ah, no!,' the man exclaims, 'I've spent enough of my life wearing myself out with work!' But this man is quite incapable of enjoying the reward of his labours, precisely because as a result of a life devoted exclusively to work he has forgotten how to enjoy any leisure-time activity.

The break with routine

This is one of the problems of adaptation to retirement: it is particularly difficult for men with a high sense of professional duty, men who are so devoted to their work that they have hardly dared to indulge in any leisure activities during their working lives. Of course they have taken time off, but always in snatches, furtively and guiltily, as if it were time stolen from work, not allowing themselves to put their heart into it for fear they should be led astray by their passion. They have enclosed themselves in a restricted world, in a blind routine, and when retirement comes to draw them out of it, they are at a loss.

Often, for example, some very active man tells me that he hardly ever has time for reading. Just a glance at a newspaper or a short magazine article. A friend has recommended a book to him: he hastily reads a page or two – not enough to arouse his interest – and then he has so much to do that he gives it up, and will never go back to it because he has lost the thread. Later on, in retirement, if he is bored, you will perhaps suggest that he should read something. A good book, a favourite author – what a wonderful treasure of quiet enjoyment! But he will by then have lost the habit of reading. After going half-heartedly through the first few pages, he will close his book and go back to his boredom, as he used to go back to his work. And he will say to you: 'What's the use? I'm no intellectual.'

Habit? The word is too restrictive in its meaning, indicating mere passive conditioning. The problem goes very much deeper. It concerns the attitude of that individual towards life and towards the world. Reading is by no means, as he believes, an occupation suitable only for intellectuals. It is a window on the world, on its extreme diversity and its inexhaustible riches. By immersing himself in the narrow world of his work, interesting though it was, that man had lost contact with the wider world, had been cut off from any dialogue with other thoughts and feelings, other subjects of interest, so important in the stimulation of our evolution of persons. Moreover, when one grows old, as Mauriac remarks, I believe one finds a special pleasure in re-reading old books one has read in the past.

I could quote many more examples. Like reading, all leisure activity is a kind of initiation into new aspects of life. And if that initiation does not take place beforehand, we will find that when old age is come many of the riches of life are foreign to us, misunderstood and unattractive. Take the case of a woman who is approaching retirement. Unfortunate administrative changes compel her to retire early, rather than suffer a reduction in her income. Throughout her life she has disliked her job, which she did not freely choose for herself.

Now, far from looking forward to her retirement, she is in a state of deep anxiety. She realizes that in the atmosphere of rebellion in which she has lived, she has turned in upon herself, cutting out almost every activity other than her work. Her only escape has been her love of mountaineering, which she has already had to give up with advancing years. 'I beg you,' she says to me, 'to find me something I can do when I retire.' She has even forgotten what her real tastes are, they have been repressed for so long.

A few days ago we went to see a couple of excellent friends. My colleague is the director of a large clinic; he has still a few years in front of him before his retirement. Naturally we talked about this book that I am writing. 'Had you thought,' he asked me, 'of talking about retirement by stages, on the instalment principle?'

This is what he has been attempting to do in his own case over a number of years, by increasing the number and the length of his holidays. With his wife he goes on caravan tours lasting several months. It is a sort of training for retirement!

He has qualified colleagues who are encouraged by his long absences to take on greater responsibilities, unlike other chiefs who behave as if they were irreplaceable right up to the fateful moment of their retirement. He himself is cutting free from the routine of his life, a routine which in the case of so many others exhausts their spirit of adventure and arrests their personal development.

There is that word routine again, which expresses so exactly the problem we are dealing with here. There are large numbers of people, especially in administrative posts, but in other walks of life as well, whose lives sink into a rigid monotony. It is chiefly in their case that retirement may bring a crisis which many of them never manage to overcome. Life is a mixture of creation and repetition, of innovation and routine. These two poles are complementary.

In my last book I used the example of trapeze artists in a circus to describe these two successive movements.[36] First, an attachment which provides solid support, and then the flight towards a new support. I have seen adventurers overcome in old age by a painful feeling of failure because they have spread themselves over a large number of enterprises, and are unable now to look back upon any single coherent achievement. Others have a sense of failure because they have been unable to detach themselves, to liberate themselves from a paralysing routine. Retirement ought now to give them the chance of doing so, but they are incapable of seizing it because they have long ago lost the capacity to adapt themselves to new situations. They spoil their retirement, because they have no resilience.

In support of this idea my friend the medical director pointed out to me that I had myself happily experienced several such re-orientations of my life, which were in effect what he termed retirements by instalments. In 1937, when I began to get interested in the psychic and spiritual life of my patients and its influence on their state of health, I engaged in what was then a quite new adventure for me. I did not realize at first that this was going to mean to some extent my retirement as a general practitioner. Later on, to my new career as a 'doctor of the person' was added a career as a lecturer, and then a career as a writer.

And so over and over again I have been jolted out of a rut by life, and this has stimulated my development. This personal maturation is the thing that counts when one comes to the threshold of old age. My wish for everyone is that they will be jolted from time to time by life, and that they will be faced with the need to make new departures. I hope that they will do their duty properly, but that they will turn aside from time to time so that they will not become the prisoners of duty.

II

TOWARDS A MORE HUMANE SOCIETY

Contempt for the old

In the first part of this book we have seen how success in retirement depends largely upon our development, all through life; and especially upon the important turning-points which take us from childhood to working life, and then from working life to old age. In addition to these personal factors there are factors external to us, social factors. This is what we must now examine: first, in this second part, factors appertaining to the way people think, to the inhuman character of our society; then, in Part III, factors due to the concrete circumstances of our existence.

The problem of old age does not concern only the old. It calls in question the whole of our society, and exposes its faults. That it is inhuman is verifiable at any age. But this is felt more especially in childhood, when we begin to discover the world and its injustices, and when we are too weak to defend ourselves. Later on, in the full strength of active life, we can at least fight, stand up to injustice, contend with fate. But when old age comes, we find ourselves powerless once again, and feel once more the pain of the faults in our civilization.

So it is the weak who feel it most, all the weak, all those whom the doctors know, because the weak need their help: not only the children and the aged, but also the sick, the persecuted, the poor, the multitudes of the hungry, the under-developed peoples. And so it is, as always in medicine, a matter of going behind the localized and visible symptoms to the hidden and more general disease, in order to make a diagnosis. And it is also in the symptoms – in this case the distress suffered by so many of the retired and the aged – that one must look for the clue that will lead to the diagnosis.

The malady of our society is a psychosomatic one, that is to say that it displays physical symptoms (material and economic) and moral symptoms (boredom and depression) whose underlying cause is psychological. Thus the cry that goes up from so many sufferers is not directed only against material injustices, but also against moral injustices. One of the gravest is the fact that the retired and the aged do not feel that they are looked upon as of equal value with the other members of society, as members 'with a full share', as General de Gaulle remarked in another context.

This problem of society's contempt for the old is going to occupy us at some length, because its importance is crucial. That is the case at any rate in the West. Professor K. von Dürckheim once asked some Japanese what was considered to be the supreme good in their country. 'Our old people,' was their reply. Alas! Our Western outlook is quite the opposite. It is not a matter only of the distress felt by the old among us, but of the effect on their behaviour of this social contempt. Anyone who feels himself rejected and a failure tends to give up. 'The psychology of the old depends in part upon the attitude of those around them,' writes Henri Bour.[1] All those who have to do with old people know how difficult it is to break through their passivity when they are turned in upon themselves. One can do something for them only in so far as they themselves react, in so far as one finds in them a desire to collaborate constructively.

On the other hand, there is also plenty of evidence of the spectacular transformation that can take place in old people once they feel themselves to be accepted as valued members of a friendly community. Dr Paul Miraillet, for example, writes of 'the extraordinary faculty of mental recuperation in old people who are brought back before it is too late into a beneficent social environment'.[2] This may be the case even with old people who are severely handicapped mentally and physically. The experience of Dr Villa, in Lausanne, is particularly telling in this respect.[3] This concerned patients so seriously ill that they had had to be admitted to a psychiatric hospital. Very simple methods, physical exercise, games and group psychotherapy in which the patients could express themselves, tell their life-stories – even at the risk of occasional repetitions! – and feel that they were being listened to with interest and attention, produced an unexpected revival of the personality, with a great improvement in behaviour and in their mental and physical condition.

Contempt for old people has, therefore, incalculable repercussions, and contributes greatly to their becoming a heavy burden on society. What is the origin of this contempt? It has been put down to the increase in the numbers of the aged. The old were highly respected in ancient society, because they were a rarity. The old man was respected, writes G. Gaillard, because he 'enjoyed the prestige of the survivor'.[4] This prestige is still found today in the case of exceptionally old people – centenarians, for example, who have the honour of being interviewed by journalists. But in the case of the ordinary old age we are considering here, we are a long way from the praise pronounced by Cicero in *De Senectute*: 'The greatest states,' he said, not without a certain political ulterior motive, 'have been upset by the young, but sustained and set up once more by the old.'

It has also been said that this modern contempt has to do with the acceleration of progress: in a static society which has lasted for centuries, the old were the custodians of tested experience which they handed on to the young. Nowadays technology evolves rapidly. The young learn its latest improvements, and have no use for the counsel of the old, who are ignorant of the new technology. Especially in the scientific and industrial fields, it is not easy for each person to keep abreast of the developments that take place in his own speciality. 'The generations are contracting, so to speak,' writes Michèle Aumont, 'resting on an ever shorter lapse of time. From a figure of fifteen to twenty years, they are falling to ten, and then to five. Nowadays, four or five years is sufficient to create a difference and to set a distance between people. It can happen that a young research worker or engineer is "relegated to the side-lines" only four or five years after arriving at the zenith of his career.'[5]

All that is true, certainly. I find it hard, however, to see what is the correct treatment that follows from this diagnosis. The number of old people will no doubt continue to increase. As for progress in technology, no doubt it is going to be speeded up and not slowed down. So what is to be done? That is what the doctor asks himself when he discovers a disturbing symptom. Yes, we ought to see a warning signal in all these old people who are bored, hidden away, no longer important to society, spending the last quarter of their lives in sterile regret for the first three.

An impersonal society

Our society is sick. The symptoms are localized, but they disclose a disease of the whole organism. Such grave symptoms ought to impel us towards a more radical re-thinking of the bases of society. My readers will already have seen that that is why I criticized with such insistence the scale of values of our modern Western world, which gives pride of place to lucrative work. Some may think that it is largely an economic problem, and that all that is needful is to improve the social services that have to do with old people, and increase old age pensions.

Of course, that must be done. But it would be only first-aid, treating the symptoms rather than their causes. If we confine ourselves to giving a bit more money to the old and do nothing to make them feel less despised, they will merely spend the extra money on drink to console themselves for the contempt of which they feel they are the object. If we confine ourselves to giving them more money so that they can cut a dash like people on holiday, it will give them only a temporary, superficial significance. What they need is something that will restore their human dignity for twenty years of their lives. Money will merely set up a vicious circle, since if they depend on that for their significance, it will only confirm the false scale of values of which they are the victims.

Social reforms are, of course, necessary, and pensions must be made sufficient. But if these things are to be effective, they must be accompanied by a far-reaching reform in the outlook of society. We shall examine later, in Part III, the question of what social reforms are necessary. However, I am not proposing at my age to enter into the political arena in order to bring about reform of our institutions. Nevertheless, the reason why I have been asked to write this book is no doubt so that I may issue a call for deeper thought to be given to the sickness of our society.

Well, this sickness seems to me to consist mainly in the depersonalization of our modern world. All problems are envisaged only as technological problems; and technology is essentially impersonal. If I discuss the exploration of space, the structure of the atom, integrated circuits or surgical technique, I am dealing with important questions which need to be studied; but they do not involve me as a person. I hope I am making myself clear. I have always had a keen interest in technical problems. I am only saying that they are but one aspect of things – their impersonal aspect; I am saying that we make a mistake if we study the manifold problems of the universe, of men and of society only from a technological point of view.

Psychology has become a technique, and the same has happened to medicine, to sociology, to politics, to art and to economics. We think every problem can be solved if only we acquire a sufficiently high technical qualification. Young people read learned tomes about the technique of sex, without realizing that they are being taught everything except how to love; for loving is not a technical skill, it is a personal commitment.

Technical competence is essential to professional success. Every profession has its technical problems. While people are still at work, technical conversations form a bond between them, and create the illusion of a personal relationship. But when retirement comes along, when we have nothing more to do with the great technical machine, when we are no longer one of the team, we realize that we no longer know what to talk about, that we have no bond with those who are in the technical society, and that we have forgotten the speech of personal relationships. That is when a man finds out the extent to which he has been conditioned by a depersonalized civilization. In Paul Ricoeur's words, this soulless world secretes boredom, a boredom which makes people a prey to anxiety.[6] Young people are aware of this. At the height of one's career the work itself provides distraction, but in retirement boredom will reappear, and become an obsession.

We have given things priority over persons, we have built up a civilization based on things rather than on persons. Old people are discounted because they are purely and simply persons, whose only value is as persons, and not as producers any more. Fortunately action has begun to be taken in favour of the old. But it seems to me today that thought is lagging behind action. Action alone is not enough. Society is sustained by both action and thought. Both must move forward, like the two legs of a walker. If he were to keep stepping forward with only one leg, he would merely turn round and round.

Well, there has been tremendous economic progress over the last century, and that ought now to be matched by a corresponding advance in the field of morality. Economic progress had to come first; as the old saying has it: live first, then you may philosophize. Duty and toil had to be stressed – less as a doctrine than as a necessity. We are just emerging from a long history through which humanity has been able to survive only by means of unremitting and exhausting toil. How can civilization be built if men are dying of hunger? It is not so long ago that there were no problems concerning retired people, because there was no retirement. The lot of the great mass of humanity was to work hard from early childhood until death.

The young hippies who reject our consumer society depend upon it more than they realize. They would not be there, with leisure to protest, if their elders had not enriched the world by their labour, and if their contemporaries were not continuing to enrich it. The same is true of our protesting students. I have great sympathy with them. I understand why they criticize our society. What I am concerned to do is to see more clearly what it is that society lacks. Reading their manifestoes, it is not clear to me what they are advocating.

Thus I have read Professor Marcuse with great interest.[7] He, too, looks to poverty to give back to 'one-dimensional man' his second dimension. In many respects I am in sympathy with him when he denounces the Cartesianism and the exclusive rationalism of our technological society, and the new alienation of man, who is enslaved by it. But what does he propose in its place? He does recognize the merits of our civilization: 'We are not fighting a terrorist society,' he writes. 'We are not fighting a society which is in process of disintegration. We are fighting a society that works extraordinarily well, and what is more ... one that has succeeded in eliminating poverty and misery to an extent which the preceding stages of capitalism never achieved.'

Why, then, does he attack it so intransigently? For he seems to be preaching not its evolution, but its overthrow. This is indeed the attitude of the young people who claim him as their authority. Is this no more than a difference in emphasis? I do not think so. I think our way of life will be fundamentally different if we consider our industrial civilization to be a great blessing which merely presents us with fresh problems to solve, rather than wanting to make a clean sweep of everything that it has brought us.

The mission of the old

I can illustrate this difference in concept by the example of medicine. For a long time I have been fighting for a more humane outlook in medicine, for a medicine in several 'dimensions'; against a too exclusively technical and rational development of medicine, in which there is a great risk of 'alienating' the patient, of losing him in a great treatment machine, extremely efficient, but impersonal. Colleagues of widely differing outlook have given me their encouragement. Unfortunately, among the keenest there are some who seem to be unjust in their criticism of 'official' medicine, to which we owe so much of the progress that has been made. They practise homeopathy, Chinese acupuncture, naturism, psychoanalysis, spiritual healing, chiropractice, or some other unorthodox discipline, and systematically criticize the teaching given in our medical schools.

I do not want to be misunderstood: it is not my intention to criticize these colleagues, whose experiments enrich medical practice with effective methods often misunderstood by orthodox medicine. For example, I have myself on two occasions been cured of sciatica only by means of acupuncture. What I dislike is the partisan spirit which these colleagues sometimes show, especially when their enthusiasm leads them to denigrate official medicine. Actually, I have treated several of them when they have been ill themselves, and have noticed that they are very glad of the relief afforded by the most orthodox of methods.

To denigrate scientific medicine, to suppose that one can hold back its technical progress, would be naïve and utopian, but above all it would be a mistake. On the contrary, when I remember the effective weapons it has provided for us in the fight against disease, even since my own student days, I can only hope that it will make further – and rapid – progress. That is not the problem. The problem is how to keep the sense of the person at the very heart of medicine at its most scientific, how to make sure that our understanding of the human person and of our spiritual needs advances hand in hand with our technical knowledge.

There seems to me to be an important analogy between the two domains, the particular sphere of medicine and the more general field of our technological civilization, as I outlined it just now in connection with the thought of Professor Marcuse. This industrial civilization also has taken a great leap forward, of which it would be foolish not to wish to take advantage. But progress has also brought with it the same danger, which must be guarded against. It is the danger of losing the sense of humanity, of subordinating man to things.

It is therefore a civilization based on the sense of the person that I pray for. For this it is not in the least necessary to reject our society and its benefits. What we must do is to introduce a personal relationship between man and man into the very heart of this society. Indeed, such a step forward becomes all the more feasible precisely because increased productivity has just freed men from poverty. One may be permitted to hope that the growth in prosperity which the second industrial revolution has brought us will favour, as Louis Armand maintains, the rise of a new humanism.[8]

All the same, we need people who will devote themselves to the attainment of that end, men who see the contrast between the wealth of our technological progress and the poverty of our personal relationships, and who will try to improve the latter. Now this is where I see that the old have a real job to do. It is a terribly important one: the restoration to our impersonal society of the human warmth, the soul that it lacks. When we are young we have to build our careers and carve out a place in society for ourselves. Later on that career absorbs more and more of our time and energy. We have little leisure in which to take any interest in the persons of others. We are caught up in a network of formal relationships.

Those about us are our business partners, our superiors, our subordinates, our competitors, our customers, our fellow-workers or our adversaries. Our course of action as well as theirs is dictated by the requirements of our work and of our role in society. Their persons and ours, their hidden suffering, their secret tragedies and their intimate solitude, have no part to play in that. In fact it is better to know nothing about them in order to do our job better. When we are old, and when we are retired, either partially or completely, our job no longer absorbs all our energies, and our experience and our understanding of life has been enriched, and so we have the time and the qualifications necessary to a true ministry of personal relationships.

Let us once more take medicine as an example. Shortly before his death, in a conference on the medicine of the person, Dr Henri Mentha spoke of the direction that the activity of the doctor may take when he is in advancing years. While still young he had realized that it was not enough to concern oneself only with the disease, but that one ought also to help the patient as a human being to reconsider his life and reform it, to accept his life and its laws, and to discover its more lasting and valid meaning. However, over-loaded as he was with work, weighed down by his responsibilities, the doctor found to his distress that he had no time for a more personal and more meaningful dialogue.

In time, Dr Mentha said, the day may come when the number of patients diminishes, because they can get more effective help from younger and technically more up-to-date doctors. Sometimes this makes the older doctor feel a little bitter, and he grumbles at the ingratitude of the patients and of his own profession. But also he has a chance of giving a new character to his work, making it more humane and interesting, if he takes advantage of the extra time he has on his hands in order to listen at greater length to his patients and to get to understand them as people. In doing so he will be moving away from the specialization which has been forced upon him in his busy youth.

Then it is the doctor himself who will as a consequence dis-cover that his personal life has been enriched. He renews himself, and breaks out of his professional routine. The older one is, the more value one places on human dialogue. With advancing age the doctor, like his patients, begins to ask all sorts of questions which previously seemed unimportant. Has life a wider meaning than the performance of a technical task? Death is approaching, in all its mystery. He has been a success in his job – has he been a success in his life? It is not a good idea to turn over such problems all on one's own. If he enters into dialogue, the old doctor introduces a bit of humanity into our dehumanized world. This man he is talking to may never before have had the chance of a really frank, serious and confident exchange of ideas.

The medicine of the person

Many doctors go gradually through this change from the technical to the personal attitude. For others, of course, the process is more sudden. Take, for example, one of my closest friends. He has had a long and brillant career as chief surgeon in a big hospital. He has just retired. It is no small matter for a surgeon to lay down his scalpel. And surgery, of course, is a profession that demands perfect adherence to routine. This can be seen in any operations block, where the whole team has to be right on the mark, able to function with clockwork precision. It has to be so well trained that should an emergency arise in the middle of an operation, one word from the chief will be sufficient to direct it to the carrying out with equal exactitude of an alternative plan of action.

But my friend is also something of a poet. He has always been attracted by the mystery of the human person, and has sought to understand it. He has guessed that there are secret dramas played out in every life, even in those cases where the patient refrains from talking about them; that there are personal problems which no one has helped them to solve or to shoulder, of which they have perhaps not even become completely aware, but which have undermined their strength and opened the door to illness. But the technical responsibilities of a surgeon are heavy. It takes time for a patient, once his trust has been gained, to open his heart on the subject of his most intimate problems.

Retirement, then, is indeed the end of my friend's career as a surgeon, but it also marks the beginning of a new career, as a 'doctor of the person'. Now he has the time to listen at leisure to those who have never spoken freely about themselves because they are inarticulate, to those who have never received from anyone the welcome, the attention and the love that may be as vital to them as a surgical operation.

As I have said, preparation for retirement must start very much earlier, in the midst of a person's active life. This was true of my friend. For a number of years he had been apprenticing himself to his new career. Despite the fact that his job as a surgeon had left him little time to spare, he had been studying psychology; he had been discovering that under the influence of a religious faith any life may be profoundly changed, and in particular he had been learning that this faith is not communicated so much by teaching or preaching as by the testimony of our own experience.

I have already told elsewhere a story which this surgeon related, long before he retired.[9] He had in his hospital a lady who was old and infirm. The initial diagnosis had not, however, been confirmed, and there was no call for an operation. Clinical and laboratory observations were favourable. And yet it was in vain that the surgeon reassured her, and invited her to get up. She still lay there, prostrated, indifferent and passive. He asked her how long she had felt like that. 'It's since my daughter died,' she replied, 'three years ago. My life hasn't been worth living since then.' She was like a clock that had stopped at the moment of her daughter's death. There are retired people, too, who are like clocks that have stopped at the time of their retirement.

As it happened, my surgeon friend had experienced the same sort of bereavement as that old lady had suffered. He had lost a son in the flower of youth, and had been broken by it. He could not but remember the fact, especially since this old lady was occupying the very room in the hospital where his own son had died. Should he talk to her about it? It was hardly the job of a surgeon to do so. Nevertheless his heart told him to speak, and he did. It was an unusual kind of consultation – instead of a one-way interrogation, it was a dialogue, a personal testimony on the part of the doctor, a communion of suffering. The next day found the old lady paying some attention to her toilet, determining to get up and go out: the clock had started again!

That, in my view, is the most decisive factor in the medicine of the person – to establish with the patient so personal a contact that a sort of spark of life flashes like an electric spark leaping between two electrodes as, polished clean of all insulating matter, they are brought together. Dr Maeder, of Zurich, with his long experience in classical psychoanalytical technique, has shown in his latest book that in certain cases this more personal attitude on the part of the doctor can produce the same results in a much shorter time.[10]

There are many illnesses which are due to a localized lesion in a particular organ, or to a disturbance in a particular physiological or psychological function. In such cases the first requirement is the technical intervention of the doctor. But there are other cases such as that of the old lady, which belong specifically to the field of the medicine of the person, since they do not have so much to do with a particular function or localized lesion as with a blockage of the life-force. Our person is not just the sum of all our organs and functions. It is a global unity which as such has a destiny and a meaning to give to its life. People may fall ill at any age because they fail to see their lives as having such a destiny and meaning. But there are still more who suffer in old age from a sense of failure, who brood painfully on their past. They turn in upon themselves, becoming gloomy, passive and bitter. They are for ever going over the injustices they have suffered and which have blocked their progress. The more clear-sighted among them go over the errors they themselves have committed.

Consequently, the medicine of the person has an important part to play in the prophylaxis and treatment of old age. The textbooks on geriatry set out, far better than I can here, what our technical task is in regard to the ageing person. It is important, naturally, to see to the conservation of his visual and auditory acuity, to treat any organic and psychical affections, to show him how to feed himself correctly and how to avoid dehydration of his tissues, to prescribe for him the physical exercise that is appropriate to his age, and to stimulate his activity and his social and cultural life.

But what is proper to the medicine of the person is personal contact, personal dialogue. The patient must be given the opportunity of expressing himself freely and deeply, of talking openly about his rancour and his remorse, and the questions that he asks himself in secret. This means allowing him to discover a certain unity in his life, an overall pattern which transcends the detail of particular accidents; to discover that our reactions to successive circumstance are governed by a set attitude to life, and that the same behaviour patterns are inexorably reproduced so long as they are not recognized and admitted.

A wider vision

The aged person has a special need to talk about all this to his doctor. I have always got on well with old people, and have enjoyed treating them. For some fifteen years at the start of my career I was the doctor for a Catholic institution for aged and ailing women. Some of my colleagues found this difficult to understand. 'What interest can you have,' they asked, 'in looking after old people? Medicine can't do much for them. There are so few remedies you can use. Whatever you do the results are mediocre, and you are always having to listen to the same old complaints.'

No doubt a psychoanalyst would have explained my sympathy for the aged by the fact that my father was very old when I was born, and that he died soon afterwards. I was probably unconsciously projecting on to every old man my need to find the affection of which I had been deprived. But I think there was another reason. Long before formulating the idea of the medicine of the person, I

became interested as much in the person of the patient as in his illness. And the fact is that in old people, where technical medicine
is less effective, personal contact becomes increasingly important.
To enter into dialogue with them is to face in more acute form the
problems of the destiny of man.

It is not that I discount the value of technical medicine, or that
I am insensible to the joy it gives us when a judicious intervention
brings victory over disease. As a young doctor I was an assistant
in a medical laboratory, and it was there that I studied for my thesis.
I grew quite fond of the rabbits and guinea-pigs which I could put
so wonderfully to sleep with injections or morphine derivatives,
without any danger of the addiction which is so fatal to humans.
And while they slept I tried out all the medicaments in the pharma-
copoeia. True, my teacher, Professor Wiki, professed great scepticism on the subject of therapeutics. But since those days the science
of therapeutics has made great progress, which I value highly.

It is no part of my purpose to belittle modern techniques in
favour of the medicine of the person: the two are complementary. In
the course of a Protestant Medico-Social Conference in Strasbourg,
Dr Théo Bovet was speaking on the medicine of the person.[11] The
philosopher Georges Gusdorf suddenly called out from up in the
gallery: 'Well, doctor, I've got acute appendicitis. You come and
examine me. Instead of calling in a surgeon you suggest that I
should meditate on the faults in my life that may compromise my
health?' The whole assembly burst out laughing, and waited for Dr
Bovet's reply: 'Of course, professor,' he said, 'I will hand you
over first of all to the surgeon. He will operate, and you will recover.
But what then? It will be salutary for you to meditate and to consider what use you ought to make of your good health, having recovered it.' And now the laughter was on his side.

Technical medicine deals with those things that are most urgent.
It has priority in time because it has to attend to the urgency of the
disease. But what then? Then other problems arise, not concerned
with immediate action, but with action in the context of the
patient's whole life. The medicine of the person goes further and
deeper; it addresses itself to these problems, and aims to lead men
and women to a better life.

It is the same in the life of nations. One eloquent example is that
of Germany on the morrow of the last war. A German sociologist,
M. Schelsky, has stated it clearly.[12] In the collapse in 1945, amid

the general ruin and the sense of insecurity that accompanied it, the Germans experienced a profound lack of interest in public and political life. There was only one concern uppermost in everyone's mind – a concern for the social advancement of the individual and the family, the only means being success in one's job. If prosperity collapses, only the primitive instincts are left, with which to rebuild it. But if prosperity is re-established, to what use is it going to be put? That is the question.

The reader may have noticed that M. Schelsky's description – family, work, professional and social success – corresponds word for word with that of C. G. Jung, of which I spoke at the beginning of this book, and in terms of which he defined the first phase of a person's life, which he called the 'natural' phase. So we find at the level of collective history the very same pattern as that which Jung outlined on the personal level. Jung himself never spoke of the two phases of human life as being contradictory or incompatible, but rather of their complementary nature and their continuity. It is after he has completed his natural tasks in the realms of sex and work, and only then, that a man asks himself what use he is going to make of the free time that his successful achievement of these tasks has procured for him.

Of course the analogy must not be pushed too far: the human race will never wholly retire, since economic prosperity is the first requisite for the progressive increase in free time. But the question we asked ourselves at the beginning, with Jung, about individual life, can still be asked in exactly the same terms on the wider scale of history, in the context of Marcuse's criticism of our consumer-orientated society. We are faced with the same thought: so long as free time remained very restricted, it had to be used only for rest and relaxation. But what if it is considerably increased? Then, it can be used for something else, 'for personal culture, for the development of the person in all its aspects,' was Jung's reply.

It seems, then, that humanity, in the West and in the Communist world, has reached in its historical evolution the point which Jung called the midday of life. The point at which man's strivings bring him to the attainment of his first goals, his natural goals, as Freud defines them: love and work. But it is a point also at which that very success gives him a new opportunity, which demands new thought about the meaning of his life: is he to plunge into an ever-greater frenzy of work, remain the slave of his old idea that labour is the sole basis of his value as a man, or is he to grow as a person, to cultivate other values, and realize his personal potential? Everyone is wondering what is the meaning of the wave of protest that is breaking on our world today. Is it not the need to rediscover a more complete and living concept of the nature of man?

The irrational dimension

This rethinking could be worked out in a real dialogue between the most lucid thinkers of our time. This was in fact what was attempted by the International Encounters in Geneva in 1969, which brought together personalities as diverse and as forceful as Paul Ricoeur of the Sorbonne, Professor Herbert Marcuse and Cardinal Daniélou. Unfortunately, by the time Herbert Marcuse spoke, Paul Ricoeur had already left, and Marcuse was no longer present when the time came for discussion on the Cardinal's paper. Of course these great men are very busy. But also, perhaps, this indicates that a dialogue of that kind is not easy.

I read with emotion and interest the inscriptions with which the French students of the Sorbonne and Nanterie covered the university walls during their sit-ins of May 1968. One had written, with evident enthusiasm: 'At last! 2 and 2 no longer make 4.' What did he mean by that? I have no idea. But what I saw in it was a *cri de coeur* against the excessive rationalism of our civilization. It seems to me to be a way of asserting that there are in the human heart needs which neither reason, nor the science and technology that are based on reason, nor even the prosperity which they procure, can fulfil.

I know well these irrational needs, because I find them in all those who come to consult me. Men or women, young or old, rich or poor, they all play as well as they can manage the rational game that society demands of them: work, duty, routine, reasonable conduct, all that is necessary for professional and social success. But behind this official facade is hidden an intense thirst for something different: fantasy, spontaneity, love, happiness. Tremendous and unsatisfied emotional needs haunt the hearts of all of us. They are difficult to formulate. They can be expressed only in the intimacy of close friendship, or in the psychotherapist's consulting-room. In addition there are even more secret and more agonizing spiritual needs: the need to understand, not only the way one thing leads to another by the rational law of cause and effect, but also the meaning of things; whether this universal interplay of phenomena is leading anywhere, and where; whether it has any meaning at all.

We have in fact come back to Marcuse's problem of 'one-dimensional man'. There are two dimensions, two worlds. One clear, apparent, fully elaborated and perfected dimension; and one obscure, vague, subjective dimension, filling men's imagination and colouring their dreams, those dreams in which their repressed aspirations come to the surface. Two dimensions, one rational and the other irrational. We have come back also to the question I raised at the beginning of this book in connection with the remark by the sociologists Dumazedier and Ripert about the difficulty of combining 'the creative imagination and scientific objectivity', poetry and technology.

I see the proof of this in the fact that the protest movements of modern youth always go along with an emotional claim, a demand for love; either in the narrow sense of sexual freedom, or in a wider sense, as for example in the remark I often hear: 'I want to be loved for myself, and not for my work or my usefulness.' Clearly what is being expressed here is a criticism of the idea of the primacy of work over the person. Another remark often made by young people underlines the point: 'I don't want to be like my parents and work like a slave all the time. Where's the sense in that? There are other things in life.'

What I find striking is that these things are not said exclusively by young protesters, or older people weighed down to a greater or lesser degree by the demands of society. Similar remarks are sometimes made by men who are in the prime of life, men who are professionally and socially successful, who have seen, a little late, that their very success has confined them within only one dimension of their being. The other dimension, that of emotion and the spirit, has remained undeveloped. They have been so wrapped up in their work that their wives, starved of real love and attention, have drifted away from them, and their children have grown up without their ever having any real contact with them. Such is the price of the prosperity they have attained.

That is why prosperity, like liberty, can make people afraid. What are we to do with our liberty, what are we to do with the prosperity acquired through work, when we have spent our whole lives thinking only about work, valuing people only in terms of their labour, and condemning idleness as a vice? This is a basic problem, which underlies and aggravates all the other more conscious problems of retirement. Retired people hide themselves away, and make themselves as inconspicuous as possible. They feel themselves to be a dead branch of society, like the remnant at the end of a roll of cloth, sold off cheaply after all the best of the material has gone at a good price.

They keep themselves to themselves in a corner of the café, playing cards to pass the time, taking no part in the noisy conversations of the other customers, proud and exuberant workers just out from their factories or offices. They do not fully live, their lives are muted, as if they were in debt for their useless lives to the others who create prosperity. They no longer participate actively. They are waiting for the end. Inevitably they suppose others to make the same value judgements as they themselves used to make during their own working lives, when they, too, valued men less for themselves than for their labour.

Prosperity? They have done their bit towards it. They have devoted themselves to it as if it were an end and not a means, as if it were the goal of life and of society, as if it were the meaning of life and of society. I invite them all to reflect now, both old and young. It is man who gives meaning to labour, and not labour which gives meaning to man. Prosperity is going to go on increasing, production will continue to rise, since all economic plans are based on a growth index of 5% or 6%. The whole system would collapse if production were to remain stationary. We are in the grip of an ineluctable process. Blessing or curse? It is at this point that I must part company with Professor Marcuse.

Overcoming old prejudices

For this rapid advance may also be used in the service of man – man as he really is, with several dimensions: not only the dimension of work, duty, and reason, but also the dimension of love, of poetry, and of the spiritual life. The economists announce the arrival of the affluent society. For the first time in its history, humanity is going to be able to live by working less. Two days, three days off per week, more frequent and longer holidays, an earlier age for retirement, a childhood prolonged in more advanced education. But what is it all going to be for? For boredom? The regressive mental state of far too many retired people is not calculated to make us widely enthusiastic.

You remember the first motor-cars, in my childhood: they were like horse-drawn carriages without the horses. Imagination does not move as fast as technology. Are we going to continue in the affluent society along the same lines as we did in yesterday's society of poverty? Are culture, personal life and spiritual life going to remain the privilege of a tiny minority who turned culture and the spiritual life into a bread-and-butter profession, while the remainder sink into boredom because they have never learnt to do anything other than earn their livelihood? To think otherwise is to free ourselves from this notorious prejudice that work is more important than man.

I am indeed writing this book for the future, in order to prepare for the future. The economists are already preparing for it after their fashion by building the affluent society. It is no exaggeration to say that there is a messianic spirit abroad in some of our university departments of economic science. I understand the emotion felt by the economists. For them the old doctrinal argument between laissez-faire and a planned economy is outdated. They are doing their sums, and in the answers they get they are beginning to read the data of the emerging affluent society, just as modern astronomy emerged from the calculations of Copernicus, the theory of relativity from Einstein's equations, and the quantum theory from those of Planck.

Think of what the term 'affluent society' means. The ancient dream of a golden age. Better than that of the alchemists, the enrichment not of a few individuals only, but of the entire human race. Liberation from the crushing age-old burden of a toil so demanding that it filled the lives of the masses and left so little spare time to do anything other than keep poverty at bay. I am far from blaming the economist for harbouring the almost mystic feeling that animates their hearts and their researches, since I certainly think that if their calculations are correct, and if the future is indeed to be as they predict, that will be a wonderful and merciful gift from God, who already foresaw it when in creating man he gave him the right, the duty and the power to dominate nature and to exploit it intelligently.

Who does not see that the advent of the affluent society is going to change completely our concept of man, and that we ought to be preparing for it? In parallel with the work of the economists, therefore, I have come to play my part in that other preparation in which psychologists, sociologists, philosophers and churchmen are collaborating. If through its very success economic labour can one day be reduced to its proper proportion, it will stop being the only serious thing in life, the thing that gives life its meaning; and it will be necessary to pay greater attention to cultural life and to its role in the development of the personality.

What we must do, therefore, is to put an end to the way we all tend to discriminate between those people who work and those who do not work, between those whom we value because of their work, and the others, whom we disparage; it is a form of discrimination which we make even in our own lives between the time we spend at work, looked upon as important, and the time we spend in leisure pursuits, which we consider to be valueless. This is bound up not only with the restoration of their true value to the old, on whom this discrimination weighs particularly heavily, but also with the dignity of the whole of society: a civilization which despises the old is inhuman.

This disparagement of the old is, of course, pure prejudice. The way we all still value working for a living as against all the voluntary activity of our spare time and retirement, is also pure prejudice. This has got to be brought home to us. But what can be done against an age-old prejudice? I imagine many of my readers calling me utopian when they see me taking up arms against such a solidly established prejudice. Does not sociology show us how strong is the inertia of public opinion? The results of opinion polls are published, and they are taken by those who read them as being scientific truths, as objective and incontrovertible as the statement that water freezes at 0° C. 'That's the way of it,' we say, and along with this goes the corollary: 'That is necessarily the way it is, and nothing can change it.'

Not at all! Sociology also teaches us how volatile public opinion is, how subject it is to passing influences. I am quite persuaded that any prejudice can be overcome if men of conviction are prepared to denounce it. The strength of a prejudice lies in its acceptance by everybody, an acceptance which is accorded without thought, simply because everybody agrees. There is, therefore, a universal complicity, for which each of us bears responsibility – the young who do not honour the old, and the old who have doubts about their own value. Public opinion may seem powerful, unshakable, because of its massive anonymity. In reality it is extremely fickle.

Consider the efficacy of commercial publicity. Consider the capriciousness of politics, the way in which alliances can be made and broken, so that nations which despised and hated one another can rapidly turn round and show mutual esteem and even friendship.

I might also point to the fluctuations of fashion. Consider the incredible speed with which the miniskirt spread all over the world, liberating women as if by magic from reflexes of modesty which seemed to have the immutability of an instinct. Think of those bathing costumes which strike us today as being so ridiculous, in the photographs from the period of my childhood. On the other hand, a thing that struck me then as being ridiculous was my grandfather's side-whiskers, which came all the way down his cheeks to his lower jaw and stopped there for no apparent reason. I never imagined that in my old age young people would not feel themselves to be in the swim unless they wore just such side-whiskers.

If the prejudices of fashion can change, social prejudices can change as well. And they must change, because this is a serious matter which poisons relations between individuals and social groups. People always sincerely believe themselves to be objective in their judgments. The person who shows contempt for the opinions of others does not realize that his contempt really arises out of prejudice. The one who does realize it is the other person, the victim, who is intensely conscious of the contempt of which he is the object. When one is the recipient of people's confidences, as I have been for half a century now, one sees clearly how vital it is to a person to be accepted by others, to be valued, to be welcomed, to be taken seriously, to be listened to with attention, respect, and kindness.

Overcoming contempt

Contempt in all its forms is extremely harmful and inhibiting. There are, of course, many shades and gradations of contempt, ranging in a subtle gamut from haughty disdain to secret scorn. It is not perhaps always open brutal contempt that is the most harmful, since it arouses in its victim a powerful defensive reaction. Such contempt is, for example, that felt by the Jew in an anti-Semitic environment, by the Negro in a segregationist society, by a businessman who has gone bankrupt in a capitalist system, or the illegitimate child surrounded by middle-class respectability.

But there are many lesser and more subtle forms of contempt, which slowly weigh down those on whom they fall, without exposing their flank to an active riposte. There is the mischievous little girl, bright and pretty, who teases her plain clumsy sister. Or the girl who pretends to be a little saint and so gets all the praise from her parents, and shames her more rumbustious sister. There is the big, tough boy who teases his weaker comrade because he cries instead of standing up for himself. There is the husband who lives with his wife almost as if she did not exist, except in their brief moments of sexual intimacy. She does not even know whether he is listening when she speaks, and when she insists he shrugs his shoulders as if she were incapable of saying anything sensible. There is the pity shown by charitable people towards those less fortunate than themselves. Their zeal is sincere, but it is humiliating to those who are the objects of their generosity – they never talk to their equals in the tone of voice they use towards them.

All this can change as a result of a deeper awareness. Consider, for instance, the astonishing change in the attitude of the Roman church towards us Christians of other denominations. Only a short while ago we still felt we were looked upon by the Roman Catholics as heretics and schismatics. All that was needed was a man filled with the Holy Spirit and with true humanity, such as Pope John XXIII, and everything has changed. We have passed quickly through the stage of being 'separated brethren', to find ourselves accepted now as true brothers. What a victory over ancient prejudice! May we Protestants be as quick to shed our own!

One point seems to me to be worthy of attention. However sudden and spectacular the event may seem, the way for it has in fact been prepared over a long period by numbers of Catholics who have been suffering because of the intransigence of their church towards us, and who have shown us their esteem and their fraternal friendship. It is thanks to them that the prophetic voice of John XXIII found such an echo in the church. In the same way a profound change in public opinion in regard to the aged is being prepared for now through the efforts of numerous doctors, psychologists, sociologists and thinkers. In writing this book I am joining my voice with theirs.

I have been able to quote this example because, as St Thomas

Aquinas says, grace does not suppress nature, so that it is permissible for us to study a religious event from a psychological point of view. Nevertheless, the action of the Holy Spirit is so manifest in this case that many of my readers will consider it a questionable example to take. We shall therefore return to non-religious examples. The attitude of society towards the mentally sick has undergone a radical change. For centuries they were the objects of real scorn. It is to the credit of modern psychiatry that it has put an end to this, beginning with Pinel, who removed the chains in which such patients were kept.

It has indeed been a long, slow task. The public, and even many doctors, listened only with a prejudiced ear to the voices that were raised in support of more humane treatment of mental cases. So ingrained was the prejudice that no one saw any sense in anything such patients said or did. Only gradually was it realized that it was much more senseless not to try to understand them. Today it is no longer true to say that they are an object of scorn. There does remain among the general public a certain reluctance to enter into communication with these people, who do not play the conventional social game. We address only vague and superficial remarks to them, in an attempt to avoid any real dialogue, because we do not know how to set about it.

Dr Paul Balvet of Lyons gives an excellent description of the recent development of psychiatry.[13] When he was a young doctor, he says, all teaching tended to suggest to the psychiatrist that there was a strict barrier between the two camps, that of the healthy, to which he belonged, and that of the sick. This was very reassuring for him. Dr Balvet goes on to refer to the crisis through which many psychiatrists have passed on discovering that the idea of this barrier is a mere prejudice, and that their own mental and emotional reactions are not so very different from those of their patients.

Despite the lingering prejudice against the mentally ill, it is fair to say that there has been a great change in the attitude of the public. This is even more striking in the case of neuroses, since Freud. Remember the derisive laughter that used to run through the audience at Salpêtrière mental hospital when the young Freud was a pupil there under Charcot. It was not that Charcot was lacking in charity towards his patients, but that as a scientist he looked for an explanation of his observations only in his own science and in his own theories, and more or less suggested to his patients the behaviour that he expected from them.

The young doctor Freud set himself to listening carefully for hour after hour to those people, to whom nobody else had ever really listened. For centuries not even those doctors of the soul, the churchmen, had listened to them anything but perfunctorily, being mainly concerned with giving them advice. If today the psychotherapist has in large measure taken the place of the minister of religion in helping people with psychological difficulties, if the most outstanding churchmen are coming to the medical schools to learn from their lecturers, that is because theology has in the past been a mass of prejudices.

Freud took these patients seriously; he tried to understand their strange dreams, the experiences they had undergone, the ideas they expressed, and all their imaginings, which until then had been simply dismissed either as perverse and wicked thoughts, or else as silly fantasies. The whole of modern psychology, notwithstanding the divergences between the various schools, has arisen out of the hundreds of hours Sigmund Freud spent listening seriously to what those patients said, thought and felt. They felt they were being taken seriously, and that, more than anything else, is what helps such people to grow and to liberate themselves. Both the sick and the healthy go to the psychotherapist in order to speak to a man who will really listen.

The development of the child

This brings me to another example which is more relevant to the question of the aged, as I should like to state it here. Paradoxical though it may seem, it concerns the attitude of society towards children! The analogy is rather surprising, and I do not expect all my readers to go along with me. But some, I hope, will understand: those who have been led by their own personal experience to think deeply about the meaning of love; to realize that it is not just a sentimental feeling or sexual attraction, but real acceptance of and respect for another person, for his otherness as a person in his own right.

It is only since Jean-Jacques Rousseau that the child has been taken seriously in this sense; more precisely, since his book *Émile*, which unleashed the irony of Voltaire, was severely condemned by

Archbishop de Beaumont, and was publicly burnt by order of the Geneva government, so contrary was this new attitude to the spirit of its time. That does not mean that people did not love children before then, but that they loved them in a different way. Of course people wanted what was best for children, but in accordance with what the adult thought was best, without listening to the child's point of view, without trying to understand him as he was, his feelings, his emotions, and his fantasies as he himself imagined them. The child was by definition ignorant of everything, and so had to be taught everything – knowledge as well as behaviour – and nothing was to be learnt from him.

The debate begun by Rousseau is far from being closed. Despite all the progress that has taken place in education, school is still a powerful machine for bending children to adults' views, and for rejecting those who cannot be bent. This argument lay behind the Nanterre and Sorbonne student revolts in 1968, in which the students were demanding more seminars and less *ex cathedra* lectures, more research in common and less of those monologues in which the professor holds forth and the only right his audience has is to listen in silence. Even today there are few parents who recognize their own ignorance and their mistakes with their children and who do not always claim to know better than their children what is good for them.

I have already mentioned my fellow-citizen Jean-Jacques Rousseau in my last book.[14] He was one of the spiritual fathers of the French Revolution and of the Declaration of Independence of the United States, because the cry that he uttered from his heart against tyranny overturned the world. He still remains the distant precursor of the modern movement for the liberation of the working class and of the peoples oppressed by colonialism. I come back to the subject now in order to underline the details of his experience which throw light on the problem of respect for others: of respect for the child in his day, and respect for the aged in our own day.

I often think of Rousseau because my wife and I have built for our old age a villa called 'The Grain of Wheat' in Troinex, on land that belonged to my grandfather, on the banks of a little river called the Drize. I picture Jean-Jacques Rousseau at the age of eleven, already in love with Nature and with botany, coming here often to walk among the trees and bushes on the banks of the Drize, where I myself used to dream dreams when I was a boy, and where my grandchildren come now. He lived not far away, in the same parish, in the neighbouring village of Bossey, which through the caprices of politics stands today on the other side of the frontier, in France.

Doubtless he was already brooding on his misfortunes. His mother had died when he was born. His only brother was dead. He had grown very close to his father, but had just been rudely separated from him, since the latter had had to flee from Geneva as a result of an unfortunate quarrel. Left alone in the world, Jean-Jacques had been placed in the care of the pastor at Bossey, M. Lambercier.

The pastor was perhaps a good man; Rousseau has very little to say on the subject. But he was weak, and it was his sister, Mlle Lambercier, who ruled the household. She did not care for the young lodger, a sentiment which the latter amply repaid. One day she had accused him of having broken her comb, which in fact the child had not touched. The pastor took his sister's side. He had refused to listen to the young Rousseau's protestations of his innocence, and had forced him to apologize. The incident had a profound effect on the little defenceless orphan.

Poor lad! I can imagine him sitting here on the river-bank where I now live, going over the whole affair in his heart. How hard life is! How wicked and unjust men are! They don't love me, he was thinking. Grown-ups stick together; they don't believe what a child says, even when the child is right and they are wrong. They don't even listen to him. Children are better than grown-ups! In fact Jean-Jacques made friends in Bossey with a boy of his own age. He had the wonderful experience of friendship: he found someone to whom he could tell everything, someone who would listen to him and believe him, someone who would not betray him, and whom he could trust!

M. Lambercier had planted a walnut tree, and a short distance away the two friends planted a willow. Then they secretly set to work on a great project: they constructed an underground irrigation channel to divert a little of the water that fed the walnut towards their willow-tree. It was by no means an easy task, but it was exciting to help each other to succeed. Imagine their glee when the water began to flow through the tunnel! Alas, their triumph was short-lived: when M. Lambercier discovered the secret channel he took a pick and demolished it, and scolded the boys severely.

And young Rousseau began to think. Children are better than grown-ups, and that is no doubt due to the fact that they are closer to Nature. They have not yet been perverted by civilization. Nature! The great consolation when one is disgusted with men. And Jean-Jacques strolled along the edge of the Drize, as he was to dream, in the evening of life, as a 'solitary stroller'. 'I walked quietly along,' he was to write, 'looking for some wild spot in the forest, some lonely place where nothing showed the hand of man and spoke of slavery and domination.'

You see how Rousseau's teaching was already being formulated in his mind as a child. It sprang from his own experience. You see, too, how I come back to the same idea that I referred to just now in writing of the sick who go to the psychotherapist: that they are looking for someone who will really listen to them, without prejudice. To be listened to with attention and respect, to be taken seriously by someone who tries to understand, is a vital need for every man, and it is much more unusual than is generally thought. Before Rousseau, children were loved, it is true, but they were not listened to. The whole of modern educational theory and child psychology has developed since people began to listen to children, to observe them, and to try to understand them instead of claiming to know everything about them already.

In Geneva at the beginning of this century, Dr Edouard Claparède and M. Pierre Bovet founded the Institute of Educational Sciences, an institution which has since been honoured as the scene of the researches of Jean Piaget and his school. As a matter of fact the first name the founders gave to it was 'Institut Rousseau', since their aim was to study the child on the basis of what the child himself says and feels, his own reactions and experiences. They realized that the child is not an empty sack that is to be filled with all the things that adults have learnt and the things they think, but a sack quite full of treasures already.

Looking at those treasures and studying them, discovering that the child's mind works very differently from that of the adult, asking the child himself to explain how he sees and feels things, in this way a true science of childhood was built up. This science was learnt from the child, just as Freud – and all psychologists after him – constructed a new science by listening to the sick. And just as the sick are healed through the very fact of people listening to them, and because they feel they are being understood, so at the

Institut Rousseau it was observed that the child grows and develops spontaneously if he is surrounded by an atmosphere of love and respect. Is it not a fact that what we really need today is an Institut Rousseau for the aged?

Personal contact

The analogy seems to me to be a good one. The discovery has been made that the child is not a miniature adult, that he has his own psychology, differing from that of the adult, and that it can be understood only by entering into personal contact and into dialogue with him. In the same way the aged person is not a shrunken, amputated, wrinkled and dried-up adult. He, too, has his peculiar psychology, his evolving personality which differs from that of the younger adult, and like the child he needs to feel that he is listened to, understood and loved, if he is to develop further. In the past, children have had no right to be heard; all they have been able to do has been to adapt themselves to the world of the adult. In the same way today the aged feel that they have been put on one side; their opinions are not asked for.

Perhaps this is because they are no longer producers, because they no longer participate in the consumer society. But children are not producers either. There was a time when they were appreciated for their services, when they used to begin work at a very tender age. Happily, social progress in our countries has put an end to this exploitation of children. It is to the credit of modern psychology that it has taught us to love children for nothing except themselves. I am sure you will know some retired people who beg a little love for themselves by rendering such services as they are able. Really to love the child or the aged person means loving him for what he is and not for what he does.

Really to love is to listen. It is not so long since in some circles it was the custom to forbid children to speak at table. The adults' conversation flowed around them, and they were unable to take part in it. The same thing still happens with old people. There are families in which both children and adults give noisy expression to their views, arguing and answering back over the heads of the old, who are given no opportunity to speak, because nobody bothers to think that they might have anything to say. They feel that they are looked upon as worn-out and of no further importance. Or else they are spoken to in a particular tone of voice, as used to be the case with the children, condescendingly, kindly, perhaps even affectionately, but in a way which indicates that no valid reply can be expected.

I have just read in a local paper, the Geneva *Messager social*, a well-written account of an interesting little scene in a teashop. A couple had kindly invited the wife's mother to have tea with them. The writer of the article, seated at the next table, was observing them. The husband and wife were in animated conversation with each other, but without ever addressing a single word to the old lady, except perhaps to say sweetly: 'Another cup of tea, mummy? Have another little piece of cake.' They were doing a kind act; they were bothering about their mother; they were taking her out with them. They seemed surprised that she remained passive, that she was not more effusive in her thanks. But doubtless a personal word would have meant more to her than fancy cakes.

Are there not many old people who can say to themselves, like Jean-Jacques Rousseau: 'These people do not love me'? Unfortunately, it is too true. I have been preparing this book, and studying the problems of retirement and old age, for the last three years, and I have come to the conclusion that there is one essential, profound, underlying problem, and it is that the old are unloved. They do not feel themselves to be loved, and too many people treat them with indifference and seek no contact with them. We have learnt to love children better and to take more interest in them. Now we must learn to love the old better.

Perhaps you protest at this – there are so many social services and societies that care for the old, and you are thinking that I am forgetting about them, or discounting their zeal. Not at all. But the trained social worker's visit cannot take the place of the sort of daily, ordinary, spontaneous, kindly homage that children receive from their smiling parents. First-class social service organizations can function impeccably, in rather the same way as a plane can land successfully when there is no visibility, guided by instruments alone.

Efficient medical care can function in that way, saving lives, and I do not under-estimate it, even when there is no direct communication, when valid decisions are taken on the strength of X-ray photographs and laboratory reports without any real contact between doctor and patient. Personal contact, personal love, consists in the looks and the words exchanged, the hands clasped. It also means giving the patient the chance to express his secret emotions, and explaining carefully to him what is being done for his welfare, because he is not a thing, but a person.

I think that our old people are far from having that warming, vivifying, health-giving love. I myself have love heaped upon me: in my family, among my patients, my colleagues and my friends. What I say is listened to, what I write is read. I am pressed to speak and write. It is very easy to stay young amidst so much affection and encouragement. But I am well aware that in this I enjoy a rare privilege. I think of the multitudes of retired people who hold aloof, who do know that people are concerned that they should have, as we say, decent living conditions, but who know that no personal interest is taken in them. Reading the reports of surveys made in old folks' homes, I was struck by the numbers of inmates who never, or only very rarely, receive visits from family or friends.

In our modern world, it is youth which is all the vogue. Oh! I am not demanding that less attention should be paid to the young. I have just been using as an argument the welcome change in the attitude of society towards young people, the attention and under-standing that are now directed towards them. With all my heart I call for a similar change in attitude towards the old. Not only in the interest of the old, for them to feel that they are loved, but in the interest of society as a whole, so that it may grow still more in love. Love is peculiar in that the more one gives, the more one has to give. The young will not be less loved when the old are loved more – quite the contrary.

To the example of the young and that of the old there should be added a third which is too well known for me to need to spend a long time upon it. I refer to the improvement in the position of women. It was not only the right to vote that the feminist move-ment claimed for women, nor their right to election, nor the right to study and to entry into all professional and public walks of life. It was their right to recognition as persons, as equal partners in the conjugal and social dialogue. Even in the churches, women were but the servants of men. 'Women were always on their knees,' a woman now elected chairman of her church council remarked to me recently.

Young and old

So for centuries, apart from a few periods of matriarchy or geron-
tocracy, the only people taken seriously have been the adult males.
The most recent change has been the improvement in the position
of women. Since Rousseau, the true value of the child has been
discovered. That of the aged remains the least well understood.
Nevertheless, there are signs of greater awareness in this direction
already. They are to be seen not only in the social services directed
towards the needs of the old, of which I was speaking just now.
There are signs of a profound change in the public attitude. There
is an awakened sensitivity to the lot of the aged. Articles appear
frequently in newspapers, and I am sent large numbers of them by
kind friends. These articles are full of wise counsel for old people,
but they are also directed at the awakening of public sympathy
and interest.

There is one very widespread notion, namely that the old used
once to be had in honour, whereas they are now despised. That is
mere legend! Contempt for the old does not date from modern
times! A study as well documented as that of Simone de Beauvoir[15]
clears away all illusion in this respect. The author reveals the
cruelty with which the aged could be treated in olden times. According to her, it seems that this brutality reached its culmination in
the seventeenth and eighteenth centuries, and that it took place
especially among the peasantry. Contempt for the old, therefore,
does not necessarily follow upon the establishment of industrial
civilization and the growth of concentrated urban populations. We
must be fair! It is only quite recently that any interest has been
taken in the fate of the old.

The serious factor in our day is the increase in the numbers of
the old, which creates, in Ménie Grégoire's apt phase,[16] 'a sort of
racial problem'. It was possible to be hard on a few isolated individuals. But when they became a multitude, the very foundations
of society are called in question. A wise remark made by Michel
Philibert throws light on the problem: 'What makes growing old
socially, economically and politically important is not the multiplication of the number of old people, but the fact that this
multiplication is taking place in a society which looks upon the
devaluation of the old as being a law of nature, instead of seeing
it as a feature of its own culture.'[17]

Michel Philibert brings home to us the importance of the problem of the old. He is a sort of witness for the prosecution in the trial of our civilization. He has just become editor of the *Revue française de la Gérontologie*, to which he has given fresh impetus. In his book *L'échelle des âges*, he sets the problem of the aged within a philosophical theme which has as its object man and his continual growth. Thus he calls in question at one and the same time both our conception of man and our present-day society and its culture. That 'feature of its own culture' which he denounced in the passage I quoted above, is what I have described as a prejudice, the absurd idea that the old are good for nothing. Taking his stand on the work of Alfred Sauvy,[18] he demonstrates the stupidity of our position: at the very time when the number of old people is increasing – and they are much more healthy and alert than they used to be – instead of having adequate use made of their services, they are thrust into idleness, while the age of retirement is lowered, and in this way the disproportion is increased between the inactive and the active fractions of the population. They are thrust not only into idleness but also into solitude, and the demoralization of alienation and contempt. For this society, with its conventionality and anonymity, is also a feature of our culture; personal relationships give way to mass relationships.

Perhaps those who understand this best today are the young, who criticize their elders because they feel that they themselves are being criticized. What is their essential complaint? That is not yet altogether clear. But it seems that they accuse their elders of presenting them with a civilization which, though rich in technical resources, is poor in tenderness and in real contact between people. A friend who knows them well said to me yesterday: 'They feel intensely the lack of love in our modern world.'

So, if one of them, despite his age and the title of this book, which must seem not very attractive to him, should chance to read it, I could say this to him: go and talk to these old people, and listen to what they have to say. Overcome the prejudice that they are not 'with it', that they have nothing interesting to say to you. You will be in for some surprises. You will discover them. You have conflicts with your elders, with the adults who lord it over our society, and who defend it because it is 'their thing'. But the aged are beyond such conflicts. Like you, they feel the lack of love which you complain of; they are the victims of it, just as you are.

Just after the Sorbonne disturbances of May 1968, I was visited by a very old Parisian lady who came from a very formal and traditional family background, the sort of person who carries an air of 'old France' about her. You might well have expected her roundly to condemn the rebellious students who had been turning Paris upside-down. Not a bit of it! She had taken their side with an extraordinary enthusiasm. She even made to me a whispered remark which would have made their leaders smile: 'It seemed to me,' she said, 'to be the work of the Holy Spirit!' She had talked it all over with her granddaughter, who had exclaimed: 'How young you are, grannie!'

Yes, you young people may well get some surprises if you make contact with the old, and enter into real dialogue with them. You may find that a mysterious bond of sympathy is established between them and you, over the heads of the adults who, for their part, identify themselves much more readily with the society which you are challenging. The old are more able to see things in perspective, and will understand better than younger adults the questions which you are raising. They will no doubt remember better than your parents do, caught up as they are in the rush of life, that they themselves used to ask the same questions when they were your age.

And then, adults do not have much time for loving, they are so busy fulfilling their obligations, making a livelihood and earning money. They sincerely think that all this great effort is being made for your sake, and they are astonished if now you refuse their money and tell them that you would have much preferred them to give you more of their time and their love. Once upon a time they found time and love for you, when you were little; they were only at the beginning of their careers; and then, you were so sweet, so docile and easy to love. But now you are adolescents who behave in ways they do not approve of; and so their sense of responsibility for you weighs heavily upon them, and they find it harder to love you. The grandparents, on the other hand, are relieved of the responsibility of your upbringing.

Grandparents and grandchildren

I am well aware, of course, that what I have said does not apply to all grandparents. There are some who do not abdicate, who continue to act as if they were experts in the bringing up of child-

ren, and continually criticize their dress and their behaviour. But
such old people are in fact suffering from a real psychological
disease. It is very difficult to cure, because it really means that they
are refusing to grow old, refusing to hand over, to accept that they
no longer have their former almighty position. They do not only
criticize the young; they criticize everybody, every change in
customs, and the whole set-up of society. And when they declare
their grandchildren to be badly brought up, it is really the parents
of the grandchildren that they are criticizing, for having brought
them up so badly!

A harmonious intimacy between grandparents and grandchildren
can very often be an incomparably precious blessing for both. For a
retired person there are few activities more wonderful than taking
an interest in his grandchildren: going for a walk with one of them,
teaching him to observe Nature and life; making a kite or an aero-
plane with another, and trying it out; or else putting together a
stamp collection. And what an event for the child – to be given
such a personal welcome, to be taken aside, away from his brothers
and sisters, and to be listened to and understood.

There is plenty of evidence of the truth of this. I questioned an
old professor of medicine about his experience since his retirement.[19] I could publish his reply at length, because it was a real
lecture, well-ordered and complete, such as only an experienced
lecturer could give. He speaks, of course, of the difficulties, the
sudden deprivation of work, the deaths of friends, failing health.
But he also speaks of the joys, chief of which come from the family:
'The development of grown-up children is a great experience, and
grandchildren are a very special gift and a task.' Father Leclercq
also insists on this point: 'The old need the young as much as
children need the old.'[20] And Dr Paul Miraillet: 'The answers to all
the questionnaires underline the importance of grandchildren in the
lives of the aged.' In the same conference, in Lyon, Dr André Berge
gave an interesting talk on the psychological role of grandparents.
He stressed, for instance, that there are times when a child 'may
need to have "only child" treatment, and this he can be given if
there are grandparents available'.[21] A little further on he speaks
of the advantage to the grandparents of having known one of the
two parents 'when he was little'. This 'makes it possible for them
to talk about him in a way that brings him closer, and consequently
makes him an easier model to imitate'.

Among the life-stories and the memories of childhood that I have listened to throughout my career as a doctor, there have been numerous moving confidences that illustrate this theme. My own wife treasures a glowing picture of her grandmother. To be like her, to be for me what her grandmother was for her husband, has been her life-long ideal. My wife loved nature and the open air; she preferred the garden to school, whereas her parents were proud of the scholastic success of her less imaginative sister. And so her grandmother used to take her out to help in the garden; and gardening is still one of her greatest pleasures.

The main thing was that she felt that she was understood. And indeed she was, by her grandmother. Later on, when we became engaged and I was introduced to her mother, the latter said to me, with touching humility: 'I hope you will understand my daughter, because I never have.' Happily that was to come later, when my mother-in-law was herself aged, and when she had rid herself of the rigid concepts of duty and of social conformity which had long dominated her outlook. It is true that grandparents can often understand their grandchildren better than the parents do, and give them the acceptance they need in order to grow up.

The age of the patriarch is past. Because of changes in habits, and the small size of dwellings, it is becoming a rarity for grandparents to be living with their grown-up children. Journeys can afford valuable opportunities for re-establishing contact. In the summer of 1969 we took Gilles, our oldest grandson, with us to the International Congress of Christian Physicians which took place in Oslo. He enjoyed the trip, but we enjoyed it much more. For him it was an important step in his discovery of the world. He met doctors from many different countries, and their wives and children, all of whom welcomed him warmly. For us the great thing was to be present and to share with him in this stage of his development. And then for the first time in his life he heard me giving lectures, and recounting events in my life of which he was unaware.[22]

Recently we were in France, in Saint-Etienne, attending a teach-in on the problems of the aged. Professor Philibert had just returned from America. He told us that there exist now in the United States organizations of retired people to which parents can apply when they need baby-sitters. That is a good idea: I hope it will develop in America and spread to Europe. It is not just a matter of making sure the children are looked after and not left to themselves. It is much more a matter of making good the absence of grandparents from modern homes, of restoring to children some contact with old people, which is useful in their development. It is a contact which is perfectly natural, and which does not replace that which they have with their parents, their teachers, and with other young adults.

But for retired people it is much more important. It is a less artificial occupation than others, it is the exercise of a natural function of which they have been deprived, it is a form of social reintegration, a breach made in the progressive segregation which is imposed upon them by the way we organize our modern society. The fact is that all the different age-groups need each other. The development of each is impeded if contact is not kept alive with all. Old people need adolescents as well as children; they need the love of both.

Make contact with the old!

Teenagers are sometimes better able than adults to overcome the distrust behind which some old people barricade themselves. Yesterday I gave a short talk on the problems of old age as an introduction to a discussion in the Ladies' Group of the parish of Eaux-Vives, in Geneva. Pastor Mobbs then told a story. There was in the parish, he said, a lonely old man whose very appropriate name was Solitude. He unsociably kept his door closed against all visitors, including his neighbours and, especially, the pastor. He was the typical recluse, who sets up in himself, in his own heart, an impassable wall. Such people never set foot in the old-folks' clubs which happily are increasing in number nowadays.

At Christmas time the parish distributes small gifts to all lonely people. But who could take M. Solitude's gift to him, and be sure of being admitted? Then the pastor had the bright idea of sending three quite young girls. 'What a surprise!' exclaimed the old man on the doorstep. 'What have I done to deserve such a charming visit? Come in, then, Mesdemoiselles!' He opened his present, and conversation soon got going. He had met Napoleon III, which seemed fantastic to the teenage girls. And he told them things about him which do not appear in history books! I was shown a fine projection screen which M. Solitude had left to the parish in his will, and the pastor who conducted his funeral service chose that beautiful text from the prophet Isaiah: 'The solitary place shall be glad for them' (Isa. 35.1).

This is why I was saying just now: Go and talk to the old! You know so little about them now! So, go and discover them. You young people have a much better idea than your parents of what personal contact means. You want to reject all that is merely convention in human relationships. You are not going to be content like the rest of us with an empty phrase: 'Good-morning, old man! Your rheumatics all right?' He would give you the same answer as he gives to everybody: 'Well, one manages.' Neither of you would really have said anything. It is this social game which you are no longer content to play.

Nevertheless, from reading a book by Dr Berne,[23] I have realized that these stereotyped phrases have more value than we suppose. This author sees them as mutual 'caresses', caresses which adults can exchange without inconvenience, and which they need in order to live, though they may not fully realize this. Simply because it does involve social interplay, that dialogue, however rudimentary, signifies that each recognizes the other as a social partner. However, it does not go very far! I am with you when you demand a less dry, less cold world, a world in which there is more love; a world in which people of all ages and conditions really meet each other, no longer like personages acting a conventional part, but as persons building personal relationships and engaging in real dialogue.

So you will make contact with the old, but you will not talk to them in the usual offhand tone that most people use – bright, perhaps, but devoid of any real personal commitment. You will talk to them of the things you really care about, as you do to your friends. You may be met at first by a moment of astonished silence: They are so unused to being spoken to like that. They had never learnt the habit even when they were still in active life – they were so conventional, so thoroughly imbued with bourgeois reserve. Now old age has made their isolation far worse. Listen to them talking amongst themselves: their speech is so impersonal, using the same set phrases over and over again, as if it had all been recorded on tape.

But behind the unchanging facade there is a mind – a mind which lives, a mind which suffers and feels pleasure, a mind which thinks and feels. It is a mind fashioned by the multitudinous experiences of a long life, its successes and failures, its joys and disappointments. That is something which cannot be manufactured, it cannot be invented, it cannot be replaced. It is unique, because it is the accumulated experience of a unique life. They hide this unique mind of theirs because they feel that no one is interested in it, because they think that what they could say about their lives is of no interest to anyone, because they do not feel themselves to be loved.

But maybe you will work a miracle of love if you persevere, if you talk to them in a way that is really personal, if you engage in the dialogue with your most intimate thoughts on life. It is then that you will discover, I think, that they are better qualified to enter into this sort of dialogue than people in the prime of life. The latter are determined, much more than the old, by the social system, which instils its traditional slogans into them – 'It is work which gives life its meaning.' The old will not say that to you. It is just because they are able to see things in better perspective that they have to make that very revision of values which you young people demand so passionately.

And then, listen to them; listen to them with attention and love. People say that they just like to talk stupidly about themselves; but it is not true. With age the mirage of fine theories becomes blurred. What remains is the reality that has been lived. And do not you young people say that you want to have nothing more to do with fancy artificial doctrines, that it is authentic life that you are looking for? Then listen to these old people in order to learn what life is, from the mouths of those who have lived it fully.

If an old man sees that you are really interested in his personal life, you will see a wonderful transformation take place in him. His eyes that seemed dull will light up with a new fire; his face will come alive with unexpected emotion. He felt that he had been thrown on the scrap-heap, and all at once he comes to life again, becomes a person once more. Just like the child, the old man needs to be spoken to and listened to in order to become a person, to become aware of himself, to live and grow. You will have brought about something that no social service can ever do of itself: you will have promoted him to the rank of person.

Respect for the person

And you, adolescents of today, will have done for the old something that has been done for you. You are, in fact, the ones most recently promoted to that rank. You have only recently won your right to recognition as persons. I have already described the evolution of public opinion in regard to children since Rousseau. More impressive still is the transformation that has taken place over the last half-century, and which has given you a recognized place in society – a place of honour, too: you are princes in our modern world.

I do not say that we were despised as adolescents when we were your age. But we hardly counted at all. We were not an age-group. We were no longer children, and we were not yet adults. We were no longer young enough to be treated as children, and yet we were not old enough to be treated by adults as equals. We were like people waiting awkwardly in an antechamber for an important interview. Which is as much as to say that we were not looked upon as fully alive.

You have now won your place as a recognized age-group. You have achieved your revolution. It is that revolution that I now demand for the old in their turn. Throughout all my books I have maintained this idea of a civilization of the person, that all those human beings who have in the past been treated as things should be recognized as persons: the weak, the sick, the infirm, workers, children, adolescents, and now the old. In our international conferences on the medicine of the person we have constantly come back to the same problem, that of the achievement of a truly personal relationship between doctor and patient. This, however, is merely a particular instance of something which should be characteristic of a civilization of the person – a bond that is no longer conventional, a personal bond linking all men together: linking black, yellow, and white, linking men and women, teachers and students, young and old, manual workers and intellectuals.

You young people have been able to get from your parents the money without which no one is given any consideration in this world. In this way you have made a breach in the wall of money. It was by means of money that your parents held you in subjection like little children. They could even stop you from marrying in accordance with our own inclination before you were earning yourselves. 'He who pays the piper calls the tune.' In order to pay, one has to earn. This principle has reigned supreme in our society until quite recently. It conferred the right of command upon adults old enough to produce and earn. The rest, the young and the old, only had to obey. You even spend thoughtlessly, at random, in order to savour your freedom. Seeing your parents' reactions to your conduct, one realizes how difficult it is for them to accept the change that has taken place.

Thus it is not just a matter of penny-pieces. The fact is that you have won recognition as persons. You have acquired the right to demand explanations from those who give you orders before you obey them. You have won your place. But it seems to me that it is still too much a place apart. You live among yourselves, in bunches, sticking all together. You are a society within society, rather like a foreign body. You have your own coffee-bars into which adults scarcely dare venture, much less old people. In order to safeguard your new-found autonomy you draw away from your parents, but that shuts you up within yourselves. You have obtained your personal promotion, but you have not put an end to that social segregation which still partitions off our society into age-groups that are strangers to one another.

The notion of the person has two interdependent faces like the two sides of a medal. On the one side there is the assertion of the irreducible originality of the individual personality, which imposes respect; and on the other side there is the assertion that man is not man if he is isolated, but only in relationship with others, with the world, and with God. You want authentic life, and you cannot discover life if you only know a small fragment of it, if you associate only with young people of your own age. You are like people who claim to have looked over a house when really they have only looked round one room and have not been in the others at all. I invite you to be more inquisitive. How can you discover what life is, and its meaning, if you do not consider it in all its diversity, in all its length and breadth? In his inaugural lecture to the French Academy, Paul Morand exclaimed: 'These adolescents, I should like to cherish them, but I feel weak before them. I do not know where to bestow an affection which they reject. . . . They ask us what future is there for youth. How are we to tell them that the future of youth is old age?'[24]

Life is movement, evolution, progression and not stagnation; it can be comprehended only in its incessant becoming, in its total continuity. You need a sense of history if you are to make sense of life. If you look only at the point where you are, you will see neither where you came from nor where you are going.

One of the dimensions of your consciousness as a living being is missing if you do not enter into relationship with all age-groups, and more particularly with those who are nearing the end of their lives. If, as young people, you despise the old, you are preparing yourselves to be despised when you are old.

Real contact with all

You are the same age as the Buddha when he discovered the fact of human suffering, which his father had tried to hide from him. Simone de Beauvoir begins her latest book with the following anecdote (it is a book whose dynamism ought to please you: she aims, she says, to 'break the conspiracy of silence' which still surrounds old age in our society and prevents us from looking it in the face):

> When the Buddha was still Prince Siddharta, shut up by his father inside a magnificent palace, he slipped out of it on several occasions, and rode about the countryside in a carriage. On the first occasion he met a man who was infirm, toothless, wrinkled, white-haired, and bent, leaning on a stick, muttering and shaking. He was astonished, and the coachman explained to him what an old man was. 'How sad it is,' exclaimed the prince, 'that weak and ignorant beings, drunk with the pride of youth, do not see old age! Let us go quickly back home. What good is there in games and pleasures since I am the future abode of old age!'

You dream of revolution. The young Buddha brought about a revolution that is far from ended: the abolition of all segregation among men. I invite you to engage with all your youthful ardour in this great enterprise, the founding of a more humane society. It is possibly paradoxical of me to address the young when I am writing a book on old age. But I believe they will understand me better than their elders. Think of the work of Gandhi, who with fine courage laboured not only to liberate his country from foreign domination, but also to overcome the age-old prejudices which within that country of his set up impenetrable barriers between the castes. He paid for that with his life.

Less than forty years ago my wife and I were in England for a religious meeting. In our traditionally democratic Swiss manner, we did not hesitate to enter into conversation with the maids responsible for the room service in the college where we were staying.

Well! We were severely reprimanded by an English friend: 'That is not done here,' he said, coldly. It was a relic of the Victorian era and of an imperial glory for which Britain has paid dearly since then.

Among the ancients, in the time of Æsop, there was much more familiarity between the slave and his master than there often is today between those who give orders and those who obey. Since Abraham Lincoln, slavery has been abolished. Since the French and Russian revolutions the claim for equality of rights has been made all over the world, though it has been satisfied only in part. Our era ought now to add a further claim, which goes much further: the claim for true contact among all men, of all races, of all conditions, of all cultures and also of all ages.

Contact between people of different ages used to be possible in the street, because people walked about peacefully on foot. They were able to greet each other, and stop for a chat. An old man would know who the child was he met, and he would chat to him about his parents whom he used to know well when they were little. He would talk of the things he remembered, and so the child became aware of a living link between the past and the present. Nowadays the traffic makes it impossible for the old as well as the young to stroll in the street. We cram into buses or the underground, in solid, silent masses, in which the promiscuity of our bodies is equalled only by the solitude of our spirits. The old are not there, and the children are stifled.

The work of the artisan also lent itself to human contact. I have already spoken of the hours I spent in the blacksmith's shop in Troinex. But there is no longer room in the modern factory for contemplative, unoccupied visitors. In the deep country one can still see, around the craftsman at his task, a group of onlookers of all ages. The old men identify themselves with him, give their advice, and enter into endless discussions: they still feel themselves to have a part in life. The children can learn there lots of things that are not taught in school. The group is there, like the chorus in a Greek tragedy, whose role was no less important than that of the main actors.

Contact between generations could also be made quite naturally within the family, because the grandparents lived on in the home of a married son or daughter. One of my father's poems used to be popular in Geneva. The children used to recite it at Christmas, as was the custom of the time then. It was entitled 'Grandfather's Corner':[25]

> This corner by the fire, I remember, is where
> My grandfather loved to sit in his old armchair.
> With his feet on the fender, he would read all day,
> Then, still in his corner, nod the evening away.
> I can see him there still . . .
> He held open heart for all. And clear on his brow
> Tranquillity was written, goodness in his eyes.
> When a smile touched his lips, I well remember how
> It seemed that there shone a ray of light from the skies.
> And then, he was so good to me! . . .

Elsewhere,[26] he recalled his grandmother, and the stories she used to tell – legends, fairy-tales, and Bible-stories which passed on from one generation to another the great verities of life, at the same time expressing its continuity and its meaning.

It is not possible, nor indeed would it be desirable, to go back to the patriarchal family system. The evolution of customs is irreversible. We must look to the future, not the past, for the new concepts that will provide the solution we need. In one way or another it is incumbent upon us to reintegrate the old into our society and recognize that they have a part to play in it. This is especially important now that the age of retirement is being lowered, and the health of the old is better, so that they are removed from their daily work some twenty or more years before they are reduced to spending all day in an armchair by the fire – which also is becoming rare.

In our society the old have no longer any part to play. It is terrible for them to feel themselves discarded. But it is also bad for the younger members of society, who are thus deprived of an influence which is indispensable to their own development. It is unfortunate for the whole body of society to have as it were one of its members amputated. Left without the counter-balance provided by the old, society is impelled into the frenzied whirl of youth. Everyone is in a rush, everything is urgent, and no one has time to think about the overall problems. Until the day comes when suddenly these feverish toilers stumble into void. The old must be given a valid place once again in our world.

III

THE CONDITION OF THE OLD

My privileges

In the first part of this book we saw how much the fate of the old depends on themselves, on the way in which they have lived their whole lives right up to the threshold of old age. In the second part we have seen how much it is bound up also with the moral climate of society, with the acceptance and love that they find or do not find there. It is my task now, in this third part, to study the role played by the particular circumstances in which the old are placed. According to whether these personal circumstances are favourable or not, their fate is radically different. As Henri Bour writes, 'men are very unequal as they face old age'.

There are some old people who are happy, and others who are so unhappy that they die of it. In this respect, among men of my age, I am one of the most highly privileged. For three or four years I have been preparing this book by reading works and surveys on the destiny of retired people and the aged. I soon realized that an inventory of the difficulties which most of them have to contend with was making me more aware, by way of contrast, of the nature of my own privileges.

Thus, to describe the troubles of my underprivileged contemporaries amounts to confessing the favours I enjoy. Generally speaking, people carefully avoid talking about their privileges. They feel that it is in bad taste, even offensive, to do so in front of those who are deprived of them. So a rich man is careful not to talk about the advantages of wealth in front of those who do not enjoy the same affluence. I, who am what you might call one of the spoilt children of life, often experience the same feeling of unease. It embarrasses me, for instance, to talk about my happy marriage in front of a woman who has just told me how she suffers from being a spinster, or in front of a man who is deeply disappointed with his marriage.

But sometimes, instead of hiding it, I admit my unease, as if to exorcize it by being frank about it. Now, I have noticed that those who suffer from such frustrations, far from being offended by my confession, feel comforted instead. They are less unhappy as a result of meeting happiness, of being assured that happiness exists. Basically, they are well aware of my privileges. What hurts them is that privileged people so rarely express their thankfulness, that they seem so ungrateful. To speak of the advantages I enjoy is in fact to recognize them and to express my gratitude. That is what I want to do now, and in so doing I can turn this book into a testimony of gratitude.

In the first place my publishers have asked me to write it because they thought that at my age I could speak, not in the third person plural of 'retired people', but in the first person singular of what I myself am experiencing. Now, at seventy-three, I am indeed at an age when people are retired, but my circumstances are not those of retirement. I am not retired. I am not even in semi-retirement, as I sometimes call it for want of a better expression. My age actually gives me an extra privilege: especially since I have been seriously ill, it confers upon me the right to turn down patients who ask to consult me. I have given up particularly those whose condition requires prolonged treatment and frequent consultations.

I have never liked being hustled, over-loaded, hurried. That is why as a young doctor I preferred night-time visits, when there was plenty of time available. That is also why my present mode of life is a comfort. But I can still take a few patients, especially those I have looked after for a long time, and become attached to. One single person opening his heart to me with that total frankness that is invited by the intimate, secret, and welcoming atmosphere of the doctor's consulting-room, is sufficient to give me the feeling of being still hard at work.

We doctors enjoy the quite rare privilege of being able to prolong our professional activity indefinitely, progressively reducing it in accordance with our wishes. The same is true of a few other professions – artists and writers, for example, and small shopkeepers, or big businessmen, whom their colleagues often would like to see retire, and taxi-drivers, because the old ones have less accidents than the younger ones. For some twenty years I have looked after an old colleague of whom I was very fond. The greatest service I ever rendered him was to persuade him to take up consultations again, despite his infirmities, because that was the best form of therapy for him, and also a benefit to his patients, who profited from his great experience. He was still at work up to a few days before his death, when he was over ninety years of age.

It is a great privilege to be in a position to slow down gradually instead of having to give up one's work abruptly. However, it does have its difficulties. In the first place, there is the question of motivation. Does not this hanging on to work express a refusal to grow old, a refusal to give up a flattering role, a need to cling to the past instead of growing towards the future? And then, is the slowing down justified? Or is it just being lazy and using one's age as an excuse? I have plenty of scruples about it, because it suits me very well.

And then, it has always been hard for me to refuse a request for my services, to refuse to see a patient or give a lecture. Now I feel I have some excuse, because my age gives me a valid reason. A few years ago a serious illness brought me up short in the midst of my work. After I had recovered, my doctor urged me to learn my lesson from the event, and not to let myself be drawn back into a life of such intense activity as before. It was a chance to ease off the pace of my work, a thing which so many people – especially doctors – do not manage to do in time.

But it was not easy. I had to give up my patients whom I particularly wanted to keep on, because they needed more intense care than I would henceforth be able to afford them, but for that very reason they were the ones who would feel my desertion of them most acutely. I found that very hard, because I have always set store by loyalty. It is a principle I have taken some pride in. Naturally the calls that must be refused became more numerous and more pressing. I sometimes find myself giving way, wrongly, to those who are most insistent. And what do the ones who accept my refusal think? Accepting one and refusing another smacks of arbitrary favouritism. And the lectures: I have just agreed to talk to a ladies' circle who timidly apologized for asking me because they thought I was very busy.

No, I am not so busy, and that is the privilege of my age. The more free time one has, however, the more difficult it is to organize it properly. My friends say the same. Dr Théo Bovet has written a delightful little book entitled *The Art of Finding Time*.[1] Yet he told me recently that all his working life he had looked forward to retirement as a time when he would have leisure to read and write more. In fact he has less time, because when one is retired there are all sorts of little tasks to do which one was excused when one was working. It is rather like the unmarried woman having to perform for the whole family services which are not expected of her married sister.

Professor Karlfried von Dürckheim[2] is about the same age as I. Being opposed to Hitler, he left Germany when the Nazis came to power, and spent the whole period of the Third Reich in Japan. There he learnt something of the wisdom of the Orient, and understood the error of our intense activism in the West. On returning to Germany, therefore, in order to escape from the crush of university and urban life he went to live in a mountain chalet in the Black Forest. But this chalet soon turned out to be too big, and it was invaded by too many people who wanted to meet a hermit. He had to build himself another tiny one, hidden in the woods.

He, too, has told me how difficult it is to organize one's time if one wants to avoid being worried. Doubtless it is still more difficult for him than it is for me, because he is a widower. My wife is a great help to me in this respect. And yet I make a lot of mistakes which make me feel that I am life's victim rather than its master. Sometimes a dream may warn me of this, or an inspiration received in a moment of prayer. I decided some time ago, therefore, to keep three days free of appointments each week, and now I keep one week out of two free. There are exceptions, of course, and difficulties arise. In reality, the proper programming of one's time and one's various activities is a problem that nobody ever solves.

Easing retirement regulations

At all events, the rules imposed at present on the majority of wage-earners are deplorable, involving a fixed age limit, on reaching which a person is put into complete retirement all at once. This must obviously be emphasized here. At the seminars organized by the Swiss Societies of Gerontology and of Preventive Medicine, in Lausanne, Professor Eric Martin of Geneva put it very well: 'Life is continuity; to thrust into inactivity at sixty to sixty-five or even seventy years of age a man who until then has been completely active, to remove all responsibility from him overnight, is a mistake on the psychological and medical level, and wasteful on the economic level.'[3] It is unnecessary to quote further examples. All the writers on the subject, Dr André Gros,[4] Jean-Marie Arnion,[5] Suzanne Meyer,[6] Roger Mehl,[7] Mlle Magnin[8] and many others, protest against the brutality of these regulations. It is not surprising that they bring on a serious crisis in large numbers of their victims, which in turn results in premature ageing, as M. Menschen, of Stockholm, in particular, pointed out at the Gerontological Congress in Copenhagen, in 1963.

'With his work,' writes Michel Philibert, 'the subject loses not only the content and framework of his daily life, but one of the mainstays of his personal identity and of his self-esteem, the principal – sometimes the only – source of his relationships with others (colleagues, clients, superiors, subordinates, rivals, competitors . . .), his livelihood and one of the guarantees of his independence. That is too much all at once.'[9]

Dorothy Wedderburn calls for the abolition of the rules which in some countries forbid retired people to work.[10] According to this expert, in Great Britain 30% of those who retire do so against their wishes. According to Thomae, 72.6% of men and 67.5% of women aged from sixty-six to seventy-two would like to continue working.[11] Paul Miraillet quotes a survey conducted by the British Ministry of Pensions which puts at 60% the workers who would like to go on working after retiring age. He describes the many psychological consequences of enforced retirement, and the family conflicts which result. Denmark has put back the age of retirement from sixty to sixty-five, and then to sixty-seven. The 'functional age' ought to be determined. At least the regulations ought to be made more flexible, as Daric proposes.[12] This is not impossible, since it is already done in Sweden.

Moreover, 'the proportion of aged persons who continue working is much greater than is generally supposed: 70% of men are still at work at sixty-five; 60% at seventy, and more than 45% at seventy-five' (J.-M. Arnion). According to Mrs Wedderburn, two-thirds of professional and managerial workers continue after the age of sixty-five. Studies carried out in Britain and the USA have revealed 'unsuspected aptitudes on the part of aged workers. Their slower rhythm of work is compensated for by its better quality.'

It is often advocated, on the other hand, that the age of retirement should be lowered. This is the general tendency among trades unions. One may wonder whether this is a blind perseverance in the efforts they have had to make up till now to obtain a proper reduction in the age of retirement. At what point must the movement be halted? That ought to depend on the category of worker in question. French National Railways have more people retired than active workers on their pay-roll.[13] One survey has established that 82.5% of men wish to retire at sixty.[14] The Mosaic law fixed the retirement age for Levites at fifty, and it does not appear that their work was particularly arduous (Num. 8.25).

One thing that might justify a lower retiring age is that the younger a man is, the better able he is to adapt to a change in his life and to undertake new activities. We saw this very clearly in surveying leisure occupations. It would therefore be necessary to combine lowering of the age with a vast programme to initiate these younger retired people either into valid leisure occupations or into new and less demanding jobs. The contradiction between the idea of retarding the age of retirement and that of advancing it is more apparent than real, since the most important thing is to institute a transitional stage either during the final years of work or in the first few years of retirement.

You will remember my friend the psychiatrist who is preparing himself for retirement by taking more frequent and longer holidays. In our Geneva Social Studies Commission, a social worker, Mlle Combe, suggested that discussions should take place with employers with a view to the institution of supplementary holidays during the last two or three years before retirement. But in this case, naturally, some attention would have to be given to the question of what the workers would do with these supplementary holidays. They ought not to be looked upon as ordinary holidays, but rather as special leave, granted so that the employee could follow courses in preparation for retirement, courses in leisure activities or in retraining.

With similar ends in view suggestions have been made 'in particular professions and jobs, for reduced hours of work, and part-time working' (Suzanne Meyer). Several sociologists, among them André Gros and Paul Miraillet, have advocated measures of this sort. Employment bureaux dealing in temporary posts are increasing in numbers, and meeting with considerable success. They are especially designed to provide temporary replacements on supply, but they are helping to accustom the public to the idea of part-time work. Forward-looking firms are more and more coming round to the idea of using permanent part-timers.

Many, however, are still hesitant over the employment of part-time workers. When I was in general practice, I often used to suggest that a patient should go back to work very soon, but beginning with a minimal time-schedule, knowing as I did how much it can assist the recovery of a patient who is convalescing after an illness or an accident. However, I often come up against resistance on the part of the employer: 'Get him quite better. We'll have him back when he can do full-time work. I wouldn't know what to do with a semi-invalid!'

This rigid administrative attitude must be overcome if we want a more humane society. This is the mentality that insists on a fixed retirement date, with no period of transition. 'Retirement ought to be optional,' writes Professor Schneider.[15] Dr Jean-Pierre Baujat[16] also advocates this idea: 'Everyone would take his retirement when he wanted to.' That would be a real easing of retirement. It would be a way of extending to all the privilege enjoyed by doctors. Especially if one also were to combine it with the possibility of a progressive reduction in working-hours, so that other activities could be begun in time.

This is what I did in starting to write, though I did not think at the time that it might turn into a retirement occupation. In this respect, I am not retired, since I am writing this book. Jouhandeau, who is a writer by profession, makes the same observation in his fine book in praise of old age: 'If you were an old man,' he says to himself, 'you would no longer be writing.'[17] As I read it, I was on the look-out for some indication that would tell me whether the author was older or younger than I. We are always comparing ourselves with other people, and our experiences with theirs. But I myself, as I go on writing, also keep an eye on myself to see if I am still as alert and lively as I used to be.

And I imagine that my readers will be observing me as well, even if it is with kindly intentions, to see if this book shows signs that I am growing old. Thus society is a mirror in which we look to see the wrinkles appearing on our own faces. The answers the mirror gives are contradictory. I meet a friend who joyfully explains: 'How young you look! You never seem to change!' A little further on

I meet another who says sympathetically: 'What's the matter with you? You've grown so old all of a sudden!' These opinions do not depend as much on how I really am, as on the respective states of mind of my friends. Nevertheless, we are always sensitive to such remarks: the first friend makes me feel younger, while meeting the second ages me. My publishers make me feel young when they ask me to write this book, thus setting me reading so many interesting books and articles in preparation for it.

That is what makes it difficult for us to ration our activity with approaching old age, the fact that we never really know what is our functional age. It is in vain that at one moment we play at being a young man, and the next at being the nice old gentleman; the one does not correct the other, and there always remains something of pretence, something of social suggestion, and something of auto-suggestion, in our behaviour. We never know whether we are just being fussy or whether we are not taking enough care. A doctor always hesitates to advise a patient to retire early. With special care might he enable him to carry on to the end? But might that not be to do him a disservice by giving him dangerous illusions about himself?

It is always a little humiliating to a man to advise him to give up his work. It is also a shock, since it means admitting to the patient that one has lost hope of his recovery, and the doctor is afraid that this may cause a sudden weakening in the patient's resistance to disease and to old age. In this connection I have more happy surprises than unhappy ones. It is often those who are most reluctant to request early retirement who are the better for it afterwards.

Financial considerations must play a big part in the decision. In my country, at least, early retirement involves a sharp cut in the amount of the pension; this is unjust, and its consequences are serious throughout all the years of retirement. I was most surprised to learn that in the United States, in 1957, 76% of those who had retired had done so at their own request, 60% of them for health reasons. When I mentioned these figures to a Swiss industrialist, he exclaimed: 'Here, that would require a total reform of the financial regulations governing retirement.' Well, that reform ought to be undertaken in order to allow a real measure of discretion in retirement.

The actuaries are expert calculators. No doubt they could apply their minds to the following systems: the pension for a given worker would be fixed at 60% of his highest previous salary, on the basis of an average age of sixty-five. This pension would be available to him at whatever age he retired, provided it were between sixty and seventy. The charges falling upon pension funds would balance out as between those retiring before sixty-five and those retiring after that age.

The resources of the retired

This brings me to the second chapter in this inventory of my privileges, namely those which money provides. Popular wisdom is right when it asserts that money is not everything. The doctor has enough experience of people to realize that. He sees very unhappy people among those who are very wealthy, and others who suffer terribly from boredom amidst their expensive amusements. All the same, there is a threshold below which the condition of the pensioner is deplorable. Everything that one can write on the problems of retirement will be no more than words in the wind or 'a cymbal clashing' (I Cor. 13.1), in St Paul's words, if a radical change is not made in the financial situation of the low-income pensioner.

Life changes entirely if the retired person enjoys a certain measure of financial ease, even a modest one, instead of having to count every penny and to go without everything except what is required merely to subsist. Even in a country like Switzerland, with its highly-developed economy, social workers find old people who hide themselves away, and whose material situation is an affront in a society such as ours. If we are to believe Simone de Beauvoir, it was in the last century, in the opulent Victorian era, that there was the most shocking contrast between the lot of the aged rich and the aged poor.

Incomes are insufficient everywhere, even in highly industrialized countries. A study by the International Labour Office evaluates the average retirement income at 50% of wages.[18] We are far from the 95% demanded by the Beveridge Report, and even from the 70% minimum of more moderate estimates. Here are the results of an inquiry carried out in France, by the Alpes District Round-table Interprofessional Fund: 58% of retired people consider their resources insufficient, only 21% claim they have sufficient, and when they are asked about their hopes for the future, hardly anything else is mentioned but an increase in pensions. All protest against having to pay tax on their pensions. Many demand exemption from the TV licence.[19]

The situation becomes more tragic when the retired person is advanced in age, when he is no longer capable of any work at all, and when his health deteriorates. For this reason Denmark very wisely increases the pension at the age of 80. That is a measure that ought to be generally adopted. More important still, pension figures show serious inequalities. In France the pensions given in some enterprises can be as much as five times those given in others. The system of 'national old age pensions' practised in Sweden, Denmark and Switzerland irons out these inequalities to some extent. Reading a comparative study of the condition of the old, such as that by G. Gaillard, I said to myself: 'Blessed is the old age of those who enjoy racial or financial privileges!'

All this is not only of material importance, in respect of food, accommodation and clothing, but even more important because of its moral consequences. The pensioner is devalued in the eyes of society because of the massive reduction in his income. He loses his independence, which is more important to the aged person than anything else. 'He no longer has anything in his own right . . . even to say thank-you with.'[20] One is made acutely aware of this in the answers given in some sociological enquiries, for instance the retired man who would like to have a little money so as to be able to entertain his friends, or another who would like to be able to offer biscuits to his grandchildren when they come to see him.[21]

As we have seen, all hobbies cost money. Before retirement, for the active man, his leisure-time occupations were chiefly a means of distraction, relaxation and pleasure. After retirement, they will take on a quite new significance, a triple significance: they are an occupation to fill the void left by the sudden cessation of work; they present an opportunity for social contact for those whom the cessation of work leaves isolated; and they are a means of continued development of the personality for those who are seriously threatened with regression.

There is, of course, nothing particularly new in this aspect of leisure occupations. But before retirement they are accessory, while afterwards they become of prime importance. One can say that before retirement, leisure occupations are superfluous, but that afterwards they are a vital need. Those leisure occupations which are most valuable from the point of view of social contacts are also the most expensive. For relaxation, one can take a walk. That is not costly. Just a little drink half-way, before turning back for home. But travel, attending language classes, serious stamp-collecting, do-it-yourself, all demand expenditure, often in considerable amounts. An adolescent can travel cheaply, by hitch-hiking and using youth hostels. But at retirement age that is no longer possible.

Here is where I feel my privilege keenly. I am in a position to lead an interesting and exciting life. I can buy myself a book, where-as one sociologist received the following reply from a pensioner whom he was questioning: 'No reading; I can't afford it.'[22] I have a car, I can travel, take part in conferences. In my workshop I have admirable little machines with which I can make nice things with-out getting tired, a power-driven cultivator to take the hard work out of gardening, and a little electronic organ whose velvety sonori-ties I love. Certainly those who have too much money too often rely only on what can be bought. As a result they enjoy neither true leisure nor true pleasure, because they put nothing of themselves into it. All the same, it is necessary to have at least enough for the creative imagination not to be sterilized through not being able to carry out any project.

Therefore, you legislators, count in the minimum living pension not only what is needed to subsist, but also what is needed to live, to lead a truly human life, interesting, active, fecund and enriching. This is going to become possible with technical progress and the gradual increase in energy resources and in productivity. The well-being of peoples depends essentially upon the raising of their standard of living, that is to say, on the global total of commercial exchanges. But then, as soon as the standard of living goes up, the question arises as to how the cake is to be cut so that the slices are not too flagrantly unequal.

An egalitarian share-out is probably unattainable, and it can only be approached at the price of a stultifyingly bureaucratic and autocratic state control. Such was the society in Ur of the Chal-daeans (Gen. 12.1) that God called upon Abraham to leave, in order to take up once again a nomadic life and to return to nature. Nevertheless, the history of the last 150 years shows that by means of economic progress adjustments are possible which ensure for everyone, if not an equal share of wealth, at least less unequal opportunities. The lion's share still goes to the richest and the best educated – and education itself is still too closely bound up with wealth – and this is due to a universal law which applies to both capitalist and socialist societies, namely that the richer one is, the richer one becomes, and the poorer one is, the poorer one becomes.

Among the disinherited, the first to achieve some betterment of their material lot have been the workers, because they had at their disposal an effective weapon which was obviously not available to the retired – the strike. In a society whose prosperity depends on productivity, those who have the power to paralyse productivity by stopping work have a powerful means of winning new privileges. Even in a country such as Switzerland, which has experienced practically no strikes for some twenty years, the strike weapon is still the decisive factor in workers' emancipation. The weapon is put away, but it is still there in the armoury. I do not deny the great merit of the few men who have conceived and negotiated on a scientific basis the social peace which we enjoy, but it is undoubtedly the fear of the strike which has ensured their success.

National pride

What is interesting to note is that, more recently, hand-in-hand with the revaluation of the working-class, has gone another, that of the adolescent. I have seen it developing within my own life-time. At the beginning of this century, the wealthiest of middle-class parents gave only a few pence pocket-money to their teenage children. They had not enough confidence in them. They amassed a fortune for them, which would be left to them on their death. But meanwhile they would not even tell them how much that fortune was, for fear that they would demand to have a little bit of it. They held their children in tutelage by means of money. They were afraid that the children would squander the money, or that it would lead them into vanity or vice.

Now all that has changed. The young people of today have their pockets stuffed with money, even those who belong to families in modest circumstances, who impose heavy sacrifices upon themselves in order to be able to satisfy the whims of their children. Now, these adolescents are not producers like the workers of whom we were speaking just now. In this respect they are like the retired people. It is not to the strike weapon that they owe their financial progress. The weapon they have used, consciously or not, is a sort of blackmail: 'What will people think of you, dad, if I haven't got a car as expensive as my friend Peter's, when his father is less well-off than you are?'

In that case the increase in revenue does not come out of the firm's coffers, as in the case of the workers, but out of father's drawer. It is not difficult to see that the improvement in the financial position of the young has given a considerable impetus to the development of our consumer society, as has the increase in workers' wages. The young are highly privileged in this new society. This is because they are impulse-buyers, customers who spend a lot without much thought, who buy sports cars and noisy motor-cycles, and a whole jingling collection of jewellery, who travel by plane, and follow the fashion more closely than their parents. They are extremely susceptible to publicity.

Basically, whether the money comes from the wage-packet, from interest on capital, from father's drawer, or from pension funds, the effect is just the same. It is always a precept upon the gross national product. The real problem is therefore that of an equitable sharing-out of the slices of the cake. That is the moral and human stake involved in the betterment of the material lot of the old.

'Nowhere yet,' remarks Michèle Aumont, 'have there been formed "trade unions" for the old or the retired to defend their claims and exercise such pressure as is possible.' They cannot go on strike, or blackmail father. There are signs now of another, more subtle possibility of blackmail which may be to their advantage – that of national pride. The reduction of poverty in old age is soon going to become, I believe, a public test of the state of civilization of a society. As the adolescent to whom I referred just now played on his father's pride by comparing him to his friend Peter's more generous parent, so we are beginning to see nations making comparisons among themselves according to the living-standards of their old people.

Concern for the fate of the old is invading public opinion in all countries. This concern is quite new. Simone de Beauvoir, with a wealth of documentation, has sketched a horrifying series of pictures of the condition of the aged over the centuries. On rare occasions, rare individuals, having preserved into old age an accumulation of wealth, have used it to make themselves respected and feared as tyrants. But one remains overwhelmed at the pitiless harshness with which the old have almost always been treated until the last century. They were forced to work until they were exhausted, and then they were rejected, despised and despoiled. They were left to slide slowly and painfully into death, or else death was hastened by means that were not always discreetly hidden. Only the church brought them some succour – just enough to prolong their agony. The only excuse for this frightful brutality is no doubt the dire poverty in which the immense majority of mankind was sunk until quite recently. Those who condemn our consumer society for its immorality and inhumanity do not know what they are saying.

It needed this general increase in wealth, which we owe to science and technology, to awaken in us a quite new sensitivity to human suffering, the suffering of the poor, of the old, of the starving millions in the world. There is a quite noticeable movement of opinion demanding an improvement in the living-standards of the old. I observe it in my own country. As you know, Switzerland's political system is one of direct democracy. This means that all important or controversial measures are submitted to the votes of the people. It means also that the people have the right to initiate legislation. A group of ordinary citizens can draw up or propose a bill to be submitted to the popular vote. Sometimes several proposals are initiated on the same subject.

That is what is happening at present in the case of the financial status of aged persons. There is competition among three different popular initiatives which are outbidding each other in an attempt to improve it. Naturally, one of them tends more towards state control, while the other two are more or less liberal, resting on what is called the 'doctrine of the three pillars', according to which the financial security of the retired rests at the same time upon a basic federal insurance scheme applying to the whole population, on the pension funds of the organization or firm, and on private savings. Each of the 'three pillars' has its advantages and its disadvantages, but the combination of all three ought to guarantee a pension equal to at least 60% of the best previous wage.

Solitude

There is a third area in which I feel myself to be greatly privileged in comparison with the majority of my contemporaries. This is the

painful solitude which afflicts them, and which I do not have to
face. I live surrounded by affection. Parsons writes: 'It is not so
much straitened financial circumstances, but isolation, which
makes the aged a social problem.'[23] Many other writers[24] maintain
like him that solitude is the commonest and the most serious difficulty with which old people have to cope. Family and friends die,
including perhaps husband or wife, and even children and grandchildren; the passing of close friends leaves a void which cannot
be filled. After the age of sixty-five there is an enormous increase in
the number of people living on their own. Whereas under that age
it amounts to 21% of the population, after sixty-five it reaches an
average of 58%.[25]

My first privilege is that I am married. In this respect the sociological surveys all confirm that there is a striking contrast between the
happiness possible in the case of aged couples living together in
love, and the distress of those who live alone, whether unmarried,
widowed or separated either through divorce or some other cause.
The marked isolation of widows has been noted.[26] Sometimes husband and wife say to one another: 'I'll be the first to go.' In saying
this, what they are really expressing is their fear of being left
alone.[27] The survivor usually prefers independence to going into an
old folks' home, but none wants to die alone.[28] It can happen that
those amorous adventures which some people embark upon rather
late in life are not just 'midsummer madness', but have as their
true motivation a desire to insure against loneliness, rather than
sexual satisfaction.[29]

'The really valuable human relationships,' says Paul Ricoeur,
'are those that exist among a small number of people, namely love
and friendship.' This becomes truer the older one is. One sociologist remarks that among the old people he questions, the only important topic is the husband or wife, whether alive or dead. The
fact is that even after his or her death, the departed spouse may
still be more present in the mind of the survivor than any living
person. This hidden bond with the dead makes the survivor feel
even more lonely. He sees his past married life as something quite
different from what it really was. This is sometimes in order to blot
out some unconscious feeling of guilt, for the most unconsolable
sorrows are those that are kept alive by a guilty conscience.

Growing old together

As one grows old one generally experiences the need for a more restricted but deeper intimacy. This need is fulfilled in the case of a couple who are happy together, in the incomparable blessing of growing old together. To reach that happy state many crises have had to be overcome. But now they are over, and those old couples radiate peace. All my readers will, no doubt, know such couples, who represent for them old age at its best.

The Swiss writer C. F. Ramuz describes a couple like that in a passage which has been reproduced in the family booklet which the government of his canton gives to all young couples upon their marriage. An old peasant and his wife come, one fine evening in the evening of their lives, and sit as they do every day side by side on the bench in front of their house, overlooking the familiar countryside in which they have worked together for so long. There is not much talk between them, because at that age a few words express a great deal. Even their silences are eloquent of their fellowship. One is reminded of an apt remark by the philosopher Georges Gusdorf: 'It is often said,' he writes, 'that silence is more eloquent than speech; but that depends on what has been said before.'[30]

I am very fond of Ramuz's well-known description, for I see it as an account of my own privileged state. But I see, too, that this blessing of being able to grow old together is the fruit of a whole married life in which one has been given the courage to face, in a dialogue of truth, a host of problems of mutual adaptation which are never easy. It is as true of a couple as it is of an individual that old age depends mainly upon the way their lives have been lived beforehand. As Paul Plattner writes, no married couple can grow without overcoming conflicts.[31] Through difficult periods and through great mutual frankness, husband and wife can each come gradually to accept the other as he or she is. Of course there will always be some problems to solve still, but the dialogue becomes less tense, without, however, becoming less fruitful.

Nevertheless, this growth together is not always possible. It can happen that one or the other, in order to safeguard the peace and the apparent unity of the couple, has to capitulate to the tyranny of the other, to avoid subjects that give rise to conflict, and hide a portion of his life. And so a trench is gradually dug between them.

They become more and more strangers to one another. Married though they are, they regress to becoming a bachelor and a spinster. This does not cause them much pain while they are still in active life, absorbed as they are in their respective activities and interests. But when retirement supervenes, and their work comes to an end, when the husband no longer has his workmates, and the children have left home, when social contacts are restricted, and they find themselves alone together, face to face, they have nothing to say to each other, and the happiness of growing old together changes into boredom together.

Another couple may both be liberal-minded. Their deep mutual respect makes each allow the other to live a life of his own, so intense and so specific to his own inclinations that they never have time for real dialogue in the heyday of their lives. When they retire they can enter upon a critical period. The wife is quite put out by the presence of an unoccupied husband who expects her to fill the void formerly occupied by his work. The wife in her turn has to give up activities to which she has been attached. They realize all at once that they have been living side by side, but have long since ceased being partners. They too have little to say to each other in this enforced tête-à-tête, apart from mutual recriminations.

Blessed are they if they can get through this critical stage, and begin to rebuild, now that they have time, a mutual relationship which they have been gravely neglecting. Blessed, if they manage, thus late in the day, to discover each other, and to discover at the same time the true meaning of marriage, which is an incessant exchange, in which each is encouraged to excel himself. They can come to know that beautiful old age which Ramuz celebrates, and which bears witness to a profound growth which working life has not sufficed to procure for them. Other authors have spoken with deep emotion of these happy old couples – notably Father Leclercq, writing in the evening of his life, a life which, however, his religious vows had dedicated to celibacy. Dr René Biot remarks that such couples 'finish up resembling each other psychologically and morally'.[32]

Growing old together, husband and wife can come to know a love which is in a way a prefiguration of heaven, for it is less tumultuous than the love of youth, being less directed towards selfish pleasure-seeking, and because a slow advance in mutual comprehension permits more authentic communication. For Jaspers, 'there is no

communication between human beings without transcendence'.[33]
This love in old age, it is true, seems like a gift from God; it has the
flavour of eternity. Young lovers feel it already, when they swear
to love each other all their lives. Witness these celebrated lines
from Ronsard's sonnets for Hélène:

> *Quand vous serez bien vieille, au soir, à la chandelle,*
> *Assise auprès du feu, dévidant et filant,*
> *Direz, chantant mes vers, en vous émerveillant,*
> *Ronsard me célébrait du temps que j'étais belle.*

> (When you are very old, in the evening, by candle-light,
> Sitting by the fire, unwinding and spinning,
> You will say, as you sing my verse, wonderingly,
> Ronsard used to sing my praises, in the days when I
> was beautiful.)

But this does not mean that sex no longer plays a part in the love
of these old couples. Of course it does not have a preponderant
role, but I do not think that sex life ceases as often or as early as
most people suppose. I am more likely to have access to the
truth of this, since it is not easy to get old people to be frank on
the subject. They are more reserved than the young in speaking of
such matters. Perhaps this is due, as Simone de Beauvoir remarks,
to the fact that people generally look upon sex in the old as being
abnormal, and even repugnant.

I do not really see why. It would seem, on the contrary, that
with age there is established a more harmonious equilibrium
among the three factors in conjugal love, namely the physical, the
sentimental and the spiritual; whereas in the young the first tends
to eclipse the other two. I even have the feeling that it is those
couples who were once drawn together by the most intense carnal
passion who soonest reject it. This is perhaps why an author like
Sacha Guitry, who has juggled in so many of his plays with the
subtle interplay of desire, has been able to write one, *Après l'amour*
('After love'), charming indeed, in which the characters, though
not yet very old, are already escaping from its hold over them.

On the other hand, one meets couples in whose early years together erotic love has not played such an exclusive role, and whose
love grows into something more lasting and complete in which a
fusion of the physical and the spiritual bond has been fully achieved.

One thing that has struck me is that this may happen in cases where the wife is older than the husband. This ought to be of some assurance to women who hesitate to marry a man younger than themselves. One might quote Alexandre Dumas the Younger at this point: 'A woman whom one has watched growing old is never old.'

Dr Paul Chauchard and his wife have together written a book[34] on this beautiful theme of 'growing old together'. Dr Sébillotte is surprised that they have nothing to say about the tragedy of separation occasioned by the death of one of the spouses. I do not wish to lay myself open to the same criticism, but I well understand what has held the two authors back. Their book is a personal testimony. They are affirming in this way that the personalist teaching which informs the whole of Dr Chauchard's work is not mere abstract theory, but that it has been lived out in practice in his marriage.

Neither he nor his wife has any experience of widowhood, any more than I have. It seems to me that, in regard to the greatest trials of all, one cannot say very much while one has no personal experience of them. Usually I remain silent, privileged as I am, before those who are undergoing them. I feel some embarrassment when someone, in his anxiety to console them, says to them: 'I can imagine how I would feel in your place.' One cannot know until one has been there. As Kierkegaard insisted, suffering is incommunicable. It is for this reason that all great personal suffering is made worse by a tragic feeling of solitude.

A loving husband and wife may well have experienced other cruel sorrows: the death of one of their children, for instance. But at least they will have been through it together. Widowhood is not just a sorrow, it is a solitary sorrow. I do not think that anyone can foresee what will be his own reaction to it. It is no use my saying that I feel that I am a solitary sort of person: I still do not know how I should react. One is often surprised at how people do react. Nevertheless, I have observed that it is often those who have been closest in marriage who bear their separation best.

Family and friendship

It is also part of my privilege to have a family. There are our two sons, our daughter-in-law, and our four grandchildren. I am particularly privileged in the strong, happy relationships which bind us to them. There are old people who have children, grandchildren, or at least nephews and nieces, and yet feel more lonely than if they had lost them, because the young folk have turned away from them.

Our own children have all spent a long time abroad, but they have come back to their own country. We do not live far from them, though retaining our independence. Doubtless this is right; it is the modern way. Only a third of all old people with children now live with them.[35] Our grandchildren can drop in to see us without any difficulty. We are passionately interested in their lives, and they are interested in ours. With their parents, as with our unmarried son, we have maintained and developed the most trusting and intimate relationship.

Another of my privileges is my circle of friendships. Sometimes one hears it said that it is not easy to form new friendships once one is no longer young. If this were really the case, my luck would be exceptional. My closest friends from the period of my child-hood and youth are nearly all dead and gone. My wife, too, has lost many of hers. But we have lots of new friendships, wonder-ful friendships with men and women who are mostly younger than we, and who certainly play their part in keeping us young in heart and mind. Some of our closest friends we have known for only a few years.

To what do we owe such a privilege? I must try to answer the question, for the answer has something to tell us about our modern world. Why is it that the only close relationships so many old people have is with a few of their contemporaries, who are dis-appearing one after another? Why do we make friends in childhood and youth? It is not only because we live together, sit together on our school and lecture-room benches, or play football or tennis together. Later on one can work, during one's whole career, in the same office or factory, or join a sports club, without forming such close associations.

It is, I believe, because in one's youth one has the wonderful experience of the first sharing of confidences. Take young Michael here, for example: as a little boy, when he came back from a walk during which something had upset him, he would climb on his mother's knee and tell her all about it. For a long time his parents were his privileged confidants – parents whom he had not chosen, and who claimed to have certain rights over him. But the time came when this claim began to be irksome to him, and the more his parents reproved him for not telling them everything, the less he felt like doing so. In this way he was becoming aware of his own person and of his freedom.

Then one day Michael goes walking in the woods with a comrade. They sit down on a tree-trunk and, spontaneously, begin to talk more intimately. Michael's parents know all about his life, or think they do. But his comrade knows nothing of it and listens avidly to what he says. Michael goes on talking, talking, and soon he is saying things that he has never said to his parents, and which he would have no desire to tell them. A strange happiness invades him. He has chosen a friend for himself. He experiences anew that limitless confidence which he had in his mother when he was very small. He is almost astonished to be speaking like this. As he expresses it out loud he discovers within himself a rich world of feelings and experiences of which he has been hardly conscious.

And then his friend talks to him as well, and shows the same exciting confidence in him. With him he finds himself in a state of reciprocity which he has never experienced with his parents. They demanded that he tell them everything, but were careful not to be equally open with him about themselves. Little by little, Michael had guessed things. He had discovered lots of problems, lots of worries, lots of conflicts which his parents had carefully been hiding from him. His friend, on the other hand, lays bare to him his life and his soul, his joys and his sorrows, without reticence. Michael discovers that it is a life other than his own, a very different one, but just as rich in feelings and thoughts. He listens to it all with burning sympathy. A door has been opened which will not be shut again. The two friends are going to be inseparable. They will readily tell each other about everything that happens to them, and be sure of being understood. They will be lifelong friends, on condition that neither betrays the secrets of the other.

Later on, Michael will find innumerable comrades, at school, at work, in his leisure occupations, on his military service. But society will already have left its mark upon him. It will have taught him to keep quiet about what he cares about most, it will have instilled into him a certain caution in sharing confidences; it will have trained him to play its conventional game. He will have learnt to argue, but not to open his heart. He will talk about the things that go on around him in the world, but not about what they mean to him in his heart. He will talk about the ideas of this or that writer, but not about his own ideas, which people might laugh at. When he falls in love, he will talk about love, rather than about the woman he loves and the intimate feelings she arouses in him. And then his life at work will provide plenty of material for his conversations. He will speak with his friends about his work, about technical problems, about the interests they have in common; he will be contaminated by our impersonal world.

Job relationships only rarely suffice to create personal bonds. You may see two partners spend the whole of their working lives together, in close collaboration, without there being any relationship between them other than conventional and worldly ones. They may even take the greatest care not to allow their private lives to enter into their business. Sociologists have pointed out how rare it is for retired people to maintain contact with their former work-mates. A school teacher retires – she used to belong to a group of friends who met regularly, and of whom she often spoke to me. I expected that this group was going to be even more valuable to her after her retirement. But no, she never goes there at all now. I ask her about it. 'Oh!' she says, 'they are all teachers; they only talk about their work. I feel out of place now among them.'

Social integration

I was talking just now about the fate of Michael. My own story is different. I was orphaned as a child, and as a result I was very withdrawn. True friendship came to me later than it usually does to others. But, late as it came, it came all the more intensely, and I was able to measure its human importance better. I realized that another person cannot be reached from outside, through objective observation, through an intellectual or technical dialogue, but only when a man opens his own heart about the things he alone knows because he has lived and is living through them now. I saw, too, at once what a rare thing that is.

I have become more and more interested in this search for the person, which always remains something of a mystery, even for each one of us to himself, but which one glimpses through the mask of the social personage. I have been attracted by this never-ending search, not only in my consulting-room, but among my friends and colleagues, on holidays, and on lecture-tours. I have realized that truly personal contact has to be reciprocal; that other people open their hearts more profoundly if I am doing the same, or at least am ready to do so, to surmount my own feelings of resistance.

It is not that I find it easier than others to lower the barriers – quite the contrary. I am still very shy and unsociable. All personal encounters frighten me. If I could, I should hold aloof. But I know that this is the price of being able to bring to others a kind of help that goes deeper and is more vital than the aid provided by medical and psychological technology. Both are necessary, of course. But in our modern world, impersonal as it is, so many people remain essentially solitary, despite the care we give them, the services we render them, and even in spite of affection we show them. It is necessary, even in a book, to give something of ourselves if we are to sound that intimate chord that will resist the passage of time. Many of my readers have said to me: you have not told me anything new, but you have put into words things that I only vaguely felt.

That is certainly why it has been given to me to make so many deep and durable new friendships. They have had their effect on me, too. They have helped me to develop, to get through crises and to be able to start again. They have given me a purpose in life which has gone far beyond my job as a doctor. They have bound me closely to all those who are struggling like me to make the world in which we live more humane. The loneliness which gnaws at the hearts of so many old people is not just their problem alone. It is characteristic of the whole of our civilization – and it condemns it.

The reason why these old people feel so lonely is that they were already lonely, without knowing it, before they retired. In this, as in all other respects, old age reveals what a man really is, though he may not wish to see it. Professional and social life deludes us, hiding from us the fact that it is the whole of society which is sick with loneliness, because it involves only conventional and superficial contacts. When, in retirement, we leave this great machine behind, there is nothing much left. A gear-wheel separated from the machine is a poor object, but fit it into the machine, and it works in with the others, even though it is not permanently attached.

This image of the gears is quite apt when you think of people working on the conveyor belt in big factories, and you can understand the moral as well as economic repercussions of retirement on the worker who is forced to give it up. But society life, even love in its physical aspect, is also a vast machine, with all its parts working together, even when the sexual side of it remains unfulfilled. That seductive woman who queens it in whatever company she happens to be in, who derives carefree enjoyment from her worldly success, which she takes as personal homage to herself, may suffer a rude shock when she is forced by old age to withdraw from it all into social isolation. She has already had a premonition of it, and that is why she is so afraid of growing old, even before the marks of age show in her face.

Freud defined psychological health under the double heading of aptitude for love and for work. But in order to resolve the problem of human loneliness, something more is required than this working of the instincts whose power and subtlety Freud has so clearly demonstrated. The superficial relationships of working life and of sexual attraction must be made the opportunity for a deeper personal commitment. And I believe that no commitment can be truly personal unless it takes on a transcendent dimension and becomes love, in the biblical meaning of the word.

How rarely this happens is shown by the great loneliness of the old, even among those who have been churchgoers. It reveals that it is possible to spend one's whole life meeting a multitude of people, living for years side by side with people at work or in one's family, acting out a professional or social role with them, without having much that is durable to show for it. Add to the enforced separation from workmates the death of the marriage partner or the last close friend, and loneliness becomes catastrophic. There follow regression, passivity and withdrawal upon oneself. Much has been written on the subject of the isolation of the old, and their social disintegration.[36] But it seems to me really to prove how little society has done for them beforehand to provide opportunities for deep personal relationships.

If social integration has not taken place between the ages of thirty and forty, say Dumazedier and Ripert, it becomes impossible between fifty and sixty. 'It is possible to be very much alone in a crowded tenement.'[37] Then, after retirement, social withdrawal is the great phenomenon that is recorded.[38] It is in face of this that geriatric social work has expanded so greatly in the United States,[39] and is about to spread to Europe. One investigator[40] notes that 31.5% of the retired people whom he questioned were never visited by anybody. The striking thing about this is that it was among the retired employees of a single corporation who were hospitalized in a well-run home, and that he remarks that 'being in the same profession does nothing to make social contacts easier'. He emphasizes the isolation suffered by foreigners: the home is in the south of France, where many Spanish nationals come to work. 'You never see a Spaniard and a Frenchman out walking together,' he writes.

Health

One factor that is important in this problem of social withdrawal is the feeling many old people have that they are physically unattractive. Often it is not so much that they are afraid of growing old as that they are frightened of seeming repellent, and so they hide. Dr Hugonot has set up an old folks' beauty salon in Grenoble.[41] He has obtained some notable psychological results from this. With teeth, hair, skin, hands and feet properly looked after, an old person may be freed from reticence in his social contacts.

This venture is part of a comprehensive and systematic project to assist old people undertaken by Dr Hugonot.[42] I have already referred to the courses he runs in preparation for retirement. There is in addition an Aged Persons Office, which seeks out and brings aid to lonely and abandoned old people. This work is carried on by a whole team of volunteers and salaried workers, among whom are a number of retired people who find it an excellent way of using their leisure time. There is a certain piquancy in the fact that in a country where social security is state-run, the office retains its private character, since if it were taken over by the state, it would have to do without the services of retired helpers. In France, retired local government and civil servants are not allowed to work!

There is also a well-equipped geriatric service, with facilities for kinesitherapy and ergotherapy, and old folks' clubs and homes situated – an important point – near the centre of the town. My wife and I have also attended several seminars organized by the Grenoble AP Office in different parts of the Rhône-Alpes region, aimed at bringing the problems to the notice of the local authorities and providing a stimulus for social workers.

Another innovation which is of particular interest is the formation of medico-social teams. These are a sort of travelling dispensary, which visits isolated old people and gives them a medical check-up in their own homes. No one will disagree that good health in old age is an important privilege. I am not concerned to write a book on geriatry. Those of my specialist colleagues who read this will know more on the subject than I do, and the rest would derive no benefit from several pages of necessarily summary medical matter. The real subject of this book is the reactions of all of us to the fact of old age. From this point of view Simone de Beauvoir's perceptive remark should first be noted: 'When we consider old age we dismiss the thought of illness; we avoid the thought of old age in considering illness, and so we adroitly manage not to believe in either of them.' From this point of view also, apart from incurable diseases which involve the threat of death, but which are not peculiar to old age, the affections and infirmities which weigh most heavily are those which compromise communication with others, when eye or ear are affected, or which make meeting other people difficult, when mobility is restricted.

Progressive deterioration, followed by loss of eyesight, hearing and memory, plunge the old person who may be healthy in other respects into acute isolation. All this is too obvious and too well-known for me to need to dwell upon it. One observation in particular that has been made is that 'the aged deaf person is much more disturbed than the aged person with poor eyesight'.[43] But there are blind and deaf old people whose state is pitiable, especially when their mental faculties are no longer good enough for them to learn to read Braille. There are grounds for insisting that Braille be taught as soon as there are signs of failing eyesight, when the person is still young enough. A certain false sentimentality often holds back doctors and families from insisting in time for fear of worrying him.

We have here a phenomenon which may be observed over the whole field of medicine, namely that the way in which people bear their ills depends much more upon their state of mind than on the gravity of the ills. You can meet blind and deaf old people who radiate peace, and even gaiety, whereas others who are only a little hard of hearing are always grumbling, and pretend to be deafer than they really are. They give up trying to hear, and as soon as they see people laughing they persuade themselves that they are the objects of the laughter. It is a universal law: those who are

most in rebellion against their misfortunes put up less of a fight
to overcome them than those who accept them.

The same is true in the case of loss of mobility. A little while
ago, in Spain, we paid a visit to an old friend, a Dutch colleague
who is younger than I am, but who is prevented by arthritis from
sitting down or standing up without his wife's help. It is a great
trial to become entirely dependent upon someone else, and it is in
great trials that one can measure people's spiritual resources. We
found my friend on the terrace of his house, busy painting a bunch
of flowers, enjoying the beautiful countryside, the flowers, the light,
the tender care of his wife and the fact that he was able to paint
and write. He had just published a new book. Despite his handicap
he travels, and he is happy. He greeted us warmly, and did us a
power of good.

That reminds me of a near relative of whom I was very fond.
When I visited him, at the terminal stage of a progressive muscular
failure which had struck him in the prime of life, he could hardly
move anything but his eyes. His bed had been wheeled out on to
the verandah of the hospital. Having been a keen amateur yachtsman, he knew all about winds. As soon as I was near enough, he
said to me: 'I follow the clouds with my eyes, and observe them;
it's most interesting. People always talk about the *vaudaire** as if
there were only one. But I have discovered that there are two,
quite distinct from each other.'

Hospitalization

Nevertheless the loss of one's independence is always a very
great trial. Before it happens, all old people fear it. It is for that
reason that so many old people stubbornly refuse to be transferred
to an old people's home. One cannot say that such a refusal is
absurd, as is claimed by those who are trying to persuade them to
agree. The hospitalization of the aged precipitates physical and
mental decline. Statistics drawn up by Dr Pequignot, in France,
show that more than a quarter of the old people die within the first
six months, and more than half in the first year after admission. It
is frightening! Simone de Beauvoir, quoting these figures, adds:
'The regulations are strict, the routine is rigid; they get up and go to
bed early. Cut off from their past, their environment, often forced

**Translator's note*: The name given in Switzerland to the strong south wind.

to wear a uniform, they become depersonalized, and are no more than numbers.' This is the triumph of the impersonal society I mentioned just now.

They have already suffered a serious shock merely by being up-rooted: 'The change is one of the worst traumas that the old person has to undergo.'[44] At an advanced age, the mere removal may have tragic consequences.[45] Gardeners know it well enough. They prick out the seedlings to encourage growth, but will say of a tree: 'This one is too old for transplanting.' One sociologist advises: 'Do not withdraw them from everyday life.'[46] And a journalist, Walter Weideli,[47] at the conclusion of a debate on the housing of the old, held in Geneva, remarked: 'Do not uproot old people. It is a crime!'

All the specialists agree on this point: the old folks' institution must be avoided wherever possible. 'Compulsory and unprepared transplantation of an aged person,' writes Dr Hugonot, 'is harmful, and often fatal.' It is especially important, he goes on, to avoid the transplantation of country folk. 'The maintenance of the old person in his family background, or simply in the place he is used to living in, is highly desirable,' writes Dr Miraillet.

In the family background, in the home of the children? Not all are in agreement. The sociologists Pacaud and Lahalle, follow-ing upon an enquiry into the personal relationships between grand-parents, parents and adolescents, come out against their living together.[48] The best that can be hoped for is intimacy at a distance, with the old folk living near by.[49]

But a day comes when it is difficult for the old person to remain on his own because of his state of health. Professor Townsend recommends the development of home help services in preference to that of old persons' homes.[50] This is also the conclusion arrived at in an enquiry conducted by the Centre National de Retraite des Ouvriers among its inmates. It involves more complicated organiza-tion, but that does not necessarily make it more costly. At the Grenoble seminar I met some members of a lay community from Paris called the 'Little Brothers of the Poor'. They have branches in Chicago and in Canada. Their spirit and zeal struck me as being quite remarkable. They dedicate themselves to the assistance of aged persons in their homes. They do housework and shopping for them, as well as performing many other services, which make it possible for the old people to go on living in their own homes. Clearly they derived real joy from this effective service. In Geneva the Hospice Général has for a number of years organized a 'meals on wheels' service which is much appreciated.

So in a large number of cases hospitalization can be postponed and even avoided. This is important. Apart from the uprooting involved, the old people's home has the serious disadvantage of segregating its inmates from the rest of the community. Even among animals the mortality rate is raised when they are put in cages. We know what are the results of experiments carried out at the other end of the age scale. Babies kept in hospital behind glass walls, in the best conditions of asepsis and feeding, have a higher death-rate than those left in a normal environment.

Of the life of old people in institutions, I have read some horrifying accounts. One must be fair, however. Great progress has already been made, both materially and morally, particularly in the smaller countries such as Scandinavia and Switzerland. In France, also, certain undertakings have set up friendly and comfortable residences for their former employees, where they are treated not as numbers but as persons, and where an effort is made to occupy their time. They are located not too far from the town, have individual rooms or at least rooms with only a few in each, and sometimes there are little bungalows in a park, with a common refectory and various services laid on.

In Grenoble, and also in Geneva, as well as many other cities, old people's residences are being built with small flats for couples or single persons, with a common kitchen, a resident nurse, and facilities for medical care in cases of minor illness. Unfortunately this does little to reduce the ill-effects of segregation, but it does do a little to counter the tendency to depersonalization. Surveys show, however, that the pensioners still tend to remain very reserved in their relationships with each other. 'I say good morning, that's all . . .' 'There are some trouble-makers.' It is a little world of its own, like any other society, with its cliques, its bloods and its stool-pigeons. And yet . . . 'the things that bind together the various elements in the block ought to be respected because their psychotherapeutic value is immense.'[51]

With regard to psychotherapy, it must be admitted that the old people who until recently had to be evacuated to psychiatric hospitals were given no moral assistance. 'It is not so long,' writes Dr Balvet, 'since aged psychiatric cases were among the most abandoned of all.' He says, further: 'To his double misfortune – of being both aged and mentally ill – there was added that of being rejected.' One dares to mention it now because, happily, a healthy reaction has begun under the impulse of doctors enlightened by the progress made in psychoanalysis and social geriatry. In association with psychiatric hospitals, but separate from them, comfortable geriatric units are being built, with sitting-rooms, cafeterias, gymnasia and facilities for games, group therapy and ergotherapy. The results are sensational.[52] In his *Manuel de gérontopsychiatrie*,[53] Professor Christian Müller describes the unit he has set up in Lausanne, the first in Switzerland. Another is at present (1971) under construction in Geneva, under the direction of Dr Junod.

What count also are those little personal attentions. When Professor Hugonot showed me round his geriatric organization in Grenoble I noticed an old car standing in the hospital grounds, covered with a plastic sheet. 'It belongs to one of our pensioners,' the Professor told me. 'He was very much attached to it. So I suggested having it put there. Every day he comes and takes the sheet off, climbs in, and sits behind the steering-wheel, as happy as a sand-boy! Then he puts the cover on again until the next day.' There's medicine of the person for you!

Living quarters

My readers will have realized that all I have been writing in these last pages on the need of the old for independence, and on their housing, has been a way of pursuing the inventory of my privileges and of talking about our villa. Three years ago we were able to sell the town house in which we had lived for more than twenty-five years. It had been a happy background for my professional and family life when I was working full-time, and our son was still at home. But it had become too big, too difficult to keep up, too noisy in a part of the town that was being redeveloped, and there were too many stairs.

We were able to build 'The Grain of Wheat', a new villa quite near the town, but in the country, and of a size more suited to our age. It stands in the shade of a fine oak-tree, between the river and a cornfield that separates us from our grandchildren, but which makes them also quite near. We were lucky in that one of our sons is an architect, and especially lucky that we see eye to eye with him, so that he really understands the sort of home we have and our needs, so that he was able to create a house that exactly suits us.

At every stage in our lives it is important that our dwelling should suit the sort of life we live in it. Transfer from town to country in itself involves a change in the rhythm of life which is very suitable to old age. And then, it meant coming back to the haunts of my childhood, in the parish in which we were married and to which we had always remained attached. When I was a child there were cows which I knew how to milk, vines with their harvest of fruit, and crayfish in the river. All that has gone! But the parish still celebrates Christmas with wonderful fêtes, in which the schoolmaster, the Catholic priest and the Protestant pastor all work closely together with the mayor, with whom I used to cycle to school.

It also meant for us a return to Nature. The garden is more my wife's domain, but we both derive a great deal of pleasure from it. There we find that 'contact with nature that is friendship, poetry, and not exploitation', of which Jean-Marie Domenach speaks in connection with leisure occupations. Many workers are eager to go and live in the country on their retirement.[54] Sometimes they are disappointed in it, and fail to adapt. Never having lived in the country before, and never having even come to the country to get used to it in the years leading up to retirement, they feel rootless and bored.

Arrangements for retirement must be made in good time. Take, for instance, the case of a school-teacher who was approaching her retirement. She had not had much happiness in her life, despite her interest in her vocation and her constant effort to improve her own cultural education. Her father had been killed in the war, and amidst the disaster she had had to flee the country as a little child with her mother, to come to the latter's home country which was to her a foreign land. She had been marked for life by this tragedy, despite the help she got from a qualified psychotherapist. All her hopes of marriage vanished one after another. Now retiring age was upon her. She longed for it and feared it at one and the same time.

Could she after a life of hard work find some happiness in her retirement? Wouldn't she just find herself going round in circles in her little flat, with nothing to do? All she loved was nature, flowers, the garden. A house in the country? Ah! She had been thinking about it for years. But to buy a country villa is not an easy decision for a woman on her own, whose only resources are what she has saved from a village school-teacher's salary! Was she going to get herself into difficulties, allow herself to be cheated into paying the price at which one house she had her eye on was offered? Her friends did not fail to discourage her, telling her the garden was too small, the house was in poor condition and the price too high.

Then my wife and I went to have a look at the house. We were quite surprised to find it charming, well-built, just the right size, with a room or two she could let, and so not be too lonely. That was all the teacher needed to give her the courage to buy the house – which she was longing to do anyway. Now her retirement has begun. She happily cultivates her little garden. She has just planted a wild cherry-tree in it. Will it take and grow well, and bear fruit? So there! Our retired schoolmistress is looking towards the future instead of brooding over her past misfortunes.

So many people do not know how to think in time, and prepare themselves a framework for the last years of their lives. Later on they are sorry, but it is too late, they have grown old. 'What's the use?,' they ask themselves sadly. There are few places more suitable than a house in nice country, not too far from somewhere to shop for supplies, for the years of retirement when one has more time for contemplation. There are few activities that are easier for the old person to ration in accordance with his abilities than the natural activity of cultivating a garden, provided it is not too big, and watching the flowers and trees grow.

Do it yourself!

In our own villa the architect has provided two spacious rooms in the basement: one for my wife with plenty of big cupboards in which a good housewife has always lots of things to put away; the other is for me, for my workshop. In all our houses I have had a place reserved for this purpose, but never as good as this one. My workshop is as important in my life as my consulting-room. That is another of my privileges, and one of the most precious as old age advances and my professional work leaves me more and more leisure time. I thought of it at once when I was asked to write this book, because I am interested in everything, and find as much pleasure in manual work as in the exercise of medicine and psychology, or in writing.

When I was a child, a withdrawn, shy orphan, my school work was deplorable. At that time it was not understood that the emotional life of the child plays an important part in determining his aptitude for study. Academic failure was still put down either to idleness or to stupidity. 'The boy will never get anywhere in his school work,' my uncle used to say; 'he must at least be clever with his hands.' And so he sent me on days when there was no school to the village carpenter's shop in Troinex. Monsieur Petrus Sallansonnet, the carpenter, was an awe-inspiring figure: he was the captain of the fire-brigade, a position of considerable prestige in the hierarchy of the village. But he treated me kindly, and took a personal interest in me, a favour of which I was very sensible. 'A workman must know how to prepare his tools,' he told me the first day. And he taught me how to assemble the frame of a bow-saw and fit a saw-blade into it – an operation which gave me a lot of trouble. But I still have that bow-saw today.

Quite soon I was making a table and small pieces of furniture which I learnt to cover with material. I soon saw that the glue-pot was of vital importance in the workshop, and that it made it possible to hide many of the faults of manufacture. Then I was given a lathe, and lessons from a wood-turner. Further lessons were given by a wood-carver, in reality very elementary ones. But I was getting to like the work, and found it a great compensation for my scholastic disappointments. This keen interest in manual work has never left me throughout my life. From woodwork I moved on to metalwork. I cannot enumerate all the practical activities I took part in, always enthusiastically: bookbinding, radio-construction – fascinating at first, when one had to make one's own coils, condensers, and resistances; histological sections in paraffin, made with a little microtome and a whole arsenal of dyes. How excited I was when I first started a piece of work in masonry! Manual work is so varied. There is always something to learn, and so much pleasure in success. I am quite convinced, as Dr Villa writes, that 'individuals can get as much satisfaction out of a hobby as out of their work'.

When the war came I was mobilized in a surgical field ambulance attached to a Mountain Brigade. Switzerland was not attacked, thank God. But the army had to man the frontiers and prepare to resist an invasion which seemed imminent. From the very first day I won the friendship of my captain and my comrades: when we put under pressure the fine mobile sterilizer that had been issued to us, the tubes exploded. I set to work at once to dismantle it and organize the repair work. That earned me the nickname of mechanic-in-chief. With the approval of the captain and of the specialists of the unit, I then undertook the construction of an articulated operating-table which could be dismantled, and which could be set at any angle. Then I made a scialytic lamp with a ship's lantern and aluminium reflectors. Then some Ombredan masks for anaesthesia.

It was then that I learnt to do oxy-acetylene welding. The news spread to other field ambulances, and we got more orders than we could fulfil. After the defeat of France, Switzerland found itself completely encircled. In these serious circumstances, General Guisan formed a corps of lecturers charged with the task of keeping up the morale of the country, and I was asked to take part. My lectures were mediocre, but they were a real school for me, in which I learnt a new career altogether. The army, too, had to become more profoundly aware of its mission and of its virtues. I remember with emotion a certain Sunday one summer, when I had been put down to speak on the wide terrace of a mountain fortress, under a superb sky and looking out towards the Dents-du-Midi. The subject given me was courage, a theme which at that time was anything but academic for the unit and for me, gathered up there in impressive silence.

Thus, in my military service as in my civilian work, I engaged in both manual and spiritual activities at the same time, and I experienced through this plurality a real sense of fulfilment as a human being. This feeling of human fulfilment is of vital importance to the subject of this book, the subject of retirement. I should like to cultivate the desire for it in my readers – both in those who have retired already and have time to take up new activities, and also in the young, who are preparing for their retirement, without even realizing it, when they take up something other than their professional speciality.

I am not, however, failing to realize that as an intellectual I am specially privileged. It is true that the better educated people are the more chance they have, generally speaking, to enjoy their retirement, because they can still carry on with their education. In the first place, because intellectual work fits in with physical repose. You can read for hours on a chaise-longue. Secondly, because the capacity for intellectual work is retained longer than physical ability. It can even go on increasing in old age so long as disease does not affect the mental faculties. But most of all, because the more one exercises one's mind, the more pleasure it gives to exercise it; the more one learns, the more one wants to learn, and the easier study becomes.

All those who have tackled the problems of preventive action in the field of gerontology point out this great privilege which the intellectual enjoys – Mme Denard-Toulet,[55] Dr Daniel,[56] and many others. Even if I had no liking for manual and practical work, to read interesting books, to write, as I am doing now, to maintain a considerable volume of correspondence, to initiate myself into sciences about which I know very little, such as modern physics, sociology, or history, to talk with my wife and with my friends, to study a foreign language, would suffice to fill my life and make it passionately interesting. There are so many books I ought to have read, and which I should still like to read, even in spheres which I know fairly well, such as medicine, psychology, theology, and philosophy, and which I shall not be able to read before I die.

Educate yourself!

This is why what is called continuous education is being rightly advocated. Men ought to go on educating themselves throughout their lives, whatever academic level they reached at school. Throughout their lives they must be given the opportunity and invited to take advantage of it. It seems that the greatest progress in this direction has been made in the Soviet Union, through centres of popular culture and especially through the factory libraries, which are used by one out of every two workers. In all countries adult courses are increasing in numbers, covering all subjects, and given by excellent teachers, and also language-teaching by means of radio, gramophone records, and tapes.

There is no doubt that this is a growing movement, and that it is making a great contribution to the solution of the problems of retirement through raising the cultural level of the whole population. In America the churches have played a great part through the Christian Education movement, which organizes discussion and development groups for all ages. In Europe one of the most success-ful movements has been the 'Parents' Schools' which began in Paris. It used a simplified form of modern psychology, applied to child education, marriage problems, family and social relationships, and group psychology.

This cultural effort ought to continue into old age. The Bonn Institute of Psychology has carried out an interesting survey of the dominant interests of people aged between sixty and eighty.[57] Travel was put first by 40.27%, the family by 22.62% and house and garden by 17.65%, whereas only 1.81% put cultural interests first! 'Activities in societies and clubs attract only 0.9% of old people; 0.45% give first importance to reading and music.'

It would be a mistake, however, to give a purely intellectual meaning to the term 'level of culture'. The decisive thing is the desire to learn and the desire to understand, the willingness to undertake something, to try, to persevere, to correct one's mistakes, to strive to improve, to gain experience and learn the tricks of the trade, to enlarge one's horizon, to broaden one's mind by seeking new paths – at bottom, to grow in love, because to be interested is to love, love persons and love things.

I have sometimes made a distinction between the world of persons and the world of things, because human beings need to feel that they are loved personally, loved for themselves as persons, and because too often in our modern world they feel they are being treated as things, as tools of production. But the person is not pure spirit: it has a body which acts and feels; and man is one with his work; he reveals himself quite as much by his acts as by his ideas and emotions; and his ideas and emotions are but the inner echo of his encounter with the world through action. The person lives within the world of things, and gives it life. You cannot love people without loving things. I love sawing, filing, grinding, turning, nailing, glueing, soldering, and cooking. And I love true dialogue, personal encounter, communion with my fellows. The same life-force drives us towards ideas, persons, and things.

The important thing is the desire to do things, to understand and to know. To know people and science, and the diversity of human activities, drawing, painting and music, flower-culture and fruit-growing, and mechanical and electrical construction. Old age and retirement are a wonderful opportunity to widen one's field of knowledge and experience by undertaking things that one could not do when one had to concentrate on one's job. But the seed must be there already; this pleasure in learning and knowing must have been cultivated already throughout one's life.

And throughout one's life one can achieve growth through mixing intellectual and manual tasks. I get as much pleasure out of my workshop as out of my library, in my garden as in my consulting-room. But I think that there is more to this than personal taste. It is a matter of the deep springs on which one draws. Ploughing and sowing, milking, building, sewing and cooking have always been, along with his words and his smile, the primitive gestures by which man has manifested his humanity. In hunting, sex, suffering and feeling, he was not yet distinct from the animals. But the joy of being a man he experienced through these primitive gestures, long before he thought, before he thought that he was performing them, before he thought that he was thinking.

This original joy remains inscribed in that sub-soil of the mind which Jung called the collective unconscious. It is set vibrating once more when he performs those gestures again. I often think of it, even when all I am doing is frying an egg. In doing so I feel I am united with my remotest ancestors, those whom God decided to differentiate from the animals, to create them in his own image. Was it not God also who taught man to sew when he made him his first garment (Gen. 3.21), as the Bible relates? Was it not God also who taught him to make his first tools and use them? So, in my workshop, I feel that I am returning to the springs of humanity and of civilization. And since I am also passionately interested in technical progress and its latest inventions, I feel I am holding both ends of the chain, embracing the whole of man in his entirety.

It is a kind of fundamental emotion, an awakening to the realization of my humanity. I realize it from this very fact, that in my life and in my heart the spiritual and the temporal are joined, that I can both read theology and manipulate matter. I am a regular customer in the 'Do-it-yourself' shop, and I keep finding new tools which I am impatient to handle, just like a child at Christmas-time. Those who have learned while still young to be useful with their hands all know this longing to do things one has never tried before. But those who have never touched a tool soon let go of it again, discouraged because it is too late to learn.

Of course, it is not possible to be an expert in every field, and in order to do anything worthwhile constant practice is necessary. But with a little good will and imagination, with a little application, perseverance and the will to 'have a go', one can initiate oneself into all kinds of disciplines, both manual and mental. This is extremely good for our personal development, keeping us mentally agile and young.

Though one may not be able to do everything oneself, one can take an interest in everything, and try to understand the experience that all men have in every sphere. There are even employers who do not take the trouble to study closely how their employees work: a foreman mechanic used to tell me how he despised his boss because he confused a shift-key with a calliper square. Everything is interesting to the person who tries to understand everything. I always remember a pig-breeder who talked to me about the problems of his job in a way that fascinated me.

In this respect I have to admit that I have been helped by the direction taken by my own work. I have become the confidant of men. And because I take an interest in them as persons, I am fascinated by their experiences, not only by their psychology, but by everything they do. I talk technology with engineers, cookery with housewives, philosophy with professors, fashion with dress-makers, business-planning with industrialists, law with jurists; or again, with marriage counsellors I talk about the difficulties they meet in their own married lives. I think they like to talk to me about these things, because they feel the pleasure it gives me, and that I am really interested in all the technical problems they have to solve.

The happiness I find in my old age is in large part due to this readiness of mind which has always been natural to me, and which my career has done much to develop. Other jobs, on the other hand, are so monotonous and mechanical that they gradually stifle all one's spirit of adventure. Happy are they who are able to react against the effects of routine by taking up exciting hobbies. The trouble is that so often what happens is that the job affects the person, restricting his mental horizon to such an extent that the worker loses the will to take up anything other than his actual job. And when retirement comes, his life is empty. The aged person is incapable of interesting himself in anything at all, he is bored all the day long.

Boredom

This problem of boredom merits our full attention, such is the suffering that it brings to the hearts of many of the old. But of course it is very late to be tackling a tendency to boredom which has been aggravated all through a person's life by a powerful combination of circumstances. I will try to illustrate the way these vicious circles work. Take two children – even so early in life there is often a marked contrast between them. The first, John, is never bored, whereas the other, James, often says to his mother: 'Mummy, I'm bored. What can I do?'

Innate dispositions obviously play an important part in the behaviour of both boys. John has plenty of creative imagination: a scrap of paper, a piece of string suffice for him to invent all sorts of games; his imagination lends them life. James, on the other hand, needs an external stimulus for everything. His mother must get a game out of the cupboard, explain its rules and show him how to move the pieces. She must play a game with him, and after that he will drop back into his boredom.

For John, the pieces are not just pieces. He projects his own inner fantasy upon them and transfigures them. For him they become by turns stars in the sky, lions in the desert, firemen dashing to a fire, soldiers in a war, horses in a show and a thousand other incarnations. In a world so vast, so varied, so marvellous, how could he be bored? All his life he will throw himself eagerly into all sorts of enterprises and will never be bored. His danger is that he will spread himself too much, and never submit to the persevering discipline of routine, which is necessary to any specialization.

Soon the effects of their upbringing will reinforce the innate determinism of their natures. John manages so well on his own that his mother can leave him to play as he likes, and so his curiosity, his ingenuity, his ability and his initiative continue to develop; he discovers and learns by himself many things that it will be necessary for James to be taught and to have explained to him. James, simply because he does not know how to play on his own, has to be taught games to play – and this will be done by his mother in her adult way, conventionally and rationally. He will progressively lose his creative faculties; he will always have to depend on somebody else, and will get more and more bored when he is left to himself. His mother may one day be blamed for mollycoddling him, for not having left him to exercise his own initiative. This reproach, however, will be unfair, because she could not have done otherwise.

At school this determinism will be even more accentuated. This boy James will be a very good pupil. He will play the game of 'school' (an adult game, after all!) very well. He will not be distracted by his inner world, like John who is always lost in his dreams. His academic successes will compensate for the sense of inferiority which he feels beside John, whose triumphs are all in the field of recreation. James will accept without revolt the academic routine which dictates what he must do. He will be happy at school, but lost when he leaves. Fortunately the routine of his job will set him right again. He will be a punctual and exemplary employee, and will of course choose a routine type of employment which will set its mark on his character even more.

As for John, he may encounter some difficulty in finding his place in our rational civilization. He will change jobs. He will be looked upon as unstable. At the office he will be dreaming up some new electronic lay-out at which he will eagerly work in his bedroom during the evening. He will be lucky if he is taken on in an electronics firm. But even there he risks censure, because he will be spending his time thinking about a canoe-trip down the river which he is planning for next week-end.

When their time for retirement comes, John and James are going to be more different than ever: John free at last to undertake all sorts of exciting activities, James all at sea because he has no precise job to do any longer. The differences between them will be multiplied ten times over by the incessant repercussion of temperament on behaviour, and of behaviour on character. It is clear, however, that in our society there are more Jameses than Johns, because society teaches methodical work in preference to the creative imagination.

Of course, in reality the evolution of mankind is much more varied, has much more light and shade in it, than I have described in this too diagrammatic picture, in which I have painted everything in broad strokes of black and white. Personally I am interested in all the tiny details of each person's life, rather than in crude classifications. I have oversimplified the future of John and James, in an attempt to explain a phenomenon which cannot fail to catch our attention.

Retired people do, in fact, seem to be divided into two quite distinct categories as different as black and white. The one consists of people who enjoy their retirement wonderfully, spontaneously find useful and interesting things to do, and are never bored. The others are like a car that has broken down. Without that motive power in their lives that has been hitherto provided by their work they are depressed, resigned, or in revolt. Between these two extremes there are very few intermediate types. The first do not need us and our advice, and their retirement presents no problem. But how difficult it is to advise and help the other group! What a problem! The best of advice, even if it is followed, is often ineffective, because it comes from outside without arousing much in the way of an inner echo.

The explanation of these facts is to be found in that law of the vicious circle which I have always found remarkable. A person's characteristics tend to become more accentuated as his life goes on. The solitary soul creates a void around himself and becomes even more lonely. The sociable person attracts a crowd of friends and spreads himself more and more. The aggressiveness of the individual in revolt provokes unjust reactions which make him all the more rebellious. The shy person does not know how to assert himself properly, and feeling himself still misunderstood he becomes even more awkward and shy. The person who is too wilful is condemned to becoming more and more authoritarian in order to overcome the resistance he arouses.

And so, generally speaking, old people seem to be divided into two well-defined categories, with few intermediate shades. There are wonderful old people, kind, sociable, radiant with peace. Troubles and difficulties only seem to make them grow still further in serenity. They make no claims, and it is a pleasure to see them and to help them. They are grateful, and even astonished, that things are done for them, and that they are still loved. They read, they improve their minds, they go for quiet walks, they are interested in everything, and are prepared to listen to anyone. And then there are awful old people, selfish, demanding, domineering, bitter. They are always grumbling and criticizing everybody. If you go and see them, they upbraid you for not having come sooner; they misjudge your best intentions, and the conversation becomes a painful conflict.

A decisive change

It would be pointless and unfair to pronounce a moral judgment on these facts. Both these groups of old people are determined by their past, and old age is only a kind of detector, a magnifying-glass which shows up the tendencies that have been there over a long period. These tendencies have become more accentuated with each succeeding stage in their lives, although perhaps they have not been really visible until now. All at once they come to the surface in old age, and nothing seems to be able to be done about them. The kindly person becomes more so as he advances in age. The critical person now never stops grumbling. This is what Mme Marcelle Auclair says in her book *Vers une vieillesse heureuse*.[58] 'When one is young, grumbling can be a form of vitality, even though serenity alone dominates events and brings victory. But grumbling when one is old is weakness, and causes enfeeblement. Complaints, regrets and worry, when they go along with a feeling of impotence, become obsessive. The conversation of a great many old people is made up almost entirely of reasons they imagine they have for grumbling.'

Therefore, if one's old age is to be happy, there must be a change of attitude. And it is important that this inner reformation should take place early. That is why the task of the doctor of the person is not merely to cure the disease, but also to help the patient to become aware of his personal problems and to solve them while there is still time. Sometimes the patient has some intuition as to what his problems are, but is not sure how to broach them with his doctor. What he wants most is to get better quickly and take up his life where he left off. But every false attitude, all disharmony in the person, will tend to get worse as the years go by, and is pregnant with consequences for the future.

Reforming lives, however, is no small matter! The vicious circles I have mentioned are powerful. To break their determinism requires more than advice and good intentions. It requires an inner revolution, a decisive turn-round, a sort of conversion. I always remember one old man who was full of bitterness, one of the worst grumblers I have ever known. I tended him over a long period. To me, as to all his visitors, he hardly did anything but pour out all his grievances, endlessly repeated. Suddenly one day, spontaneously, without anything I had said prompting him, he entered upon a confession. He began to talk to me not about the injustices of which he had been a victim, but of the things for which he blamed himself, for which he judged himself to be responsible.

I was overwhelmed. An immense tenderness invaded my heart. He, too, was visibly transformed, his crabbed features were gradually unbending, lighting up, becoming beautiful. I do not claim that all was changed at once in him, but after that our conversations were quite different. Something had changed in him, something essential, which no exhortation, however affectionate, could have produced: a sort of new birth, of conversion. Anne Dupuy describes in her fine book *Le réflexe de vengeance chez l'enfant*[59] changes just as miraculous in irreducibly unsocial autistic children. She uses the same word 'conversion' to express what happens in such cases.

Like her, I am here using the word 'conversion' in a psychological sense which is not strictly religious. Of course it can be religious. Of course it can be a religious experience, an encounter with God which overturns a person's life and casts a new light for him upon everything. But a political conversion, a great love affair, a psychoanalytical cure, an artistic emotion, a really personal contact, even a simple remark that goes straight to the heart, can transform a man and give him this conviction that his life hereafter is to be quite different from before, and more free.

It is religious, I think, in the least formal meaning of the word, for it is always God who acts upon men, and his means of acting are unforeseeable. This is why attempts at the medicine of the person can be disappointing if one does not rely upon God. They become too burdensome, a laborious search for a synthesis of a number of sciences which no one could master all at once. And even if some scholar managed to possess them, the essence of the human person would still escape him, because it cannot be subjected to objective scientific examination. Dr Jacques Sarano has very clearly explained this in his book *Homme et sciences de l'homme*.[60] Whatever our knowledge of man, of ourselves, or of any particular person, the unexpected can always supervene, perhaps in the form of a reaction that surprises us and tells us more about the person.

Sometimes it is a decisive event which will open the way to a quite new direction of growth. What has always struck me is that such events usually take place in some unforeseen and unforeseeable manner, without calculation, as if they were springing up spontaneously from the depths of the being, and their consequences seem disproportionate to the thing that has triggered them off.

Take, for example, the case of one of my patients, who had the terribly depressing feeling that her life was nothing but a succession of failures. She was caught in the vicious circle of failure: she undertook nothing outside her professional duties, because she was unsure of succeeding. I had a deep sympathy and a good relationship with her. Over a number of years I had taken a lot of trouble to restore her self-confidence, but without much success.

Then, all at once, without my doing anything in particular, an unexpected idea came to her, which astonished her as well: the idea of learning to drive a car. It was not a very exciting idea, and would have been quite natural in other people. But in her it seemed to me at once to be a real miracle. Of course, it was not all plain sailing! There were moments of despondency. Driving instructors have nerves like the rest of us, and can let slip an unfortunate remark: 'Come on! Have a bit of confidence! If you go as slowly as this you are a public danger!' When things like that were said to her, she got upset and lost the little confidence she had. But I was sure that she would succeed, and my confidence sustained her. She had the courage to buy her car before she passed her test – a good sign, don't you think?

Even after receiving her licence, she still hesitated to do a journey long enough to get her to Geneva. Then my wife had a happy idea. She suggested that I should go to Geneva and back with her myself, in her car. I saw at once that she was a very good driver. But the most important thing was that for the first time in her life she had the joy of having succeeded in something. You can imagine how happy I was, too!

I have a very lively appreciation of experiences of this kind. It seems that every profound change in a person's life must spring first from within that person himself, not as an effort, in obedience to advice or in some other artificial way, but spontaneously. The movement may still be timid and limited, but it is real. We must be on the lookout for it, and grasp the opportunity when it comes, and then help the person who has entrusted himself to us to take himself seriously, to trust this new life which is rising within him, and to accept the consequences of it.

Since I wrote this, that patient has retired. Her retirement threatened to be a lamentable period, but instead it has been a rediscovery of life for her. The car plays an important part, since it has given her an independence which she has never known before. Most important of all is the fact that one step leads to another in this life. She has other ideas now, and the courage to put them into practice. Her life has become wonderfully enriched.

IV

A SECOND CAREER

A place for the old

We are half-way through our study. Basically, in the first three parts, we have been asking ourselves the sort of questions that a doctor asks himself in making his diagnosis. What is causing the trouble? Among the ills which affect the old, there are natural causes, which belong to the field of geriatry. But there are other factors as well, and it is they which make old age the problem it is today. So, we have seen that the sufferings of old people come in the first place from themselves, secondly from the general attitude of the public, and lastly from the particular circumstances in which they find themselves.

As always, the diagnosis itself suggests the lines along which a suitable treatment can be worked out. It is this constructive aspect of our work that I wish now to define more clearly. A personal change and a change in society must go together to bring about the reintegration of the old into the community of today. They must recover in that community a life that is as happy, as interesting and as useful as possible. In short, they must recover their place in it.

But what place? In order to direct our thoughts, I shall refer to a small item of current news – the announcement of the retirement of Hubert Beuve-Méry,[1] editor of the daily newspaper *Le Monde*. It is twenty-five years since he founded his newspaper in Paris, just when, thanks to the American landing, France was waking from the nightmare of defeat and enemy occupation, when everything needed to be reconstructed, beginning with public opinion. The paper was 'exceptionally successful'. I am no judge of this myself – I am not French, and I see *Le Monde* only occasionally. But even its rivals recognize its success, which they attribute to its founder. In particular, it has attracted the support of the young, since a poll reveals that more than half its readers are under thirty-five.

Everyone stresses the independence of mind with which he runs his paper, 'without ever being afraid to take a line that ran contrary to the views not only of the powers that be – which is nothing – but also contrary to those of its readership'. In *L'Indépendant*, Henri Trinchet writes that Beuve-Méry is 'the man who has most clearly left his mark on the French press over the last quarter-century'. And now, this man is suddenly withdrawing from the scene! The immediate reaction to this resignation of a man who is at the height of his success and his powers is, as is often the case, one of astonishment: 'I cannot believe you are retiring,' writes André Fossard in *Figaro*. 'Let us say that you are retreating – that's quite different.'

Jean-Jacques Servan-Schreiber, the author of the famous book *Le défi américain*, goes further in his reflections. He has something else besides praises to write of Beuve-Méry. In particular, he reproaches him for his 'indifference – apparent at least – . . . to the problems of modern economics'. But, recognizing his merits, he thinks of the service he must still render after his retirement. 'How can a person,' he writes, 'who has completed his working life, and who has arrived at the time of retirement, renew himself for the third age of life? What can he invent in order to continue to be useful to society? . . . According to whether old age has or has not a "value" in the eyes of the community, and a part to play, our society will become humane or bestial. That is the test. And the young, more readily than we think, will judge in accordance with this criterion of civilization: the place that we are prepared to give to those who, in the autumn of their lives, are reaching the summer of wisdom.'

That is exactly our problem, it seems to me. It is not just a matter of consoling and entertaining the old by offering them some leisure occupation. It is that society desperately needs the services which the old are better qualified than the young to provide. After the end of a person's professional career, and before the age of impotence – which is coming now to be called the fourth age – is there not room for a second career? It is this notion of a second career that I should like to throw light upon here.

I realize that what I have to say is not new. Countless men, great and humble alike, have not waited for me to write this book in order to take up what I call a second career. My role is to make people aware, to make them realize the fact themselves, and to make society see that such people are doing something far more important than keeping themselves occupied in retirement. It is for them, I think, that we can say that they have a fine old age. The idea of a career suggests that of work. They are doing work because their activity is co-ordinated and planned, because it is the result of a choice, a value judgment, which gives a meaning to their lives.

My wife's grandfather, Charles Geisendorf, was a merchant. He had a stationer's shop. At the age of fifty, he gave up his business, reckoning that he had earned enough. He lived for another thirty years. Fruitful years. He worked for his church, of which he became a sort of permanent general secretary, but voluntarily and un-officially. How much time did he give to it? I have no idea. But you could always rely on him. He knew more about church affairs than anyone else. He brought to the work all the qualities which had already made him a successful businessman, and he added to that his wide experience of people, as well as his goodness, his kindness, his understanding and tact, learnt over the years. It was, to the end, a second career for him.

I should not like, however, in quoting this fine example, to give a restricted idea of the possibilities of a second career. There is absolutely no necessity for it to be confined to religious or even philanthropic activities. On the contrary, the second career may be devoted to the most diverse activities – much more varied than the regular career, and either full-time or part-time. It is not in order to restrict the idea that I use the expression 'second career', but because the word 'career' does suggest a certain coherence and continuity.

Not a hobby, but a career

In order to make clear what I understand by this word 'career', I shall take an example – that of a bank employee. He is interested and successful in his work. But for his leisure time he buys a sailing-boat, and develops a taste for sailing on Saturdays and Sundays. He joins a sailing club. He takes part in a regatta and does well. From then on his passion for sailing becomes more pronounced. He is still only an amateur. But he reads books on yachting and learns from experienced sailors. He buys himself an improved boat. His prize-list lengthens. One day he is selected for an international regatta, and wins first place. People start talking of his career. The newspapers publish lists of his successes. He is not a professional, nevertheless people talk of his 'career as a yachtsman'.

When the time comes for him to retire from his position as a bank employee, he finds no difficulty in filling the free time retirement affords him. He has been enjoying it for a long time. In the fine weather he is on the water. In winter he is repairing his boat. As I have underlined several times in this book, he has been preparing for his retirement for a long time, without even realizing it. By slow degrees he has been beginning his career as a yachtsman well before his professional retirement. Afterwards it develops and becomes a substitute career, a second career. Grandfather Geisendorf, too, was interested in his church and devoted himself to it well before he withdrew from business. A second career is like a plant whose seed has been sown in the midst of a person's active life, which has taken root, which has developed tentatively at first, but which bears all its fruits in retirement.

If our yachtsman loves his grandchildren, he takes them on board his boat, he gets closer to them, and he will be told he is 'doing a grand job as a grandfather'. So one can do several jobs at once. To begin with, several professional careers, as I am both a doctor and a writer. But even more 'second careers'. The term, however, still connotes a certain constancy of interest and action. Another man, for instance, is a sociable type. He has always enjoyed seeing his friends, especially lonely ones, and he derives pleasure from bringing them in their solitude the warmth of his affection. Comes the day of his retirement, and he multiplies his visits until it becomes a veritable career for him. His old age is a happy one, because instead of frittering his time away and getting bored, he has dedicated himself to a task which he feels is important.

The idea of a second career remains, therefore, necessarily imprecise. I cannot give a direct definition of it here. But I can try to define it indirectly by saying what it is not. There are old people who struggle to continue their professional career, which they will certainly have to give up some day. There are others who turn in upon themselves in idleness and boredom, in a sort of resignation from real life and from society. There are yet others who fill the void left by their retirement with so-called leisure activities which do not always suffice to give a meaning to their lives, so long as they remain mere distractions.

Let us take up these three points once more. The last one first: what distinguishes a second career from what are called leisure activities. As soon as you start talking about the problems of retirement, many people exclaim: 'Ah! You must have a hobby, you must know how to do-it-yourself, or take up gardening; you must build up a stamp collection, enjoy playing chess or line-fishing.' There is, as we have seen, some force in this, in so far as it asserts the value of free activities, the motive of which is pleasure, and not gain or service. But to my mind it is insufficient to ensure a really successful retirement and old age.

I have said enough about the pleasure I have always had in manual work, in reading, and in all kinds of leisure activities, for me not to be suspected of underestimating their attraction. But if such activities have to occupy the whole of every day throughout the year, they will no longer be leisure occupations, but means of filling in time. The word 'leisure' always suggests, to my mind, relaxation, rest, do-as-you-please, spontaneity and the inalienable right to do nothing. Paul Lafargue wrote a book on the right to be idle![2] At least it means the right to do what one likes, without having a bad conscience about it, for no other reason than that one enjoys it. But at the same time it implies doing the thing for a proper and limited period of time. One relaxes from some other activity, one seeks distraction and rest from something else. If leisure lasts all the time, then it loses the sharp tang of pleasure, and takes on the stale smell of emptiness. This is clear if one studies the crisis that overtakes so many people on retirement.

Let us look again at the example of the yachtsman. If he had contented himself, like so many others, with sailing as an amateur; especially if he had been content after his retirement to go on as before, not troubling to perfect his technique, but just getting out his old boat every day of the week instead of only on Sundays, he might very well have wearied of it. What transformed his hobby into a career was the systematic effort he made to make progress and to succeed.

I quite agree that leisure activities should be re-assessed, that it should be affirmed that they contribute as much as our regular work to our development and our fulfilment, that their human significance should be studied and better understood, that we should recognize them as a valid part of life and not just an optional extra. But for a healthy man of sixty or sixty-five, and often of seventy-five or eighty even, they cannot provide a sense of fulfilment, and they do not even fulfil the needs of society. 'Man cannot rid himself of the anxiety of Narcissus,' says Paul Ricoeur, 'unless he takes part in some work which is both communal and personal, universal and subjective.'

I feel that the word 'leisure' is over-worked nowadays. You hear of a 'civilization of leisure', as if civilization must not always rest on an active economic life, on pain of lapsing into famine. You hear of 'serious leisure-time activities'. Does this not take from leisure its charm, its poetry, even its incoherence? If one devotes oneself to leisure seriously and methodically, it is really no longer leisure, but in fact a second career.

When I was a student I attended the wonderful clinical lessons given by Professor Maurice Roch,[3] who knew well how to ally science, experience, common sense and compassion. I did not realize in those days how fortunate I was to have such a master, a real doctor of the person, who could use all the resources of scientific medicine, but who also knew how to teach people to live better, to recognize and correct the faults in their lives. Later on he was to give me most valuable encouragement in the reorientation of my career.

There was an old retired doctor who never missed a single one of Professor Roch's lessons. He was always in the same seat, in a corner, modestly silent. I never even knew his name. We students used to observe him with a somewhat derisive eye. We looked upon him as a foreign body, almost as a gate-crasher, and we imagined that his presence was due to some special favour on the part of our master. I understand now why he was granted that favour. Going back to being a student in the evening of life is much more than a pastime, it is a true enrichment of the person. The exemplary fidelity with which that old man followed the lessons gave to his action the character of a retirement career.

Here is another example: a retired man begins to frequent one of those old folks' workshops which are springing up here and there nowadays. He is in his element, because since his childhood he has always been a handyman, and in the club he finds machines which he does not possess at home. Soon he is giving tips and hints to the other retired people, communicating his enthusiasm to them, and helping them also towards the satisfaction of success. Now his activity at the club is taking on a new significance – it is a career. He has become an encourager of hobbies!

An interesting and useful career

You can see that the borderline between hobbies and a second career is difficult to define. It is nevertheless perceptible: that man had gone to the club for his own sake, for pleasure, in order to practise his favourite hobby. Even if he does not go more often now, he has discovered a new pleasure in going, the pleasure that comes of helping the other old folk to occupy their time intelligently. He has become attached to them. He is engaged in a career of great social value. And this second career in its turn leaves him with time to spare for other things, new things, the novelty of which will give him pleasure. Grandfather Geisendorf, too, had his leisure time along with his second church career, just as he had had before, during the period of his regular employment.

Yesterday, in a restaurant, I met an old gentleman whom I had not seen for some time. He was sitting alone at the same table where I used to see him with his wife. He has lost her recently, and so I address a few words of sympathy to him. Then I question him.

'It's a great grief, of course,' he says, 'but I never have time to fret. About ten years ago I founded a club for retired people – the "Fine Autumn". There were forty of us to begin with. Now there are more than four hundred. I can assure you I've plenty to do organizing my programmes, and getting speakers and artistes.' It is a real career.

People who advocate a new and fruitful era of leisure-time activities often quote the example of ancient Greece. Pizzorno speaks[4] of 'the leisure of the ancients, the seat of the humanities'. He thinks that the reason why the Greeks experienced a golden age of culture is that they had plenty of leisure to discuss philosophy, art and politics on the Agora. But was it really, for them, a leisure-time activity? It was much more a function, a career. They had leisure activities as well. They went to the exhibitions of Praxiteles' sculptures, they watched the tragedies of Sophocles, they read Homer and consorted with the courtesans. But when they met on the Agora, when they walked with Plato in the gardens of the Academy in order to discover the meaning of life, it was not leisure, but a career – an unpaid career, but one that was essential to their civilization.

On the Agora there were not only old people, but men of all ages, in the midst of their active lives. They had time to gather there because the economy of their city, founded at that time on slavery, was prospering. It seems to me that the notorious affluent society that the economists have in store for us ought to free us all for a second career, just as slavery in the ancient world liberated the men of the Agora for their career on the Agora. Only now, instead of slaves toiling so as to free the men of the Agora, it will be the whole population, while it is young, working in its various occupations in order that when they come to the evening of their lives its members may have the freedom to follow a second career.

In Teheran I met the French director of the Franco-Iranian College, who fascinated me with his stories. He had spent a great many years in black Africa. There, he said, it is the women who do the work, and the men are free, and gather every day for several hours in the village square – their own Agora. My friend added that he was admitted to these palavers because he liked these people and knew their language. I exclaimed:

'Whatever did they talk about?'

'About the meaning of life and death, the meaning of sickness and health,' he replied.

Those are the people we call under-developed! Under-developed economically, certainly: but more highly developed than we are from other points of view – like our ancestors the Greeks.

I believe, then, that technical progress, automation, the use of electronics and of new materials, the alteration of climates so as to permit the development of scientific agricultural production, atomic energy and other discoveries, must bring economic prosperity, just as slavery among the ancients or female labour on the Black Continent brought prosperity. Then it can bring greater liberty, not only to a single class, but to the whole of humanity. But what then? Liberty for what? Free time for what? That is the question put by Dr Riesman: 'Abundance for what?'[5] To kill time by means of organized hobbies? To be bored? Rather to allow everyone a second career when they are advanced in years, not a professional career, subjected to constraint, but a free career.

The notion of a second career is, therefore, very different from the old idea of leisure-time activities, even if they are enlarged, developed, and organized. Leisure activities must retain their imaginative, opportunist, craft-oriented character. As I write there is taking place in Geneva a hobbies exhibition, which is no more than a trade fair similar to the fair held to advertise household goods. Instead of selling refrigerators, manufacturers are looking for customers interested in buying their water-purifiers for fish-tanks or fishing-tackle. The Federation for the Development of Leisure Occupations has published a protest, declaring that such a fair runs counter to their efforts, which are aimed at the encouragement of personal initiative in the individual, rather than his conditioning by commercial publicity.

The chief motive of leisure activities ought not to be profit, or fashion, or vanity, but pleasure, pure and simple. A second career has a different motivation, one that is more social. It has a goal, a mission, and that implies organization, loyalty, and even priority over other more selfish pleasures – not in line of duty, since professional obligations are not involved, but for the love of people. It is, therefore, not an escape, but a presence in the world.

What I have just written brings me to the difference between the second career as a reaction to the fact of old age and that failure of interest which turns away not only from hobbies but from the whole world outside, a turning-in upon oneself which is too often described as serenity. There are, I believe, two sorts of serenity, good and bad. The good one is the fruit of great personal maturity, of victory over ambition, of detachment from self and from the selfish impatience of youth. But this detachment will have given place to great love, to goodwill towards men and a passionate interest in understanding them, in helping them disinterestedly and not in an authoritarian manner. The bad serenity, or rather what is wrongly taken to be serenity, is, on the contrary, supreme indifference.

The fact is that in old age we remain in general what we were before, but the traits of our character become more marked. The generous person becomes more so, the wilful person becomes a tyrant, and the person who was already passive becomes even more so. Simone de Beauvoir puts it very well: 'Those who have already chosen mediocrity will not have much difficulty in fitting themselves in, and trimming their lives. I have known one old man who was perfectly adapted to his age: my paternal grandfather. He was self-centred and superficial, so that between the empty activities of his maturity and the inactivity of his last years there was no great difference. He did not overwork, he had no worries because he never took anything much to heart: his health remained excellent. Little by little his walks became shorter, he fell asleep more often over his newspaper. Right up to his death his was what is called "a beautiful old age".'

Yes, Madame, your irony is justified. A beautiful old age is not that; it is a fruitful old age, open to the world, attentive to people, an old age that is ardent as well as serene, an old age which goes on fighting, and with passion; differently from youth, of course, but fighting nevertheless, for all life is a struggle. Too often we label as wisdom what is no more than an attitude of indifference and resignation, not to say resentment. That may sometimes be the underlying significance of solitary leisure occupations: 'I am not wanted any more? – Well, I'll go fishing!' In that case fishing is no longer a pleasure but an occupation for embittered rumination.

People talk of an age when we are exempt from passion. But the absence of passion really means anticipated death. If the frown of anger is no more, then the smile of pleasure will have gone as well; if there is no more indignation, neither will there be forgiveness; if there is no more anxiety, there will be no more hope either. That will come, alas, in the last extremity of old age, of course. But then it is not the triumph of wisdom, but rather decay. There is no further problem. There is nothing but a patient whose suffering the doctor tries to mitigate, and whose life he endeavours to prolong, and one never knows what is going on below the surface in the life of a human being, behind the appearance. The real problem arises earlier. For the able-bodied retired person, it is how to make a success of his retirement. His strength is diminishing, infirmities may supervene, but he has kept his heart, his capacity for love, his need to give meaning to his life. Is he going to fill it with endless hobbies? Spend it in sulking resentment? Or perhaps to refuse to retire and to prolong his professional career for as long as possible?

Contrast with the professional career

At this point I must clarify what I mean by this notion of a second career, by contrasting it with the first career, the 'job'. There is a great contrast. On the one hand we have organization, regulation, and on the other liberty and spontaneity – two quite different modes within the context of the human community. The work we do in our daily occupations ensures the proper working of the community's economic life, which has its unavoidable requirements. Prosperity depends upon our getting the maximum return from the economy, and without prosperity there is no liberty. It must therefore function perfectly, like a gigantic piece of clockwork in which every part works with set precision. Anything imaginative or fantastic would compromise the process. The making of exceptions, the granting of personal favours, would constitute injustice, arouse revolt or revolution, and cause the machine to break down.

The more highly this economic life is developed, the more detailed and rigorous its organization must become. The professional task of each person, the function of each person in the individual enterprise, as in the community as a whole, must be determined in every detail. Everything is provided for in advance by the law, by collective contracts, by individual contracts, by conditions of sale, by rules of procedure. There must be a recognized hierarchy; at every level one must know who is responsible, who gives the orders; and he must be obeyed to the letter. Working hours are regulated almost down to the last minute – symbolized by the time-clock at the factory-gate. The weekly rest-day, the duration of holidays, the age of retirement, are all precisely fixed, and if any easement is possible, that too must be defined in the rules.

This is the result of the successful efforts of lawyers, accountants, employers' associations and trades unions, which themselves impose discipline on their members. There is necessarily a scale of salaries corresponding to each professional function, and promotion from one grade to another, and from one year to another, is regulated. The criteria behind the scale of salaries are different in a capitalist economy from those in the communist system, but the principle of having a scale is nowhere challenged. All possibilities – accident, sickness, disability, premature retirement, unemployment – are included within this rigid system. Insurance premiums are calculated by the actuaries, and the precise degree of incapacity for work has given rise to a whole field of law.

But that is not all. The code of professional duty takes the place of individual conscience. The frontiers of unfair competition and of fraudulent bankruptcy are well-defined. You must have a diploma in order to have the right to heal the sick or preach the gospel.

There are regulations governing the levels of fatty matter in soap or cheese, or the amount of butter in margarine, of microbes in pure water, of alcohol in brandy or in eau-de-Cologne. Conditions are laid down for an *appellation contrôlée* for a wine, and for the correct nomenclature for China tea, skilled tradesmen, and senior operatives. The octane index of petrol is laid down, as is the number of hours to be devoted to geography or mathematics in each grade at school, and the master must keep to his syllabus without arbitrary digressions.

Tax fraud is taken into account in the calculations of the Ministry of Finance, and losses through shoplifting in fixing the prices of goods for sale. Legislation controls marriage and divorce, military service, and the dates for bank holidays. It is laid down under what conditions a crime is not punishable. Everything connected with work is codified, regulated, catalogued, inventoried, programmed, allowed for, inferred, provided for, ratified, controlled, certified and protected by law. And work routines adapt themselves to the patterns laid down by the regulations. All this is absolutely necessary in order to guarantee human liberty.

There is, however, another aspect of liberty which will always fascinate the human heart – the need for imagination and spontaneity; the need to be able to do, or not to do, what one likes, when one likes, where one likes, and how one likes; the need to escape from the net of obligations and prohibitions imposed by economic and social life. Men have always found this chance to escape in leisure occupations, and that was all right so long as they had so little leisure. But now there is room, and there is going to be more and more room, for something else, something which is neither a job nor a hobby, something which combines the satisfaction of doing something worthwhile which was to be found in one's job, and the pleasure of being free which one enjoyed in the pastimes of one's leisure hours.

I am attempting here to give a name to that 'something' in calling it a second career, a free career. It will have no set specifications, no contract, no hierarchy, no age-limit, no routine, no fixed wage tied to an obligation to work. It can be voluntary, it can be paid, but without any compusory relationship between earnings and output. It has nothing to do, therefore, with the idea of a second *job*,[6] which so many pensioners accept perforce, in order to better their financial position. They go and take car numbers in limited parking areas. That is fine, of course! They are in the open air. But that is still a job, and one which lacks the standing of their former proper skilled trade.

It is because the amount of their pension is insufficient that they have to add a second job at a salary greatly reduced from that of their professional career. Everything holds together, as I am sure you have realized, in that new vision of life which I have described, point by point, in this book, a life in which the retired will be able to find their true place.

The following measures are all necessary:
1. Provision of sufficient resources to retired people for them no longer to have to earn their living.
2. Restoration of the status of voluntary and disinterested work, and of leisure-time occupations considered as a creative activity.
3. Relaxation of the regulations governing retirement to make it possible for people to move at the right time, and by degrees, from the first to the second career.
4. Development of permanent educational facilities for older people, making it possible for them to broaden their minds, achieve personal maturity, and acquire a variety of new interests from which their second career may be chosen.
5. The propagation of this idea of a second career, so that the aged will have something better to do than vegetate, get bored or indulge in trivial amusements, and so that they can consciously organize this new stage in their lives so as to turn it into a true career.

A more personal career

What I have been doing is, in fact, to describe in broad outline the distinction between the professional career and the second career. It remains for me carefully to bring out two essential points of difference between them. The first is the much more personal character of the free career which may develop after retirement. Even if one has made a free choice of one's job, even if one has loved it passionately, one will have had to perform it according to the rules of the craft. One practises it in the way one has learnt it. It is, as Jung said,[7] a collective, impersonal culture.

Of course each one of us gradually learns to confer, to some extent, a more personal configuration upon his career. This is particularly the case with the learned professions. Thus I was able to move on little by little from my work as a general practitioner and house physician to that of a psychologist and a director of conscience. But it was a delicate process. There are some countries, less liberal than Switzerland, in which one cannot practise psychotherapy without first having gone through the usual channels of specialist training; in which the social security departments will not pay psychotherapist's fees to a doctor who is not on the list of specialists. His personal qualifications do not count. What counts is this registration, the conditions of which are precisely laid down.

At my door was a brass plate which indicated clearly that if you rang the bell you would be received by a doctor who conformed to what society understands by the title of doctor. A French surgeon who came to see me once asked me why my plate did not refer to 'medicine of the person'. 'Because that is not an official category; it is not a recognized name,' I replied. And then theologians, both Protestant and Catholic, have often criticized me for interfering in what does not concern me in practising the cure of souls without having studied at theological college. I am fortunate in that the career of the writer is not yet controlled by a committee of grammarians, for I should certainly not have found grace in the eyes of such an academy of experts. I could certainly follow the custom of taking on a poor patient without payment, but if I abused this tolerance I would be offering unfair competition to my colleagues. One's professional career remains inexorably bound up with money, not so much for profit as because of the economic system of which one forms part in earning one's living. That is why it is important that retirement pensions should be sufficient to free the pensioner from that need to earn which makes a professional career necessary.

The margin of freedom is thus very restricted, even in a freely chosen profession. What are we to say, then, of those who have had no part at all in choosing their job? They are the more numerous. There may be external causes for that: they may have had the misfortune to be born in a poor family and never to have been able to extricate themselves from a life of drudgery despite their ability. One hears of exceptions, but they are no more than exceptions. Another may have had a domineering father who thwarted his vocation because of social prejudice, or else in order to force him to enter the firm he ran, so as to succeed him some day. Another may have had a sentimental mother who led him into a career which she thought carried status.

There may also be interior causes: self-doubts, the fear of being unable to earn sufficient as an artist, an inferiority complex, an examination failed through nervousness, a failure neurosis; often also a lack of maturity such that at the age when a young person ought to choose his vocation he does not yet know what he wants to be, or else he still has idealistic illusions about a dream-vocation. Without intelligent external support it is often very difficult to change jobs when one has been disappointed. There are many thousands of people who put up with an irksome job until they retire, never putting their heart into it, and always complaining.

But there is something that surprises me – seeing these very malcontents making a mess of their retirement, missing the chance when it comes at last of doing what they would like to do. Chronic bitterness has gradually smothered the life force in them, whereas others who have enjoyed their work are able at once to pick up interesting activities in their retirement. The former say 'What's the good? It's too late.' It is too late to learn English or Greek, to take up painting or singing. Spending their time saying 'It's too late, I haven't the time any more', they lose a lot of time when there would still be time. It is they whom I should like to attract with this idea of a second career; which one can start on at any age, provided one is prepared to use a little determination and ambition.

It is worth thinking about seriously. We all carry about within us what Dr André Sarradon called a still-born twin, an *alter ego* which might have developed in different circumstances, and which it is worth while to resuscitate. Who knows, for example, how many people keep in a drawer pages, notebooks, whole volumes, scribbled in secret and with deep emotion long ago, which have never seen the light of day? But then, it would be necessary to go over it all, setting it in order, correcting, re-arranging, starting all over again, doing research. What a splendid occupation for a retired person, to go poring over old books in libraries and archives in order to produce the sketch of an original work! A personal creation, something much more personal than a job! Because one has to formulate one's own aim, choose one's own method of work, set one's own daily task and assert one's identity in one's work.

There is a second important difference between the professional career and the second career, which I must emphasize. I alluded briefly to it when I pointed out that the proper working of the economic life of the community requires a hierarchical organization in occupation. If you do not know at every level who makes the decisions and gives the orders, if the person who ought to be making decisions hesitates and ducks the issue, if the person who ought to be obeying just pleases himself, nothing will work properly. Production is the law of economic life, whether it be the yield from capital invested in a liberal economy, or that from the five-year plan in a communist one. Financial yield implies responsibilities, and responsibility authority. This inevitable connection between money and work applies also to gainful employment.

Whereas this hierarchy is necessary in our working life, it is its very absence which characterizes the second career, which for its part is freed from the tyranny of money. Here there is no longer any question of obeying anyone or of giving orders to anyone. The only responsibility the individual has is to himself. He may have the very greatest moral authority, but he will no longer have practical authority over people. Thus the second career demands an inner revolution, which consists in giving up giving orders. One can still be a counsellor, but not a boss. This is in fact what retirement means. A story will illustrate the point.

This is how the historian Raymond Cartier describes the end of the Korean War in *Paris-Match*.[8] After recounting the ups and downs of the conflict, he comes to 'the fourth sudden change of fortune in seven months', when General Ridgway, in January 1951, 'regained Seoul and crossed the 38th parallel once more'. Cartier goes on:

Macarthur wishes to take advantage of this back-flash of victory and press on as far as the Yalu. Truman is against this . . . Ridgway supplants Macarthur, and even tells him not to set foot in Korea again . . . Alone among the world press *Paris-Match* announces that the succession to Macarthur is open. The aureole of the victor of the Pacific is so bright that no one thinks that Truman will dare . . .

Truman dares. Using a despatch from the general as his excuse . . . he relieves him of his command. America is dumbfounded. The president's popularity sinks to its lowest ebb. The general, returning to America for the first time since 1936, is given a hero's welcome. Broadway buries him under torn-up

telephone directories. Congress invites him to address it . . .
Meanwhile Harry Truman is burnt in effigy. But the demonstra-
tions of idolatry are in vain. Macarthur is just a retired general.
Truman has imposed his will.

Obviously hierarchy and the right to command are specially
characteristic of the army, so that for a general on active service to
be 'bowler-hatted' means dismissal and disgrace. There is another
pejorative association of ideas suggested by the military's use of the
word 'retire', because they cannot bring themselves to speak of
'defeat'. 'Our troops have retired,' says the communiqué. What it
really means is that they have been defeated.

It is difficult to avoid altogether these injurious associations when
using the word 'retire'. A person who has been a master in his profession, even if it was only as an office manager or a modest foreman, often finds it very hard to accept that from now on he will be
issuing no more orders; he finds it hard not to feel his retirement
as a sort of dismissal or failure. This is particularly difficult for
those who are leaders by temperament. It is a matter of vital importance, because refusal to accept this can poison the whole of their
old age. Difficult old people are the ones who have not accepted
that they must give up giving orders.

For want of being able still to do it in their jobs, they tyrannize
their families and all those around them. They do nothing but criticize, in order to let it be clearly understood that if they were still
allowed to take charge things would be a lot better. They are like
those 'possessive' wives before whom one can only either bow or
rebel. Moreover, the word 'possessive' has a deep significance: the
avarice that one finds so frequently in old people is a defence
mechanism against the feeling they have that life is just flowing
away from them. This also explains the way they encumber their
houses with so many odds and ends of possessions.

Giving up giving orders

It is not, therefore, only a matter of the right to give orders, in a
strictly military, political, or administrative sense. It is a matter
of the dominant social situation. All the artists and writers quoted
by Simone de Beauvoir, who cry out in rebellion against old age,
are really voicing their refusal to accept the decline in their author-

ity. It is a very difficult renunciation to go through with, especially for certain eminent people who have exercised great ascendancy over their contemporaries. The more services a man has rendered to society, the more renowned and successful he is, the harder does he find it to lose his influence.

Society will evolve fruitfully only if we are prepared to trust those younger than ourselves and hand over the leadership to them, without ourselves losing all interest in the community. But sometimes the young themselves do not make it any easier for their elders to go through with this renunciation. Several years ago now I wrote that owing to my age I was giving up the post of secretary-general of the International Sessions on the Medicine of the Person. But making my decision, choosing a qualified successor who scarcely felt himself personally called to the work and considered himself as merely a stop-gap, was not enough. My abdication was more theoretical than factual. My friends continued to rely on me. There are many movements and organizations in which the refusal does not come from the person at the top, but from those who want to keep him there. It was necessary for one of my friends to come to my rescue and exercise his authority in setting up a young managerial team. Even then it was some time before the new team achieved full autonomy as far as I was concerned.

What, then, are we to say of those statesmen who sometimes stay in power to a great age? They are sometimes cited as praiseworthy examples proving that a man can still render the greatest of services to the community long after the age of retirement. Their case does not seem to me to be at all typical. Being endowed with an exceptional capacity for work, they lead a rushed existence which is not proper to their age. They are still in the full flood of their professional careers. They indeed command, they are in power. They are following that most responsible of all crafts, that of the statesman. They are not in retirement, and people who are retired will not solve their problems by imitating them.

What is it, then, that gives them such prestige? Well, I think that it comes precisely from the fact of their exceptional victory. Between organized and hierarchical society and the old there is, if not all-out war, at least a certain competition. Society lays down the rules – it fixes the age for retirement and imposes it on the old. 'That's the way it is,' it says to them, 'now you retire!' It declares them disqualified, as if for a championship. It suspends them from the game in order to make way for younger people, and ensure their chances of promotion. The majority of the old give in, willy-nilly. Some are glad to do so, happy to be able to live at last in the way they want to. Others, more numerous, turn in upon themselves in boredom and inertia, or else rebelliously criticizing the young.

But there are a few old lions who simply refuse to retire, and who fight so tenaciously to retain their dominant place in society that it is society that gives way. They have won the competition. Then society obeys the laws of such sporting competitions – it treats its conqueror with adulation, having failed to defeat him. Proof of this is the remarkable phenomenon that quite young people, who are ready enough to challenge their elders and the whole of society, who look upon men of forty or fifty as being old fuddy-duddies, nevertheless harbour a veritable devotion for extremely aged leaders such as Mao Tse Tung, for example, because such men have successfully stood out against traditional society.

That does not happen only in politics. One sees some aged businessman or industrialist defying the laws of retirement and hanging on to his directorship. They impose respect on their younger colleagues, impatient as they are to succeed them, and they themselves will get their own back later on by doing the same in their turn. Of an old stalwart of this type one says: 'Hasn't he remained young!' But that is as much a criticism as it is a compliment. Sometimes, although officially retired, he still exerts in the background a paramount influence on his successor, who is not free to direct the business as he would wish.

In the Bastions Garden I meet an old college friend. He is, of course, the same age as I, and has been a banker by profession. We have not met for a long time, and we greet each other most warmly: 'What are you doing now?' I ask. 'Well, you see,' he replies, 'I've retired.' He adds at once: 'I looked forward to retirement with some trepidation, and I am quite surprised to find that it suits me so well. I'm happy. I take my dogs out for walks, and I am never bored. And then, as you see, I've just been to my office. I pop in every day. That is very precious to me.' 'Don't you ever upset your successor by going in so often?' I asked him. 'Not at all!' he says. 'Because I've made it an absolute rule never to talk about business with him.' 'Good for you!'

And so, really to accept retirement is to accept that one no longer gives the orders, that one is no longer in authority. It is to accept that one is no longer a part of the hierarchical society. It means taking part in a different game, in which one is not taking anyone else's place because there is no hierarchy, no allocation of duties, no set function. This is quite the opposite of an unnatural prolongation of youth as in the case of the aged statesmen.

The same applies to the mother of a family. At the beginning of this book I wrote of how the crisis of retirement may affect her when her children get married. Until then her instinct has made her their guardian angel. She has protected them against all dangers, both external dangers and the inner dangers of moral depravity. But in order to do that she has had to exercise a hierarchical authority: she has reigned like a queen over her little world. Now, she may quickly find a second career with her grandchildren, one that is well-suited to giving a meaning to her life. But in order to make a success of this second career some abdication on her part is indispensable. Her daughter or daughter-in-law will the more willingly put the grandchildren in her charge if she is careful not to interfere with their upbringing and not to substitute her own authority for that of the parents.

I shall naturally come back to this theme of the renunciation of hierarchical authority when I am dealing in Part Five with the acceptance of old age. It is of supreme importance. This second career which must be built up is a new life, characterized by its spontaneity; in it one no longer does what is laid down, but what one undertakes on one's own, freely. That requires a little imagination, and the old are so poorly trained for it! During their professional careers they have had rather to suppress their personal imagination in order to do their duty docilely. And then it is so much simpler to obey than to give orders, to follow a conventional routine. So we see retired people in large numbers fall back into another routine, that of mass pastimes, 'They choose,' writes Pierre Arents, 'precisely the same leisure activity as their neighbours, which becomes reproduced millions of times.' Commercial exploitation only accentuates this slide towards impersonal pleasures.

There are people who are at a loss what to do when they are no longer receiving orders, and do not themselves have to give orders to others. Obviously they must change their habits; but the problem goes much deeper than that. It requires a certain change in one's inner attitude, a sort of de-clutching and engaging of a different gear. A de-clutching, a detachment, a quite conscious and determined breaking away, not only from the post occupied until that moment by the retired person, but also from the whole of the great machine of organized society of which he has been a part by virtue of his function as a worker. The great problem of his adolescence was how to find his proper place in that machine. Throughout his working life that place has become more clearly defined from promotion to promotion. This function, his work, has validated his existence for forty or more years.

And now he must let go of it all! Inevitably he experiences a feeling of having lost his validity as a person. All at once he is losing a complete section of the content of his life, an important section, which gave him a recognized status – his visiting card in society. At that moment he must discover that his personal value does not reside essentially in his social function, but in his own person. It is on his own person, freed and shorn of all outside investment, that he will have to base his second career. Just as in driving a car one cannot engage a new gear without first disengaging the old, so a real detachment from the old career is a condition of a fruitful retirement.

There is another striking analogy – that of marriage. One cannot make a success of marriage without detaching oneself from one's parents. What is involved is not merely a formal, administrative detachment, but a breaking of bonds which goes deep into the heart. This reconversion from the first to the second career implies an inner conversion. If there remains a secret nostalgia for the old working life, its joys and even its sorrows, its struggles and its victories, the social status it conferred, and for the exciting feeling of being part of a large-scale enterprise, of engaging in an industrial or scientific adventure – that secret nostalgia is a great obstacle to the birth of a valid second career. Imprisoned by his past, the retired person is not free enough in his mind to construct a new future.

More imagination!

His creative imagination, of which I spoke just now, and which is so necessary if the retirement stage of life is to be an exciting adventure, is blocked. The great problem of the imagination is how to apply it to present reality, to enliven, fashion and develop it. Otherwise it is only evasion, sterile day-dreaming, the empty satisfaction of a need to escape. A new analogy comes to mind, that of an irrigation channel in which one sluice must be closed when another is opened. If one dwells on one's past working life, either regretting it or complaining about it, going back to it in thought and spirit when one can no longer return to it in reality, one drains the present of its colour, and deprives oneself of the joys that may be found in a second career.

Sometimes the transition from professional career to retired career is accomplished happily. An ageing doctor like me may appeal to his younger colleagues for new courses of action, and at the same time go on receiving a few old patients himself, patients to whom he is attached as much as they are to him. Or take my friend the surgeon of whom I spoke, who has laid aside his scalpel in order to practise the medicine of the person. He is indeed still a doctor, but in a quite different way. He has abandoned the position in which, as chief of a clinic and a surgical team, he made decisions and gave orders, in order to become a counsellor, since psychotherapy is specially described as being 'non-directive'.

An old pastor or priest, having reached the age limit, leaves his parochial charge and the responsibilities for spiritual direction which it involves. But he has acquired a wide experience of the cure of souls and can still exercise it. He is much more at liberty to devote himself to it now than in the past, when he was afraid to give too much of his time to some desperate person who perhaps was not even one of his own parishioners. My old friend Pastor Arnold Brémond, a little younger than I am, is another case in point. I met him a few days ago at the wedding of one of my godsons. As we ate fancy cakes at the reception we chatted. 'I am retired now,' he told me, 'but I'm having a marvellous time: the French Reformed Church has given me the job of making contact with the Catholic and the Orthodox Churches. I have plenty of time to go and spend a few days in a monastery or a seminary, to discover their spiritual treasures and to reveal to them those of my own church.'

A retired banker whom I know well goes back from time to time to his old office to meet former customers, who are very touched that he should do them this favour. Or else – an even more personal favour – he welcomes them to his own home and gives them advice. It looks as if it were merely a prolongation of his professional career, and yet he has in fact taken the decisive step, since he takes no further part in the management of the bank, and confines himself strictly to the role of personal adviser. That is the essential criterion, that one gives up being a leader, even if one remains an adviser.

This task of adviser can of course be developed enormously, not only in the bank which I took as my example, but in all kinds of undertakings. One of the bad things about our technical civilization is precisely that those who carry responsibility, the leaders, have all their time taken up by urgent matters of the moment, and so have none to spare for the study of more general long-term problems. That is a gap that could be usefully filled by older men. They have wide experience of life, of people and of affairs. They have time to read the recent writings of economists, sociologists, psychologists, technologists and scientists of all kinds, and to distil from them the new ideas which may well be needed to help the leaders of the undertaking to make the decisions they will have to face.

Many writers[9] have insisted on this distinction between the work of exploratory study and that of leading the undertaking. They stress the advantage that would accrue from relieving the leaders of their obligations in regard to research and reflection, and entrusting this work to former colleagues who have the time for it once they are retired. 'For the majority of old people,' says Arnion, 'the functions of counselling are more normal than those of direction.' And he quotes Pitkin:[10] 'America has an urgent need for a Council of the Aged. But no aged person ought to be a governor, a senator, a mayor, or a chief of police. . . . It is the young, resilient people who ought to carry such posts. But experienced counsellors are needed alongside the young.'

A resolution by the French High Consultative Committee for Population and the Family demands that 'intellectual workers who have reached high positions accept, on reaching a certain age, an employment in which they will no longer have, as previously, directorial functions'. It would be important, then, that a serious study be undertaken of the possibility of creating advisory posts which would relieve the over-crowded grades. Arnion quotes Sauvy and Daric, who 'have proposed . . . the creation of posts outside the established hierarchy, which would at the same time safeguard the position of the older member, both materially and as to status, and also increase the chances of advancement of the younger staff'. In this way,' writes Daric, 'one could conceive of an age limit for executive posts, together with the possibility afterwards of advisory posts.'

'Outside the established hierarchy' is an apt definition of this movement from an executive to an advisory function. Obviously this movement out of the hierarchy can take place well before conventional retiring age. It will then bring about that easement of retirement the necessity of which we have recognized. It will make possible the initiation, before retirement takes place, of a second career 'outside the established hierarchy', which will be continued and developed after retirement. It is interesting to note here the distinction which Bertrand de Jouvenet has suggested should be made among men of action, between the 'trainer' and the 'adjuster'. The function of trainer would be suitable for the young, and that of adjuster for the old.[11]

We have at present in Switzerland a thorny political problem, namely the agitation which is going on in the district of the Jura, that is to say the French-speaking part of the canton of Berne which was arbitrarily attached to that German-speaking canton a century and a half ago. The problem is a delicate and complicated one because of the division in the Jura district itself between those who claim its complete autonomy, and those who prefer minority status within the canton of Berne. All sorts of local rivalries naturally come in to make matters worse.

So the federal government has decided, with the agreement of the canton, to set up a Good Offices Commission, popularly known as the Committee of the Four Wise Men, consisting of men who in fact have the authority that is conferred upon them by their age, their experience, and their independence of mind. They are good examples of men 'outside the established hierarchy', who have no decisions to make, but only a mission of study. Proof of this is the fact that as I write these lines, one of the four 'wise men', M. Graber, has just been given a post in the federal government, and that this necessarily implies his resignation from the Commission, since he is thus re-entering the political hierarchy.

This proves, too, that the frontier between hierarchical and non-hierarchical posts can be crossed in both directions. Winston Churchill as well seemed quite retired from his political career, during the war, when he was called upon to take power again because of the gravity of the situation. The same had happened in

France with Clémenceau, who was recalled by the very people who hated him, during the First World War.

General de Gaulle in 1958 also seemed to be definitely retired in Colombey-les-deux-Églises when he received another call in dramatic circumstances. Now M. Graber has been replaced by two new personalities – thoroughly retired, these – in the commission of the 'Four Wise Men', who are thus now five in number. In all countries recourse is had from time to time to exceptional measures of this kind, when individuals are recalled and charged with the task of studying a delicate problem, and not making a decision upon it. Here one can see the important part that the old can play in the community.

More initiative!

All the examples I have given up to now, however, have an exceptional character. It is not just anyone who can be invited to 'sit on a Commission of Four Wise Men', to make high-level contacts with other churches, or to fulfil a function of study, research, and advice for the organization in which he has worked until his retirement. My purpose in giving these instances was solely to make clear what is to be understood by the term 'second career'. Obviously it must take the most varied forms, and each person must draw its outlines in accordance with his own tastes, interests and talents.

The revaluation of old age and of the status of the retired person demands a far-reaching change in the attitude of the public. But it also largely depends on the initiative of retired people themselves, on the use they make of the freedom and time that retirement affords them. It is to you, my contemporaries, that I wish to speak now. It is for us old people to build our own lives, lives that are worthwhile, interesting and worthy of respect, and so to arouse fresh hope in the young that they can look forward to a happy old age. It is for us to show that it is possible in old age to live a life that is different from our working life, but quite as useful and satisfying. Dr Baujat uses the term 'second-wind employment' for what I have called a second career, and he provides a whole sheaf of ideas for use in the construction of this new life.

You have complained for so many years of being rushed, of not having enough time. Now that you have time, what use are you making of it? You feel you have been relegated, but is it not a fact that you allow yourself to be too easily relegated? Are you not conniving a little in your relegation, through your passivity? People talk a little too much to you about leisure occupations, about hobbies. I invite you to have more ambition. Unearth your repressions! Remember not only your old grumbles, but the aspirations you buried long ago. Recollect and relive the times of your youth when you had your life in front of you. You had to make choices; and choosing one career meant renouncing many others.

You all have more in you than you think. Do not expect others to do everything for you and to make room for you. Do not say: 'What's the use? It's too late!' Listen to what Dr Miraillet says: 'Experience proves that an old person whose creative faculties are dwindling, following upon the crisis of a badly integrated retirement, can still regain a measure of originality in an occupation suitable to his tastes and his capabilities.' And again, listen to what Gilles Lambert writes: 'The over-sixties are the best reservoir of talent and energy in the nation.'[12]

Do not be so lacking in self-confidence! You don't have to become as good at gardening or carpentry as the professional is. What you need is to try, to make a start, to apply yourself with care and common sense. I put forward this idea of a second career in order to stimulate you, to arouse your imagination and your zeal. I would not want the idea to frighten you.

It is not a question of excelling, but of 'having a go'. Do not say that such and such an activity does not interest you before you have tried it. Everything becomes interesting if one is prepared to stick at it for a while. You will find that it is trying it out that counts. Before he chooses his career, it is right for a young man to try out a number of things in different spheres of activity, so that he can find out by practice what he likes, and what his aptitudes are. Do the same on the threshold of your retirement career. You will gradually find out what absorbs you most. There is no lack of opportunities for self-improvement in this world, even at an advanced age. What is most often wrong is that people do not open their eyes to see the opportunities, that they fail to grasp them, and do not have confidence enough to succeed.

The fear of not succeeding is, for many people, the biggest obstacle in their way. It holds them back from trying anything at all. And for lack of trying they never give themselves a chance of succeeding – the very thing that would cure them of their doubts. It is not, after all, such a terrible thing not to succeed straight away in some new undertaking. What is serious is to give up, to become stuck in a life that just gets emptier.

Take the case of a relative of mine, a retired engineer. He is clever with his hands, patient and painstaking. He has artistic tastes. One day someone brings him a beautiful Chinese vase that has been broken, for him to mend. It is a delicate task, but he sets about the work with the utmost care. He makes such a good job of it that people bring other objects for him to restore. He has to improve his technique, think out ingenious methods, transform his little workroom, instal new machines. You see, he is no longer just a handyman, occupying his spare time – it is becoming a second career.

Perhaps you have a little garden, and love nature. For a long time you grow a few flowers like everyone else, buying plants in the market, and that of course is a wonderful activity for someone who is retired. But one day you have the idea of making a seed-bed yourself in order to grow your own seedlings. You do not require a big and elaborate greenhouse in order to do so. With a little ingenuity you manage with a few planks and some transparent plastic to make a cold-frame. What excitement when the soil is covered with a down of germinating seedlings!

Why not try a graft? Read your gardening books carefully. You will certainly fail to get some of your grafts to take, but do not be discouraged; you will get such satisfaction when you do succeed with one. A neighbour will come to see how you do it, and you will acquire experience. It is biology – no longer just a pastime. What an extraordinary thing life is, with its almost unbelievable power: a tiny piece cut from one plant can continue its own individual existence when grafted on to another, and become a tree and bear fruit!

Do you think that surgeons would ever have thought of making grafts, including heart transplants, if horticulturalists had not discovered the principle of grafting before them? But above all you will have developed your personality with patience and perseverance – that is a career in itself. And I, as you know, will be so happy if I have been able through this book to make you take up some new activity that stimulates your life and brings you happiness. That, indeed, is why my publishers wanted me to write it:

not for me to compile statistics, but to help people of my age to come back into life and to grow.

Consider the part played by amateurs in the great discoveries in the field of technology. They were the first to use short waves when the official world of radio was still entrenched in long waves, and in fact would not allow the amateurs to use them. Invent! Of course, there are people who seek and do not find, and there are others who find almost without having sought. The important thing is not to become discouraged, to be oriented towards the future, not the past, to make plans. You may come up with some original idea that no one has thought of before. Others will imitate you, because you will have shown them the way. It is only step by step that the aged will become more active once more – and more respected.

This is the way, for example, in which the keep-fit classes for aged persons began to spread, and now their effectiveness is much greater than could ever have been thought possible. I myself attended one of these courses in Geneva, and was extremely struck by it. One retired person who has had experience of them tells another and brings her along to the class, and this has a snowball effect. There are already about forty such classes in my town, and the number will certainly increase, provided there is a sufficient supply of instructresses as excellent as the one that I saw in action. As you rub off the rust you will realize how rusty you have allowed yourself to get, how rusty the rest are, and how sad that is! As you regain the use of your limbs your attitude will change; you will straighten up, become less stiff, and your whole attitude to life will change with that of your body.

And – who knows? – you may become a keep-fit instructor for other retired people, just as many patients cured and made enthusiastic by psychoanalysis, themselves become psychoanalysts. You smile? You think I am being too idealistic? You doubt if you can ever be capable of it? Well, if you cannot become an instructor, you can be an organizer. You can set about finding premises and an instructor, getting retired people together and persuading them, collecting the fees and sending out notices – that is the first step, and you have time to do that! Some day you will be astonished to see so many people congratulating you and thanking you. And you will modestly answer: 'But I haven't done anything much.'

More diversity!

The first beneficiary will be yourself. You will have had an unexpected adventure when you thought your active life was over. You
will have made new friends, experienced enthusiasm, known the
fear of failure and the joy of success. Your role may even be more
modest, but not less important – you may talk to some friend whom
you know to be better fitted than you are to be an organizer. If you
persuade him, you can start the thing together. You will be his
assistant, his secretary, but the result will be your achievement as
much as his. When you can no longer be a man of action, you can
still be an initiator. When you can no longer accomplish, you can
still give inspiration, trigger off the action, or even be a simple
intermediary link.

Thus, for example, in Holland I once met an old friend, Dr Klaus
Thomas. He had founded in Berlin one of the first 'Samaritan'
posts, which anyone in despair could ring up, and be able to pour
out his anxiety to an anonymous listener. I heard Dr Thomas give
an account of his first experiments: their success was far beyond
anything he could have imagined. I was most impressed, and when
I got back to Geneva I invited a few friends to come and talk about
it with me. Among them was a man of action, Pastor Raynald
Martin. I gave him Dr Thomas's address so that he could get further
information from him. Some time afterwards, the Samaritans were
functioning in Geneva. The *Journal de Genève* published an article
about it. A reader in Paris telephoned to make contact, and the
work started up in Paris.

The spot of oil spread. Now there is a great international federation of Samaritans, which organizes conferences, in which large
numbers of keen and qualified participants exchange their astonishing experiences. I was only a tiny link in that chain. Strictly speaking all I did was to pass on to a friend a little of what I had heard.
But I am so glad to have done so. Henry Dunant, the founder of
the Red Cross, was not a man of action. He was a shy and sentimental poet. But he wrote a little brochure in which he told of what
he had seen on the battlefield of Solferino, where he had chanced
to be quite by accident.

That brochure came into the hands of Gustav Moynier, who
gathered together a few friends. And soon the first Geneva Convention, setting up the International Red Cross, was signed by

the governments. What else am I doing in this book – an excellent retirement activity – but telling a few stories which may stimulate other retired people to take part in this great effort, so necessary nowadays, to reinstate the old in their rightful place in society? And if one of them takes the initiative in getting going another keep-fit class for aged persons, that will give this book its true meaning.

I shall even be very happy if all he does for a start is to join a class himself. Simply by joining in movements together, in time with a well-chosen record, he will discover what he lacked: integration in the community, personal participation in a living group. Any new activity, whole-heartedly entered into, sets going a new current of life that is more fruitful than one could have imagined, especially if it is an activity which draws the participant out of loneliness and forges social links.

That is also what explains the growing success of the clubs for retired people, and their considerable psychological effect on their members. Do-it-yourself in a team, in a club workshop, is quite different from doing it all alone at home. And if you have more imagination and initiative than other retired people, you will teach them all sorts of things, and make friends with them. Attending a drawing or language class is quite different from studying alone at home, by correspondence, or by listening to a gramophone record which one soon gives up in discouragement.

You also know that as a reaction against the laziness that has come with the motor-car, attempts are being made nowadays to popularize walking once more. Group walks are frequently organized, in all countries; they are not too strenuous, so that people of all ages can take part. Our older son is very keen on this simple recreation, and I can see that for him it is a community experience much more than a recreation. He has made firm friendships in several countries. In this way he is putting into practice what I have not ceased recommending in this book: making a start before retirement with activities that can be continued afterwards.

In fact you can see venerable old men taking part in these walks. When well trained, they can turn in very creditable performances. And at the end of the walk they get a lot more applause than the young ones. A splendid victory over the contempt for the old! A great feature of these events is the opportunity they give for contact between young and old, an opportunity which is fairly rare.

The same is true in the case of swimming. It has already been pointed out[13] that the swimming pool is one of the rare places where young and old meet, and there are few exercises better calculated to maintain physical fitness in old age.

This fraternization with the young is very good for the old from the psychological point of view. It is a thing that tends to be missing when they play chess or cards among themselves. Nevertheless any game, especially a team game, in the open air brings a new dimension to the retired person, because of the companionship it affords. You can drive a car? You can take a patient to hospital for his daily physiotherapy treatment. You are fond of reading? You can read to a blind person. To render a service is to make friends.

Your wife is ill? You will do the shopping, the housekeeping, the cooking. Do not say resignedly to yourself: 'I suppose I've got to do it.' Say: 'I have found my second career.' Has it not been noticed that women take to retirement much more easily than men, because they all have their second career already, that of house-wife? Why is it, then, in Europe, that men find housework distaste-ful? Cookery is an art, a creative art. You will look for new recipes, and will be quite proud of your success. Even after his resurrection, Jesus cooked a meal for his disciples.

Like him, you can do it for love. When one is young one attaches especial importance to choosing what one does. And that is right, because one has to choose one's job in life. So when I was still a child I chose medicine rather than mathematics, which I was par-ticularly good at. What was in my mind was the wish to have a more humane vocation. I know now that it is possible to be a very humane mathematician. When you are getting old you attach less importance to what is done than to the spirit in which it is done. Undertaking something that one has never tried before is always enriching.

I have a very dear friend who is a university professor. One day he was told that the illness that had struck down his wife was in-curable. He left the university, resigned from all his other duties, professional and otherwise, in order to devote himself entirely to his wife. Not only to tend her and take over the housework, but in order to be with her, to live to the full their life together, in fellowship and dialogue, during that last year of their marriage. That was his career for that year. It is so wonderful to give oneself unconditionally. He was quite young then, and a long way off retirement. What he did, in a way, was to insert a brief 'second career' between two parts of his professional career. And this period of intermission took on the character of a retirement, a sort of spiritual retreat.

Further examples

Many Americans have a right to take what they call sabbatical leave, a year away from their professional activity which they can devote to study. Pierre Arents[14] rightly hopes that all undertakings will realize that it is in their own interest to encourage this personal renewal among their staff. Mature studies, if seriously undertaken, are much more fruitful than those of youth. They favour a personal growth which thereafter renews and enriches one's career. In Denmark my colleagues proudly took me round one of the many popular universities that have been created, where men and women of all ages, including peasants, can go and spend six months studying, away from their daily work. I myself interrupted my medical studies at the age of twenty-two, when the International Committee of the Red Cross sent me to Vienna to help in the repatriation of Russian, Austrian and German prisoners from the First World War, and in international aid for children. It was a period which contributed greatly to preparing me for life.

Later on, having devoted many years to listening to people's life-stories, I am still suprised at the extreme variety of the roads along which people have to travel in order to fulfil their destiny. That is why advice is so rarely of any use. When we give advice we are always influenced to some extent, consciously or not, by our own experiences. In all advice there is a little of the 'do as I do', whereas everyone must find his own personal destiny, conditioned by his past and by what he feels within himself that he is called to do.

Nevertheless, professional counsellors of great experience, such as Dr Gros and his team, make interesting suggestions for activities by retired people, who may well find something there that attracts them: 'From park-keeper to mayor,' they say, 'from hall-porter to director of a cultural establishment, there are many jobs suitable for the retired person.' They stress particularly the services that retired people can render in the study of land use.

A former school-teacher had to retire prematurely because of ill-health. She had hesitated for a long time! I had been encouraging her to continue her career despite her poor health. But where lies the limit between this praiseworthy effort and awkward obstinacy? It is a delicate distinction. And how would she be able to bear retirement, she who was so fond of her job? No one could tell. In fact, at the start she found it very hard. Then, although she was not really keen, she thought she ought to make up her mind to do something. But what? She looked through a programme of adult education classes. Suddenly she saw 'Course in Drama'. She had never thought of that, and what she really had in mind was a language class. But why not? She had always had a liking for literature and for the theatre, and comedy is suited to all ages, since in every play there are parts for old as well as young.

What she had not foreseen was the extent to which one discovers oneself in playing a role imposed upon one, and that even if one is expressing the feelings of another character, and using words written by the author, one is really expressing oneself. And then, in a troupe of actors, people of all ages rub shoulders and are interdependent. She found herself in the company of young people, whereas in her retirement she met only people of her own age and circle. I soon found her full of enthusiasm for her experiment. She was working hard, and was highly esteemed by a first-class teacher and by dynamic comrades. What a renewal of life! Even her health was improving, or perhaps it was that she was finding her ills easier to bear.

But there it is. When you take something up and put your heart and soul into it, it always takes you farther than you expected. Soon she was interested not only in the acting, but also in the author and in the skill with which he had put his play together. In order to act well one must to some extent get inside the mind of the author. How intriguing it must be to write a play! Writing had always come easily to her. I remembered having read, long before, some very good children's poetry that she had written. As a matter of fact she was in charge of the children's Sunday School in her church. She could write a Christmas play for the children of the parish to perform.

So she set to work. The performance was a great success. It was no small task to cast the play, train the actors and rehearse the whole company. The children were keen as mustard. It was quite as good for their education as lessons in the Catechism. And as soon as the curtain was down one of the children exclaimed: 'What play will we be doing next year?' One cannot go on always putting angels, shepherds and wise men on the stage. So she began thinking about fresh subjects. She had to do some research, read history books so as to familiarize herself with the customs and usages of the chosen period. And year followed year. She wrote many plays, with increasing skill. It became, for her, a second career!

I have recently been talking it all over again with her, because I am engaged on this book. What happened? Apparently, a chance occurrence to begin with, then a chain of reactions which she had not foreseen at all, much less planned. 'I feel as if I had been led by God,' she said. An experience like that particularly moves me. I am quite certain that God reigns, that he rules the world, not only in general, but down to its tiniest details. He leads us men also, to the extent to which we allow ourselves to be led, since he has granted us free-will. He does not lead only believers, but also unbelievers. It is the privilege of us believers to know it, and to be able to ask him in our prayers to lead us, and to listen in the silence to his inspiration. But the Bible shows us that quite often it is the believers who are most rebellious against the rule of God.

I believe that God has a plan for every man at every moment. This conviction can give a new dimension to the reflection to which I was calling the retired person just now. There is no more fertile source for the creative imagination than prayer and meditation. What does God expect of him in this stage of retirement and old age? What is God asking him to give up in order to adapt himself to his age, and what is he asking him to undertake? That is what must be discovered; the natural thing is to go and ask him.

The search for divine inspiration

But after all – is it really the voice of God that we hear in the silence, the 'still, small voice' that Gandhi used to speak of? Is it the voice of God, or of the Devil, or of our unconscious, or of our personal ambitions, prompted by pride and selfishness? Who would dare deny that we all deceive ourselves, often? How many sincere and fervent believers have been mistaken, in good faith, such as those who had Christ crucified, or those who persecuted the heretics in the time of the Inquisition? Of course divine revelation, that of the Bible, that of the person of Jesus, that also of all the great religions which so clearly agree together, and furthermore the experience of believers over many hundreds of years, can enlighten us, but our interpretation of revelation and of tradition is not proof against error, as is shown by the fact of all the theological controversies. How can we protect ourselves both from sterile scepticism and naïve illuminism?

Further, how do we set about it? I am often asked this in regard to meditation. I have only one answer: try it. I was thirty-four years old when it happened to me. I was in the prime of an active life, to active, perhaps; but it can happen at any age. About that time I made the acquaintance of an old retired gentleman, who came from abroad. I became very fond of him. He, too, tried to listen to God. In the evening of a well-spent working life, he lived in a magnificent villa, the lawns, flower-beds and roses of which were beautifully kept by his gardener. He lived a life of ease and peace, doted upon by a devoted wife, without realizing that basically he was bored. He told me later that he waited every day with some impatience for the arrival of the *Journal de Genève* so that he could get on with the crossword, and he was quite pleased when it was a difficult one, because then it took him longer to do.

Naturally I am not complaining about people doing crossword puzzles; I often do them myself; they are amusing and often fascinating to do; and instructive, too, obliging me to have recourse to the dictionary. But for a man of his ability, it was a rather meagre compensation for the emptiness of his life. It happened that in a villa nearby there lived a fellow-countryman of his – the person, in fact, who first made me want to listen to God. So it was that I as a young doctor, and this old gentleman of the crosswords, had the same experience at the same time. I was present when his life was turned upside down, and what a turning upside down it was! For a good number of years afterwards that old retired man fulfilled a real mission. People of all ages and all conditions came to him with their personal problems. He took an interest in them all, listened to them, and witnessed to his faith. He discovered the immensity of human suffering, and he had not too much time to relieve it. He had a great heart.

He had his heart before, but he did not have its use. His experience of life was of no use to anyone. He was already a Christian. But it needed a kind of conversion, that inner transformation which is brought about by personal encounter with God, for his faith to become adventurous and infectious. Note that for the disciples of Jesus their apostolate was also a second career. One was an employee of the inland revenue, others were fishermen. In fact they all retired from their professional careers in order to throw themselves, at Christ's call, into the great adventure of saving the world. It is quite clear that there is no power greater than that of the Holy Spirit to change men.

It is not my intention, however, in writing as I do, to suggest that all retired people should turn themselves into evangelists. God is not interested only in religion. In any case, even St Paul, for example, continued to earn his living to the end. It is as true of him as of the rest of us that everyone must find his own way. St Paul was endowed with a strong constitution, and carried on two careers at once. He speaks with pride of his manual work. All human work is equally valid. Some work is exceptional, and some is quite simple and ordinary. The same is true of the activities of retired people.

A few days ago, at a wedding reception, I met a former neighbour of mine. I did not recognize him just at first. 'Remember,' he said, 'I was a sergeant in the police. You used to live in Bourg-de-Four, just opposite my station, and we often used to meet.' 'Oh, of course!' I said. 'Forgive me! Now you're in civvies, you don't look the same as in uniform.' I went on: 'Aren't you in the police any more, then? Yet you still look so young!' 'Ah! You know, in the police, they retire us early!' It is interesting how many talk to me about retirement nowadays! 'I'm interested,' I said to him, 'because I'm writing a book on the subject. Do you get bored? What do you do?' 'It's quite simple,' he replied. 'I've gone back to my old trade. When I was young I was a design draughtsman. A crisis came along, and I saw an advertisement for the police. I joined. I've never regretted it. You know, it's a fine job. And then, I became a sergeant!' I wondered at him: he was radiant with happiness.

'Now,' he said, 'I am back working with the firm I used to work for before; but doing part-time, it suits me fine. I don't earn a lot, but I go when I like, and I have time for my garden and for lots of other things.'

I thought straight away of Georges Guéron, who has suggested that firms should create part-time posts on reduced salary for old people.[15] I said to myself: there's an intelligent firm, putting that advice into practice.

But my former police-sergeant set going another train of thought in my mind. I had just been reading the book by Professor Arthur Jores, of Hamburg, on death as a consequence of retirement, in which he mentions in particular the case of policemen, who tend to live much longer after retiring than many groups. So now is the time to tackle the serious problem of death brought on by retirement. It will occupy our attention up to the end of this Part Four, since it colours the whole question of the second career: it is not merely a matter of banishing boredom, of remaining active and useful. Often it may be a matter of life and death.

Death caused by retirement

Just now the sergeant was recalling our neighbourhood of Bourg-de-Four. There lived also in Bourg-de-Four a master-shoemaker, M. Corbat, a craftsman the like of whom there are very few left, who used to sing as he made shoes to measure for the distinguished people of the old town. He had retired recently, and I have just learned of his death. The anonymous reporter recording the fact in *La Suisse* of 2 January 1970 added: 'M. Corbat retired only five months ago. Perhaps it was inactivity which killed him . . .'

There was also in Bourg-de-Four a lady who kept a much frequented tobacconist's and newsagent's shop. The judges and lawyers as they came out of the courthouse nearby used to stop to pass the time of day with her, in order to relax from the cold solemnity of the Court. I myself never failed to exchange a friendly word with her. I heard the news of her retirement, too, followed a few months later by that of her death. It is quite likely that she, too, died from having retired after such a sociable career. Pastor Brémond, whom I mentioned above, exercised his ministry for a long time in Oullins, a suburb of Lyons, and an important French railway centre. 'Almost all my parishioners worked on the railway,' he told me. 'They were very proud of being able to retire at fifty-five, but they did not seem to notice that very few survived retirement by more than two years.'

At a recent seminar at St-Etienne, we were also told that civil aviation pilots are retired at the age of fifty, but that they almost all die during the following five years. My readers could no doubt quote many other examples. These deaths following upon retirement are often spoken of in public, but these are only vague impressions. The phenomenon is difficult to study closely, with the necessary strict scientific objectivity. Was it really inactivity that killed the shoe-maker, as the journalist said? Or was it some intercurrent disorder that had nothing to do with his retirement? Might it not be that it was because he felt himself slipping towards death that he decided to retire? Who could claim that he would still be alive today if he had gone on working?

One has to die of something, and it is 'very rarely simply of old age'.[16] Even in these cases the doctor hesitates to declare that the patient died of old age. It does not sound very scientific; it is as if he were admitting that has not been able to make a diagnosis. He will willingly use a more scientific formula: 'progressive senile asthenia'. He may even write it in Latin, like Molière's doctors: 'asthenia senilis progressiva'! In the statistics which the Swiss Federal Medical Service sends us regularly, there are tables of the causes of deaths, but there is no heading devoted to retirement, which is not a disease.

A railway employee, for example, dies of pneumonia a few months after his retirement. Obviously that is the diagnosis which the doctor will declare to be the cause of death. Reasoning of a quite different order, not on the level of immediate causality, but on the more distant level of his whole existence as a person, permits us to presume that his retirement is the cause of his death. There is no contradiction between these two causalities. What is commonly called the cause of death in statistics comprises the phenomena which have led to death, the mechanism of death as one might call it, the true cause of which may be determined by the crisis of retirement.

So there are two determinisms, one superimposed upon another. The pathogenic process is the mode in accordance with which the death, 'decreed' beforehand, is carried out. Thus a court condemns a criminal to death, whereas the execution is carried out by the hangman. This judicial analogy seems to me to fit precisely the relationship between the two determinisms. But here is where the difficulty resides: the scientific proof of the relationship of cause and effect between the pneumonia and the death can clearly be established, if necessary by means of an autopsy, whereas that of the relationship between retirement and death remains impossible to define in any given case.

It is necessary, therefore, to have recourse to a different method. Just as Virschov and Claude Bernard, following in the footsteps of Descartes, formulated the anatomical and experimental method that could prove the relationship between disease and death, so it is necessary now to devise another method to show, with the same

strict objectivity, the relationship between death and an event in
the personal life, such as retirement. We are touching here on a
point of capital importance for the whole of the medicine of the
person. Scientific medicine cannot be content with an intuitive
interpretation of each case. It demands rational proofs. Such proofs
will be forthcoming only through sociological enquiries, such as,
for example, that quoted by Dr Miraillet, who reveals that 47.9%
of men – almost half, that is – and 43% of women admitted, in
France, into aged persons' institutions, die within the first six
months!

The work of Professor Jores

But that is part of the special problem of hospitalization. That of
death following upon retirement is a more general one, and also
one that is more difficult to clear up. This is the task that Professor
Jores and his assistant Puchta set themselves. That is why I consider that their work is of exemplary value in the formulation of the
medicine of the person. To their statistical researches they have
added, like the sociologists, systematic interviews, notably with the
widows of retired men, in order to question them about the habits
of their husbands and their reactions to retirement. We shall first
pick out from their work a few points of detail which confirm what
we have already seen. Very few men are capable of enjoying the
leisure-time that retirement brings them. Those who did not already
have, before retirement, some amateur activity, or who did not
carry on some other work, slip into idleness. 'Activity for activity's
sake never gives true satisfaction.' There is no joy to be found in an
activity undertaken on someone else's advice. Even walks are
appreciated, say our authors, only by those who are happy. You see
the problem: you invite them to go for a walk in order to be happier;
but they have first to be happy in order to enjoy the walk. Unless,
we are told, they have already acquired a liking for looking for
mushrooms, chasing butterflies, botany or geology.

But the Jores-Puchta statistical researches are going to provide
us with an important piece of information. For a sociological sta-
tistic to be valid it must be based on a sufficiently homogeneous
group. The authors have chosen that of public service employees.
But among these employees there are various professions. Now, it
turns out that death occurring shortly after retirement is frequent
among those employed in the inland revenue department; it is less

frequent among male teachers, and it is not at all so among women teachers, city policemen and employees of municipal services such as water boards, fire services, etc. Nil among the rural police! That is why I was reminded of this study when the former sergeant told me he was enjoying his retirement, and that he had been able to put it to good use.

The authors draw from these statistics the obvious conclusion that retirement is fatal to those employees who are most bound by routine and red tape – those of the Ministry of Finance, who spend all day in the office. The rural police retire at sixty, but since they do not join the force before the age of twenty-one, most of them have previously had other work, like my sergeant. In particular, they do little office work, and the same is true of council employees. It is, then, the uniformity of office work and the spirit of routine that it creates which are most likely to turn retirement into a serious crisis. Jores notes in this connection that an office career prevents the employee from maturing inwardly. Retirement is a calamity for the civil servant who has wholly identified himself with his work, and who has not attained a certain personal maturity. In that case the consequence can be death, and of this there are striking examples.

Routine! There you have public enemy number one. We had already suspected as much. But now we have been provided with a scientific demonstration of the fact. One ages prematurely in a routine existence. There are people who are already little old men at thirty or forty, because their lives are restricted by routine. What will become of them when retirement comes and deprives them of their sole motive force – professional duty? They will sink into boredom and passivity. We can see a vicious circle here, as in all domains of life: routine causes ageing, and this premature ageing buries the individual all the deeper in routine. On the other hand, to stay open throughout our lives to a multiplicity of interests is to prepare for ourselves a lasting youth and a retirement free from boredom.

The authors have other important things to say about retired officers of the finance department. Tax inspectors are not often highly esteemed by the population at large. But man needs above all to be valued by others, to be respected as a person, and honoured for what he does. Social repudiation saps the resistance of the individual. Jores observed this in the case of the civil servants of the Nazi régime in Germany, who were retired at the end of the war for political reasons. The majority of the sixty-three officials of the finance department whose cases he studied died within five years, even though they were still in the prime of life.

Bitterness, resentment, the feeling of being the victim of an injustice, seriously aggravate the difficulties of retirement. A teacher dies six months after his retirement – he was disappointed at not having been previously promoted to a post in the inspectorate to which he felt he had a right. It could well be the right thing for an organization to grant honorary promotion to a worthy employee, even in the final years before he is due to retire. It would be much more worthwhile than the traditional small present and public testimonial. He will be able to take his title with him: until his death he will be not merely a retired clerk, but a retired office manager. His morale will be higher as he turns to new activities.

The authors also point out the importance of marriage to the retired person. Often a retired man who loses his wife soon follows her to the grave. The state of mind, the social standing, the poverty of a life of monotonous routine, the lack of a real goal in life – all these play a decisive role in the crisis of retirement. These views are in accord with those of Professor Viktor Frankl, of Vienna, who denounces the 'existential void' of modern man, and sees in it the cause of many neuroses.[17] He talks of an 'unemployment neurosis'. He speaks also of the 'Sunday neurosis', the depression which assails those who realize the emptiness of their lives when, on Sunday, the week's activity is interrupted and 'the existential void' is revealed to them. In this connection he expressly assimilates the 'crisis of retirement' to a 'permanent unemployment neurosis'. As for Jores, he has returned to the subject in a number of his writings, notably in an article in which he writes: 'Among men, the one to die will be the one whose life contains nothing but his job.'[18]

I might repeat that remark to many of my colleagues who allow themselves to be too exclusively absorbed by their professional work. There is no question here, of course, of death following retirement, since doctors are not compelled to retire. What is involved, on the contrary, is premature death. I took part yesterday, at the home of a journalist, in a seminar on the problems of old age.[19] Present was M. Renaud Barde, the secretary of the Geneva Chamber of Employers. He told us that he had noticed, when organizing a benevolent fund for orphans of members of professional and employers' associations, that there were more orphans of doctors than of any other group that he had to deal with. Doctors warn their patients against overwork, but often they themselves overwork. May we not apply to them the word routine in a quite different sense from that in which we used it in the case of the civil servant?

Let us come back now to Professor Jores. In the article I have just quoted, as in several of his works (*Man and his Sickness*,[20] *A Medicine for Tomorrow*[21]), he widens the argument until it becomes a veritable manifesto of the medicine of the person. His thought starts from a fundamental distinction which he makes between diseases common to man and the animals, and those which are peculiar to man. In the first, virus diseases, or tumours, for example, only the pathogenic phenomena of classical medicine are involved. But they are not sufficient to explain the diseases peculiar to man, into which come all those innumerable functional troubles which encumber the general practitioner's consulting-room, and in face of which he justly feels himself so poorly armed with the resources of classical medicine.

He claims that all these diseases have something to do with a malaise that is specific to man: the feeling that his life is not attaining its fullness, its full growth, or, as he says elsewhere, that it has no meaning. For to man alone, he says, is life given as a task to be fulfilled. The animal, strictly controlled by its instinct, necessarily fulfils its destiny. Man, enjoying a measure of liberty and the power of thought, conditioned by his upbringing and by the ideals suggested by society, can make a success of his life or spoil it. 'If a man does not fulfil his task,' he writes, 'then death supervenes.' He goes on to point out that this death comes through the medium of a disease which hides its real meaning.

As you see, what we have here once again is what I was describing as two determinisms, one superimposed upon another, but what I called the second determinism, on the level of the person and its destiny, Jores now calls the meaning of disease and death. The expression is quite apt: classical determinism, which is concerned with the phenomenon, and which is the subject of pathogenetic study, is purely causal. The word 'meaning', on the other hand, contains the idea of a direction, a goal, an end, and hence a purpose. This is what all men intuitively feel – disease must mean something. We doctors are often asked about this, if we give our patients time to talk freely when they come to consult us.

It was to this problem of the meaning of disease that Professor Jores had devoted his inaugural lecture on the occasion of his installation as Rector of Hamburg University,[22] a lecture which aroused widespread interest. The reintroduction of the idea of purpose into medicine after centuries during which the notion had been carefully avoided in order to shake off the philosophical prejudices which had for so long stifled scientific medicine, sounded like a mental revolution. This revolution has its origin in Freud, as Viktor von Weizsäcker has shown,[23] despite all the efforts of Freud himself, and of the Freudians up to the present, to keep to a strictly mechanistic and causal point of view.

It was Jung, Maeder and other disciples of Freud in the Zurich school who came round to a finalist interpretation of physical phenomena, and so parted company with their teacher. Dr Maeder has recently devoted an important article to the history of this new discovery of the finalism of the mind, and to the progressive development of this finalist view.[24]

Like Professor Jores, he asserts that we are no longer concerned only with psychology, but with the whole field of medicine: if disease has a meaning, it must be fulfilling a function. What is the function of disease?, he asks himself. Here is his reply: everything that is born must die. In the eyes of the biologist, this is the condition of evolution, which takes place not on the scale of the individual, but over a long series of generations. Since it is necessary to die, it is necessary also for Nature to be organized in such a way that death is assured. That is in fact the function of disease – to lead the individual to death.

You will understand, of course, how new and important these views are. What is commonly thought is that men die because they fall ill. The truth is the opposite – they fall ill because they have to die. Here we have precisely the judicial analogy I previously made: disease carries out a sentence of death pronounced by Nature. Actually, men have more than a little intuition already that this is the case. Any disease is a reminder of death. Every person who falls ill wonders anxiously if the disease will get worse and lead to death, or whether medicine or prayer will be able to win him a reprieve.

Life as a task to be fulfilled

Life and health, then, are closely bound up with this feeling of fulfilment which a man experiences on accomplishing his task, when his life has a meaning, when he has an aim, and the hope of achieving his aim. When Richter carried out his well-known experiment in Baltimore in which he placed rats in danger of drowning, he observed that those which had some hope of escape swam vigorously and remained afloat, while those that had lost hope let themselves go, and drowned. Nothing is worse than loss of hope.

That brings us back to our pensioners. Those who let themselves slide – down to death – are those who no longer have a task, a goal, a hope, more meaning in their lives. There is no joy in an aimless life, no fulfilment when life seems meaningless. Now this radical despair, the veritable breath of death, is only an exacerbation of an existential anxiety which I believe to be latent in every man, ready to rise to the surface as soon as he feels himself powerless to solve a personal problem. That is when those diseases appear which are peculiar to man, and of which Jores speaks. All those functional troubles which are called 'nervous' are signs of a dissatisfaction with life, an emptiness of meaning, a personal problem that is unsolved and is without hope of solution.

A classic example, abundantly studied by psychosomatic medicine, is that of the stomach ulcer, with its recurrences every time the patient's situation reawakens his inner conflict. Here Jores makes a striking comment: quite often, he says, he has asked an ulcer patient: 'How were you during the war?' The reply never alters: 'During the war, I was fine.'

That reminds me of my visit to Liège, in Belgium, shortly after the war. Towards the end of the war the terrible V2 bombs fell at random on Liège, and against them there was no possible protection. 'During that time,' a psychiatrist said to me, 'all our nervous cases were quite well! They became ill again when the V2s went.' Jores, too, says that his patients got their ulcers back after demobilization. So, then, when circumstances are very bad, when soldiers or civilians are in constant danger of death, they are miraculously delivered from troubles against which therapeutics are powerless.

This clearly shows that the real core of the problem is not outside, but within; that the decisive threat is not the external menace – the bombs – but an internal menace; that the despair of which we were speaking is no ordinary despair, such as the fear that one is not going to save one's skin, but a dark, inner despair, the fear that one is not going to overcome a personal problem. Demobilization may mean a return within one's family, having to face a hopeless matrimonial conflict – a conflict that is much more likely to drive one to despair than the conflict of war, because it is situated in the heart and mind of the husband.

Professor von Dürckheim also reports experiences undergone in heavy bombardments, and throws upon them a more penetrating light which reveals their spiritual dimension.[25] A man tells him that just when he thought he was lost, in the hell of an aerial bombardment, he felt himself invaded by an unbelievable feeling of calm. All at once he knew that there was in him a Life 'beyond life and death'. That, says von Dürckheim, is more than a paradoxical psychological phenomenon. It is a religious experience. I am convinced that he is right. It is an encounter with God. It is the realization of belonging to a Life which transcends biological life, limited as that is by death.

I spell that Life intentionally with a capital letter. Jesus said explicitly that it was necessary to lose one's life in order to find Life. But the Greek uses two different words, both of which we translate by the same word 'life'. The first is *psychē*, the biological life studied by science. The other is *zōē*, the transcendent life, the life of God, which Dürckheim's patient had all at once become aware of during the bombing, and which the gospel proclaims.

Do not think that I am straying away from our problem of death following upon retirement. On the contrary, these facts are singularly enlightening. What kills these retired people is not a threat from outside, but a drama within. It is not the prospect of approaching death, which they are reminded of by the fact of oncoming age, however disturbing that may be; it is a problem in their lives that they are unable to resolve, the crisis of their retirement; it is being unable to see any more meaning in their lives, anything more to hope for. On the other hand, an aged person may undergo slowly and gradually the same experience which Dürckheim's patient had in a flash, the awareness of belonging to a Life 'beyond life and death'.

Then he, too, will find that strange, unshakable, inner calm. That, as we have seen, is true serenity. It is never to be mistaken for indifference, withdrawal and passivity. On the contrary, such a person is more alive than ever, because he has found Life, and it is that spiritual Life which will from then on give meaning to his earthly life. He has found the Life which is 'beyond life and death'. Dürckheim goes on to speak of other experiences in which men may perceive a 'Love beyond sympathy and antipathy, or a Meaning beyond meaningfulness and absurdity'. I cannot report in detail here all he has to say, but I wish to point out what is its significance for our serene and radiant old man. He, too, has gone beyond the tempests of ordinary emotion, because he has found supernatural Love, and passed through the arguments and controversies about the meaningful and the absurd, because he has met transcendent Truth.

We come back now to the patient who said: 'During the war, I was fine.' Jores makes some pertinent observations about him. On active service, he says, that soldier was not encumbered by his ego, his 'little ego', according to the expression familiar to Dürckheim. The meaning of his life was no longer a problem for him; a great aim had been put before him, and it galvanized him into purposeful activity, even if it was fallacious. The man was involved and carried along by a powerful current of historical events in which his personal problems became blurred. He formed part of a whole, the homogeneity of which was in fact symbolized by the uniform. Ah, that military fraternity! How many men have told me that the only real experience they have ever had of community was in the army! Even Swiss nationals who have never fought in a war.

Besides the stomach ulcer, there is another psychosomatic disease of which Jores made a special study: asthma. The classic explanation of asthma as an allergic reaction is unsatisfying, he says, in four cases out of five. He therefore set about finding a more general and more valid interpretation. He observed that all asthmatics have a very strict super-ego, a high ideal of purity. They cannot stand dirt, or even the smell of dirt; external dirt is as unbearable to them as is that in their own hearts, which Jung has called the shadow. Asthma, therefore, is a manifestation of an inability to accept life and the world as they are, to accept evil in others and in oneself; it is a pathetic cry of rejection, a 'No!' to the evil which the asthmatic feels is stifling him.

The difficulty in asthma is not breathing in, but breathing out. Breathing out is a gesture of abandonment, a gesture of relinquishment, an attitude of self-abandonment and love, loving others and loving oneself. In the article I quoted, the author reports the circumstances of the death of a young asthmatic woman. In the euphoria and thoughtlessness of a carnival she had done something wrong, and found it impossible to forgive herself. Her super-ego condemned her, and the disease was her punishment. On the occasion of a visit to the hospital by her husband, she was unable to confess this thing to him. She was in the impasse situation of which we have spoken, of radical despair; and the next day she died. The phenomenon has applications far beyond the case of asthma. Already Heinrich Huebschmann, of Heidelberg, had shown that an evolving tuberculosis bursts out in a carrier just when he finds himself in a moral and social impasse situation.[26]

Who can be blind to what all this means in terms of the problems of old age which occupy us here? What general practitioner or what nurse has not had to overcome with difficulty his repulsion at the odour of dirt which emanates from some old people? Is not death the culminating point, the résumé, of all the evil which it is so difficult to accept both in others and in ourselves? The most difficult and the unhappiest old people are those who cannot accept the world and life as they are, with sickness, old age, and death; those who cannot learn abandonment, who cannot bear to be contradicted, who are nothing but complaints and criticisms, who cannot accept themselves, with their limitations, their infirmity, and their dependence.

V

ACCEPTANCE

Who can claim to have fulfilled his task?

We are on the threshold of the great problem of acceptance. Before tackling it in its fullest implications, I should like to follow up our discussion of Jores' work by examining a particular aspect of it which seems to me to be important. At the end of his study of death following retirement, Jores says that the subject involves a serious accusation against our culture and civilization. In his other article, which I quoted earlier, Jores writes that the tremendous incidence of chronic functional disorders is a sign that all is not well with our society. It is not only asthmatics who cannot breathe. Proof of this is the number of people who dream that they are locked in, that everywhere they come up against iron-bound and padlocked doors, that they absolutely must escape, and yet there is no way out. Animals, too, can die of being shut up in a cage.

Jores concludes: 'There is a close relationship between health and fulfilment of life, and between sickness and death and non-fulfilment of life.' Life, he says, is felt to be a task to be performed, and a feeling of fulfilment is a necessary condition of health and life. A man's task is his life, his personal fulfilment. So the vocation of the doctor of the person is in the first place, of course, to treat disease with all the resources of science, but it is also to help men to fulfil themselves.

Life is a task to be accomplished. But who can claim that he has accomplished his task, that he has finished his task? The task always remains unfinished. The particular acceptance I am referring to here is perhaps one of the most difficult to achieve: it is acceptance of unfulfilment, acceptance of the unfulfilled. That is one of the great problems of retirement. This is my sixteenth book. Had I written 32, 64, 128, had I written as many as Goethe or Voltaire, I should not have completed my career as a writer. And in my income-tax return this is put down as an 'accessory profession'!

I have treated the sick – less than the majority of my colleagues, because I have never liked working at speed. Some of them I have lost; I have accompanied some of them as they went on their way to death; I have helped some of them to bear their misfortune; some of them I have healed. We must be clear what we mean by healing. Even Hippocrates said with humility that it is Nature which heals. Ambroise Paré echoed his words in the language of faith. Of his wounded soldier he said: 'I tended him; God healed him.'

Nevertheless, every time a patient gets better, we experience a wonderful feeling of fulfilment. This shows at any rate that the word 'fulfilment' must be taken here in a qualitative and not a quantitative sense. It is, however, when we think of the quality of our lives that we feel our limitations most acutely. Are we not always trying to make up in quantity for our shortcomings in the quality of everything we do? What do we really know about how much is due to our own efforts in the healing of a patient? Does the attraction of surgery perhaps lie in the fact that the role of the doctor in it is a more decisive one? But then he pays for it by endlessly going over every difficult case, such as those which fill the journal of the great Russian surgeon, Nicholas Amossov.[1] For in medicine one is never quite sure what would have happened if one had done what one did not do, or if one had not done what one did.

And then, life seems very long when one is young, and very short when one is old. One's career, too, seems long at the beginning, but short at the end. When one is young one dreams of being able some day to do all that one has not yet been able to do. The older one gets, the deeper lies the immeasurable gulf between that dream and reality. All through my professional life I have had gradually to reduce the number of my patients, in order to be able to devote more time to each one. Now I have to refuse the majority of those who come to me. Even so, it is easier to turn down new patients than to give up, with others, a treatment that is not yet completed. Plenty of limitations there!

One spends the whole of one's life struggling against one's limitations. Unlimited expansionism is the very nature of life. We attack obstacles, and overcome some, even many, of them. But though the limits retreat, they are still there; we feel their presence more acutely. Ménie Grégoire asks a girl: 'Are you afraid of old age?' 'If I have made a success of my life,' she replies, 'I shall not be afraid of growing old.' It is an excellent reply at that age. But it is the very idea of success which gradually loses its straightforward aspect. There are many successes, and at the time we appreciate them as if they were definitive. But success retreats, and escapes us. It itself is limited, unfulfilled. 'When one comes to the end . . . a man's life, it's nothing much,' writes Father Leclercq, and that in the fine book in which he speaks of the joy of growing old. Yes, in order to know the joy of growing old, one must be able to accept the unfulfilled.

This is particularly difficult when one has to drop one's work overnight, when a rigid regulation imposes an abrupt retirement. One can understand the far-reaching repercussions of the crisis that this retirement may have. There is a sudden realization of the limitations of life, which up to that time the mind has been able to avoid. Professional life is over, and it finishes unfinished. This is a prefiguration of death, in which the whole of life will finish, it, too, being unfinished. That is the dramatic contradiction of death: 'An end, but not a fulfilment – that is the face of death,' writes Roger Mehl. In retirement, there is a pitiless revelation of our human condition, more brutal even than that of old age, which comes on gently, and about which one can still delude oneself a little. Retirement, on the other hand, has a quality of finality about it, like death. Moreover, it is only through a series of definitive renunciations that a man becomes aware that he has grown old.

Accepting the unfulfilled

It is too easy to say 'old age must be accepted', and it is too vague. You can say it with a soothing smile. It is more precise to speak of accepting the unfulfilled. You can only say it seriously. And that, rather than his age, is the problem of the retired person, and it is harder the younger he is. His professional life is finished. He can do something else, lots of other things, but he can no longer add anything to his career, no longer complete anything, or correct anything, or do anything to safeguard what he has managed to achieve. He had still so many projects in mind, which no one, perhaps, will ever bring to fruition; which no one, at any rate, will be able to carry through in the way he would have done. Think of the number of unfinished works of art there are in the world, which no one would dare to complete.

And then, what is his successor going to do? I think of Professor Richard Siebeck, of Heidelberg, who had so firmly come out in favour of the medicine of the person. Having reached the age limit, he saw his place taken by a colleague who professed quite different views. He could, of course, reflect that in medicine diametrically opposed tendencies are allowable and even to be welcomed as complementary. But it was still hard.

Worse still – one of my best friends was the governor of a province in his country, which was under German occupation. He found it was more and more against his conscience to carry out the orders of the victorious enemy. He could prevaricate for a time, pretend he did not understand, delay and manoeuvre. But it did not carry him far, and the High Commissioner was becoming more and more insistent. Finally, unable to stand it any longer, he tried to play the card of frankness. He went to see the High Commissioner, and told him that what was holding him back from handing in his resignation was his fear that he would be replaced by a man who believed in the Nazi ideology. The reply was reassuring: 'I accept your resignation. That will not be the case.' But in his retirement my friend soon learned that he had been replaced by a Nazi.

My mother, who had been determinedly lied to about the true state of her health, suddenly learnt on the very day she died that she was going to leave two young orphans, and that she would not be able to complete her task as a mother. But those who lose a dear one also themselves painfully experience this feeling of unfulfilment. A relationship of love or friendship is also a creation that has the savour of eternity, but death strikes it brutally with incompleteness. Saint Augustine expressed this vividly in regard to the death of his young friend: 'I wondered yet more that myself, who was to him a second self, could live, he being dead.' Each of us dies a little in the death of those we love, and there is a part of our lives which ever afterwards we feel to be incomplete.

There are things we wish we had said, things we should have liked forgiveness for, things we should like to have heard, and comfort we should like to have received. The dialogue has come to a halt, incomplete. 'Through my horror of the silence of the departed who can no longer reply,' writes Paul Ricoeur, 'the death of my loved one pierces me like a wound in our common being.' This is the theme of Max Scheller's book:[2] he asks to what extent man can have personal experience of death. It is, he says, precisely through this participation in the death of another, which leaves incomplete his participation in the life of that other. This is a particularly destructive experience in the evening of life, especially when widowhood is involved: 'The loss of a spouse is the principal psychological trauma of old age,' said Professor van der Horst at the Gerontology Congress in Copenhagen.[3]

But the pain of unfulfilment is not felt only in exceptional and dramatic situations. It is a daily occurrence. We die a little every day in all the things we leave uncompleted. All work is a beginning which does not really finish. It is rare for a man to be able to achieve what he has undertaken to do. Especially within the time expected. Every job takes longer to complete than one thinks it is going to. Which of us does not know the feeling of guilt at always being behind in one's programme? At not being able to concern oneself with one thing except by neglecting many others? But also at the fact that we often invent unnecessary jobs to do in order to avoid more difficult tasks? There are even people, the most conscientious, who postpone their holidays or give them up, because they have so much urgent business in which they feel themselves to be irreplaceable, and at fault for not having settled it already. The unfulfilled is always felt as a failure. And when our children grow up, which of us can think about them with the clear conscience of parents who have fulfilled their mision?

Of God alone can the Bible say (Gen. 2.1) that on the evening of the sixth day of creation he had completed his work. The pain of unfulfilment is that of our human condition itself. It is the perpetual tension we feel between our aspiration towards the absolute and the unlimited, and the limitations against which we inevitably come, both without and within ourselves. When the serpent of Genesis said (Gen. 3.5): 'You will be like gods,' he was speculating on the powerful longing of man to escape from the narrow limits of his life, which close in around him more and more, until his death.

Jesus himself knew this pain, for, as St Paul says, he did not take advantage of his divinity in order to escape from any human suffering (Phil. 2.6–7). In the tragic dialogue in the Garden of Gethsemane, there is physical anguish in face of approaching death. There is also the painful problem of the slow, dark search to know God's will, so difficult to make out with certainty. But there is also the tragedy of unfulfilment. At the outset of his ministry he had responded to God's call to save the world. The beginning of his ministry was brilliant, with the miracles and the enthusiastic Galilean crowds. He had been able to resist the temptation to indulge in political activism and demagogy, but his earthly mission was in ever greater danger of unfulfilment, and for several months now the shadow of the Cross had been falling across his mind.

That he should not have been able to get his message across to the religious leaders of his people was not the worst of his disappointments. His own disciples, his intimate friends, asleep there, nearby, at this moment! He had just spent a heart-rending evening with them. All their questions revealed that they had as yet understood nothing. To Philip he had said: 'Have I been with you all this time, Philip, and you still do not know me?' (John 14.9). And now he was going to leave them! Truly, his work was not completed. All through that supreme conversation one feels how overwhelmed he himself felt by that fact. He spoke to them of peace, of consolation, of seeing them again one day. But the awful drama that he foresees for them, he himself is living through it now. A few hours later, on the Cross, he was to see his mother, and beside her John, the disciple whom he loved, and whom his sacrifice was to plunge into the cruellest distress. He said then to his mother: 'Woman, this is your son.' Then to the disciple: 'This is your mother' (John 19.25–26).

It is indeed hard to accept the unfulfilled! This is the problem which lies behind all the other problems with which we are concerned here – those of retirement, old age, and death. And even the turning-point in the middle of life of which Jung spoke, and which so many people run away from, as we saw at the beginning of this book. And already in all the little daily renunciations which mark out the stages of life, and which one did not take too seriously in childhood because one hoped to make up for them later on – either suddenly or little by little every man discovers what the philosophers call his finitude, that is to say that all his prospects are limited. He becomes aware of his finiteness.

Old age can be pleasant for some, and painful for others. But the pain of unfulfilment is universal, the same for all. Even from childhood, consciously or not, man experiences his finiteness. It is a reality well calculated to make him rebel. He will either accept it despite everything, with a good grace or unwillingly, or else he will refuse it either in rebellion or in dreams. The attitude he adopts will control all his reactions throughout every stage of his life. The last stage, which is death, is only the acutest form of a problem pertaining to the whole of life.

Must we accept everything?

Life, in itself, is characterized by a limitless potential. I am not thinking only of the way it goes on from generation to generation. I am thinking of Carrel's experiments: living cells, cultivated outside the organism in favourable conditions, do not die. We do not die, therefore, because of the death of our cells. Our cells die because we must die as an organism. 'Death is fatal for our cells,' writes Professor Chauchard, 'only because they form part of the whole.'[4] The progressive decline of the body which obsesses the old is not the cause of their death, it is the sign of their march towards it.

As René Schaerer says,[5] 'The human reality does not exist. It becomes, it is made . . . Unfulfilment is a constituent of my being. To live is to evolve ceaselessly – to evolve towards death.' Often the crisis of retirement, or the crisis through which a sick person passes on learning that he will not get better, marks a tardy and brutal realization of personal finiteness. It was no doubt because I was an orphan that I became aware of that finiteness sooner than others. From childhood I was in a world that was smitten with finiteness. I have been able to take an interest in everything, in this world, and I still do, passionately, but I have always felt the distance that separates this kind of interest from the thoughtless adherence to worldly things, even the most precious ones. I readily identify myself with the apostle who called us 'strangers and nomads on earth' (Heb. 11.13). My wife, without doubting my love, sometimes feels uneasy when she hears me quote this biblical text.

Whether we like it or not, that is our human condition, which nobody accepts easily. Acceptance! I began my career as a lecturer and writer on his theme of acceptance. I was struck by the number of people who refused the reality of their lives, and by the way their refusal could compromise their spiritual and physical health. Their rebellion made their sufferings worse, while acceptance could lighten them, and sometimes contribute to the healing of disease. Accepting one's life, one's age, one's body, one's sex; accepting as they are one's parents, one's marriage partner, one's children;

accepting affliction, illness, infirmity, bereavements; accepting one-self, one's own character, one's failures and one's faults. All that filled my first book.

A friend had devoted a benevolent article to it, but cunningly slipped in at the end a question which disturbed me: 'Must we really accept everything? Are there not many people who are too passive, and who ought to be urged to break a yoke that is weighing them down?' 'Of course!' I thought. Albert Camus' book, *The Rebel*, which I have often quoted, had made a strong impression upon me. He shows man revealing his greatness by his rebellion. My country, Switzerland, in love with liberty, was born out of the rebellion of the first Confederates against a foreign tyranny, sym-bolized by the legend of William Tell. What, then, could I say? That man reveals his greatness in rebellion, and his wisdom in acceptance? That would be absurd! Is there not often wisdom in rebellion and greatness in acceptance? Where, then, was the dividing-line to be drawn, between legitimate revolt and fruitful acceptance?

For thirty years I have been carrying in my heart, confusedly, this unanswered question. And now, in asking me to write this book, my publishers oblige me to take it up again, in all its depth and breadth. For it is no longer only a question of helping men by helping them to accept their lives, but of helping them to the end, by helping them to accept retirement, decline, old age and death. My career has brought me face to face with suffering; I have seen how sterile revolt can be; but I have seen that capitulation is no less so. Man must fight ceaselessly against all constraint. I often talk about acceptance, but I have the soul of a revolutionary. Can I find for myself some clue that will show me the way out of this contradiction?

It is only with caution and reserve that I can attempt to formulate a reply, since any answer will necessarily be an over-simplification. Life always overflows and confounds our simple formulae. Neverthe-less, I must say where I stand. What revolts me is the injustice and constraint that originate in men; what imposes respect upon me is Nature. Thus, among the ills of the aged, there are some that come from men, from their prejudices, from their lack of love, from their contempt, from the way society is organized and its inequity. Against all this I shall fight without respite. But there are others which come from Nature, and fighting against the laws of Nature only brings fresh suffering.

Of course there is no question of giving up the fight and neglecting precautions against natural catastrophes, disasters, epidemics, poverty, hunger and diseases which entail premature death or infirmity. Humanity has already won great triumphs in all these domains, and I am glad of all the progress made by medicine. But it must be recognized that the more powerful man becomes in his struggle against his ills, the more unbearable are those that he has not yet been able to subdue. This is why the horror of old age and death is greater in our Western societies than among primitive tribes, or in the Far East. It is also why it is often the doctor who finds it hardest to accept the loss of a patient – just as it is he who, in other circumstances, savours the joy of snatching a patient from the jaws of death.

I was not, therefore, speaking just now of capitulating to natural scourges, but of a profound submission to the laws of nature, which the triumphs of science are too apt to make us forget. It was just when modern science was beginning its triumphant progress that Bacon remarked: 'One commands Nature only by obeying her.' All the victories of science, right up to the harnessing of atomic energy and the epic journeys of the cosmonauts, and all the triumphs of medicine, are the fruit of this attitude of humanity towards Nature. She remains our mistress, in two meanings of the term: she teaches us and rules us. We learn from her all that we must know if we are to advance. She it is, too, who in her sovereign power sets limits to our progress and our desires. Who can deny that being born, growing, maturing, declining, and dying – all this is a law of living Nature? And so, in the same way, one commands old age only by obeying it.

The meaning of acceptance

This brings me to a second question which has also haunted me for thirty years, and which is no less difficult: 'What does it mean, to accept?' One sociologist questioned the residents in a home for old age pensioners.[6] Did they accept their retirement and their old age? The replies were pitiable. They were all summed up in the remark of one man: 'You've got to!' That is not acceptance, it is fatalism, passivity, resignation. There is no word more positive than acceptance, since to accept is to say 'Yes!' But for many people the word has a quite negative ring.

One could use a different word. One young woman suggested

'consent'. Or one could say 'resignation'. But all these words are equally ambiguous. The frontier is not in words. As always in psychology, what counts is the motivation. To accept because one cannot do otherwise, is to obey a negative motivation. It is to take up a negative attitude.

Psychotherapy is a long enterprise aimed at saving men from their conditioning, from their unconscious negative motivations, and calling them to liberty, to autonomy and to conscious positive choices. It cannot deny itself at the last moment and advocate passive resignation. Liberty is not without, but within. It is in the heart, or it does not exist. No one is free of all external constraint. But man may remain free in the midst of the severest privations. And the secret of this inner liberty is in fact his personal acceptance of his destiny. The thought is Freud's: 'Everything in Freud leads us to understand that true, active, personal surrender to necessity is the great task of life,' writes Paul Ricoeur.[7] Freud himself retained this attitude to the end, despite the thirty-three serious surgical operations he underwent during the last sixteen years of his life.

To accept is to say yes to life in its entirety. When the child cannot leave his mother's apron-strings, when he cannot assume his adolescent autonomy, he is already to be suspected of neurosis. When that adolescent cannot become adult and assume the responsibilities of the adult, he sinks into neurosis. Neurosis is always linked with an inability to evolve. The adult who cannot accept growing old, or the old person who cannot accept his old age, or who accepts it grudgingly, 'because he's got to', is in the same difficulty, blocked in his evolution against the stream of life.

Life is one-way, its law is the same for all, it moves only forwards. Normal life flows along harmoniously, without turning back in its course or leaping forward. I am not really suggesting to the young, or to young adults, that they should meditate on old age, which is not their problem, but rather that they should truly live their present youth. One prepares for old age by taking a positive attitude throughout one's life, that is to say by living each stage fully. One may indeed note, with Michel Crozier,[8] that the people who are most passive at work are the same in regard to leisure activities, and later on in retirement.

Look at those disgruntled old people who cannot accept their failing strength. Many of them have been no better at accepting

their active lives before their retirement. They grumbled then
about their work and the responsibilities they had to shoulder; and
they regretted their childhood, which also they had frequently not
accepted either. The free and convinced consent that life demands
of the old is not some exceptional burden that is laid on them
alone – it is a universal law. A single 'Yes!' goes through the
whole of life. It is successively 'Yes!' to childhood, to youth, to
adult life, to old age, and finally 'Yes!' to death. It is easier to turn
over a page of life when we have filled it right up. The Bible talks
of the patriarchs who died in peace because they had lived their
'full span of years' (Gen. 25.8).

Here is a woman who looks much younger than she really is.
She would have a right to the half-fare card which the railways
issue to old age pensioners. But she refuses it. She would rather
pay the full fare than produce the tell-tale card in the train. It is not,
however, that she is being vain. She is very shy, and being held back
by her shyness, she has never given full scope to her possibilities;
she has lived at half pressure. And already she must take in her
sails, sails which she has never been able to spread like other
people. I understand her, and I suggest to her not so much that she
should accept the coming autumn, as that she should fight more
strenuously against her shyness, so that she may still be able to
harvest a few late fruits from the summer of her life.

In any case, I do not think I have ever said to anyone: 'You must
accept' – whether it be old age or any of the other natural realities
which are part of our existence and our destiny. To exhort someone
to accept would be to moralize at him, and that always does more
harm than good, except in early childhood. One of my former
patients who is now a social worker has just told me of a remark
made to her by an old blind lady: 'When you haven't got what
you would like, you must like what you've got.' But while this is a
fine and telling testimony from the lips of a person suffering from
such an infirmity, the same remark would be unbearably smug and
worthless if it came from some healthy person exhorting her to
accept her lot.

If an old person complains of losing his sight, many well inten-
tioned people reply: 'But you still have good hearing.' To a man
who bewails his loneliness since he has lost his wife, they say: 'But
you have the children, and good friends.' Such remarks do more
harm than good. A privilege never wipes out suffering. 'Nothing

replaces anything,' one of my patients said to me only yesterday. Mme de Beauvoir is quite right, I think, to challenge the 'moralists' who preach acceptance and renunciation. I see it all as a doctor. What the doctor is concerned with is helping Nature. He tries to see, therefore, why a particular old person has so much difficulty in accepting his old age. It is not a matter of chance. There is some obstacle. The removal of obstacles to the harmonious evolution of life is the task of the doctor.

That is the question I ask myself as I read the book which this woman of letters has written on the subject of old age. She quotes, in large numbers, the confidences of famous men, writers, scientists, artists, statesmen, whose last years have been poisoned by rebellion, and more by their rebellion than by the ills against which they were rebelling. There are some exceptions in the picture she paints, but in general it remains pretty dark. Now, the men of whom she speaks were all in privileged positions, people who had known great success and enjoyed great acclaim in their lives. There are not only external, social obstacles to acceptance, therefore, but there is also an intimate, psychological obstacle.

I will not refer to the most spectacular examples, such as those of Chateaubriand or Lamartine, in which human vanity is only too manifest. I will quote a brief remark which gives one plenty to think about, a remark by an eminent man, full of wisdom, a veritable master-thinker, Paul Valéry. Simone de Beauvoir writes that to Léautaud, who was talking to him of 'that frightful thing, growing old', Valéry replied: 'Don't talk to me about it; I never look at myself in a mirror, except when I shave.' I have treated several young neurotics who suffered from this phobia about mirrors because they did not accept their bodies. But it is a far cry from these patients to Valéry, a man who has cast his penetrating eye over the world, over mankind and over himself. And then, all at once, his glance is turned away – he cannot bear to look at his old age face to face.

In harmony with oneself

Why is it that so many people have such difficulty in growing old? How can they overcome their resentment? The 'You've got to' of the CNRO pensioner which I quoted just now is not enough. His passive and negative motivation reveals resistance rather than acceptance. Can we find a positive, active, effective motivation? I think we can. For my part I see it in a very deep, existential, powerful need that I observe in all men: the need to be oneself, to be in harmony with oneself.

To play the old man when one is young or the young man when one is old; to behave like a single person when one is married; to put on masculine manners when one is a woman; to affect love for a father whom one hates, or to pretend to be brave when one is not – all this leaves behind it an ineradicable malaise, the feeling that one is in disharmony with oneself, with the truth about oneself. There is in the human heart a need for truth which one can indeed betray, but cannot get rid of.

My personal and professional experience has taught me how great this thirst for truth is. In the person-to-person conversation in the consulting-room, a man may come to a decisive turning-point. There comes back to him a memory about which he has never dared to speak to anyone. He hesitates, falls silent, becomes agitated, a prey to violent emotion. He mutters: 'I don't know what you're going to think of me.' In the end he can stand it no longer, his resistance crumbles, he speaks. An intense emotion grips us both. It is the emotion of truth. He looks me in the eyes and says: 'What a terrific effect it has to tell the truth!' I share his emotion: 'What a great thing it is for a man to have the courage to tell the truth!' He may very well have told me many things that were true already. But he has never felt what he is experiencing at this moment. It is like a new birth. Each of us has but one truth, but each truth has a savour of the absolute.

The emotion of truth can be experienced in any sphere. It was that which overwhelmed Descartes when he glimpsed the principle of his philosophy. Pascal knew it in the course of his famous night. Galileo knew it when he had the proof that the earth revolved. St Thomas Aquinas knew it when he realized the coherence which the thought of Aristotle could bring to Christian thought; Luther knew it when he was sure of justification by faith; Michelangelo knew it, as did Einstein, Kierkegaard and all the pioneers of truth.

But the truth also makes us afraid. In the intellectual, objective field, we are afraid of calling in question what we have held to be true, of losing the security of traditional concepts. Personal truth is no less frightening. Think of Paul Valéry's averted eyes. It is the fear of seeing myself clearly as I am. A scientist, a philosopher, an artist, a theologian may devote his life to a search for truth. But if he does not accept his old age, the fact is that despite his passion for the truth, he does not welcome it in its entirety. Man both seeks truth and flees from it. Though man flees from truth, he does not stop seeking it as well. We flee only from the things that fascinate us. Man needs truth in order to live. The love of truth is the source of all harmony with oneself.

This is the case, especially, with our inner truth. External, objective, intellectual truth has little influence upon our behaviour. What determines that is the extent of our honesty with ourselves, of our coincidence with ourselves. Moreover, intellectual truth is relatively stable. Only at infrequent intervals does an original thinker come to call it in question. But our inner truth is moving and fluctuating. It calls for incessant readjustment, because we ourselves change, because we integrate our experiences into our person, and also because we grow old. 'We must change in order to stay the same.'

To live is to grow old, and that is true at any age. A few days ago my wife and I were visiting some friends in Germany. They had also invited a psychoanalyst and theologian, Dr Rudolf Affemann, and his wife. Naturally we were talking of all these things. Suddenly Frau Affemann said to us: 'I remember what a shock it was when my first baby was born. I was quite young – not yet twenty. And there I was, faced with the realization that I had already gone one generation up. From then on there was a generation below mine.' The same kind of shock can be felt when the last representative in the family of the preceding generation dies. Mme de Beauvoir tells of how she shuddered, at the age of fifty, when an American girl student told her of a friend's remark about her: 'But after all, Simone de Beauvoir is an old woman!'

Thus we become aware of our slow and permanent ageing only in fits and starts, when some unusual incident or sign brings it to our notice. One may indeed pull out the odd white hair. That is quite all right provided we do not lie to ourselves. Harmony with oneself depends less on appearances than on one's inner self-consciousness. The danger is that we may start out on a road where a deeper and deeper ditch is dug between the artificial and the real, to the point where one would have the greatest difficulty in bringing them together again. It is possible, too, to adopt a nonsensical policy of ageing oneself prematurely, in order to spare oneself the emotional strain of progressive ageing. This can be done particularly by 'talking old' so as to attract flattering and reassuring protestations as to one's youth. I have heard of one lady who for more than twenty years has been in the habit of dividing up certain personal treasures into little parcels, carefully wrapped and each labelled with the name of the legateee for whom they are destined. She takes pleasure in displaying them.

There is, then, always and necessarily a certain tension, as Jouhandeau says, between 'one's real age, the age one looks, and the age one pretends to'. Even the person who is privileged to feel younger than he is, may worry about it. Gide, when he was my age, wrote in his Journal: 'I hardly ever feel my age, and it is no doubt in order really to convince myself of it that I say to myself at all hours of the day: My poor old chap, you are on the wrong side of seventy-three.'[9] Why does Gide call himself a 'poor old chap'? Obviously he thinks that to be seventy-three is a misfortune even if one does not suffer for it. I am more privileged than he in accepting my age, and in not looking upon it as a misfortune!

Nevertheless, that remark bears testimony to his wish to accept his age, to accept himself as he is, to accept his present reality. He repeats his age to himself 'at all hours', you will have noticed. That burning need for harmony with himself, for self-coincidence, is quite characteristic of Gide: he pursued it all his life with exemplary sincerity. Now, this desire also seems to me to be very much alive among young people today. And as for the old, it seems to me that it is this need which will best be able to help them to accept the reality of their old age.

Positive acceptance

There is, then, an essentially human phenomenon that we may express in two ways, one negative, the other positive. The first: there arises a malaise the moment there is disharmony between me and myself, between what I affect to be and what I am. The second: there is a profound joy as soon as I make a readjustment of me to fit my reality, as soon as I express myself as I am. This joy is the emotion of truth which I described just now, when my patient unburdened himself in my consulting-room.

There are also two responses: one is negative – it is the 'You've got to' of the CNRO pensioner. The other, the positive one, is the love of truth, the passion for truth. The second is more powerful

than the first, because it is positive, and also because it is free. I
have said that the phenomenon is essentially human, because the
animal is not free. It must necessarily coincide with itself. Whereas
man is free, free to coincide or not, to seek truth or to bury himself
in illusion. To accept is to choose the reality, choosing freely between the reality and the fiction. The reality is one, the fiction
multiple. You make the unity of your life by accepting the reality.

You are going to reply to me that one does not freely choose old
age, that it is imposed upon us by Nature. The objection reminds
me of the argument I have often had over the acceptance of celibacy
by a woman. I wrote somewhere that to accept celibacy is to choose
it. This is contested violently by a woman who suffers acutely from
her celibacy and cannot accept it. She exclaims: 'I did not choose
it at all! Nuns choose it freely in their vows, but I never have!'

It is true. And yet, by dwelling too much on her dream of a life
shared with a husband, which she does not have, she makes worse
the cleavage between the fiction and the reality, and she suffers all
the more acutely from her enforced celibacy. What I propose to her,
as I do to the aged person, is to choose the reality, so as to live her
reality to the full and thus to readjust her harmony with herself.
The same applies to each of us. That is not a matter of morality, it
is the observation of the laws of Nature. It is the same with all the
afflictions that come upon us – we do not choose them, but we can
overcome them only by accepting them. What of life itself? We
did not choose to live. But to live truly, and not to vegetate, we have
in the end to say yes to life with conviction, to 'choose life', in the
fine expression of Deuteronomy 30.19.

Does this mean that I am rejecting aspirations, dreams, imagination, and poetry? Not at all. The dream is a potential of reality. It
is the wonderful source of all true creation. This is particularly true
in the child, who works out the reality of his future in the profusion
of his imagination. Again, in adult life, in active life, the dream
may remain linked to action, and be the powerful generator of
action. But there is always the risk of its becoming too detached
from reality, being nothing but an escape, a pure fiction. And in
old age, it may be nothing more than an excuse. Dürckheim speaks
of the complicity of those around the aged person, who play a
game of make-believe in order to maintain his 'illusion that he is
still useful'.[10]

Thus, throughout his life, man faces a choice: a choice between facing reality and evasion. It is a difficult choice, and one that is not taken all at once. There are always two movements: first, a natural, spontaneous, necessary rebellion against what affects us. The glance is averted, like that of Valéry. But there may be a second movement, a movement of acceptance, a sort of reconciliation with ourselves, when we perceive that rebellion involves a divorce between our reality and us. In prayer and meditation we see what we would not, or could not see; we can look it in the face and accept it. Otherwise, a terrible vicious circle is set up. Rebellion brings more rebellion, the fiction is consolidated and return to reality becomes increasingly difficult. Thus the dilemma is accentuated until old age and its afflictions come – and old age is no matter of chance, it is natural and inevitable, and its afflictions not small.

It is no easy matter to accept that one is growing old, and no one succeeds in doing it without first overcoming his spontaneous refusal. It is difficult, too, to accept the growing old of someone else, of one's nearest and dearest. That of a mother whose kindness, welcome and understanding used to seem inexhaustible, and with whom one begins to hesitate to share one's intimate confidences, because they no longer arouse in her the warm, lively echo they used to. The ageing of a father whose judgment and advice always used to seem so sound, but whom one can no longer consult because he must not be worried, or because his faculties are failing. The ageing of a friend to whom one no longer talks as one used to, because it would be necessary to shout out loud things that used to be said quite quietly. It is hard to accept the decay of conversation into banality, empty optimism and insignificance.

Old age is indeed hard for the majority of people, and very hard for some. It must be said in all honesty. It is in fact one of those realities which must be looked at in the face. It is to the credit of Simone de Beauvoir that she has applied herself courageously to the task in her book. But right at the end, perhaps to console herself for the pessimistic impression it gives, she concludes unexpectedly: 'Old age is not the necessary conclusion of human existence . . . A large number of animals die – the ephemera for instance – after reproducing themselves, without passing through a stage of degeneration.' She starts to 'dream' of a transformation of society so profound 'that old age would, so to speak, not exist at all. As happens now with certain fortunate people, the individual, secretly weakened by age, but not apparently diminished, would

one day be attacked by a disease to which he would offer no resistance; he would die without having suffered degradation.'

Ah, dear lady! Your dream looks like pious utopianism to a
doctor who has treated old people throughout his working life! Professor Eric Martin put it quite clearly at the Lausanne study-conference on gerontology in 1970. Replying to Simone de Beauvoir's
words, he reminded his hearers that old age is still for every living
creature a 'process from which there is no escape'. He added: 'My
old dog limps, has a bad smell, and glassy eyes.' Of course, we must
better the lot of the old. The movement has already begun, with the
zealous support and devotion of many doctors, psychologists, sociologists and legislators. But old age will remain a formidable trial,
because it is part of man's nature. Man is not going to join the
ephemera.

Medical science has demonstrated that ageing begins at the
youngest age, and it proceeds very unevenly, according to the organ
and the individual, but inexorably. There are no grounds for hoping
to defeat it. At most it may be retarded. The fountain of youth is
one of those dreams that man invents in order to hide the reality
from himself. And then there will remain the fundamental moral
problem, namely that regression always seems to us to be contrary
to the very principle of life, which is expansion. Is not old age, for
many old people, the pain of disappointed love for life? I have not
yet been attacked by any of the real ills of old age. But I am under
no illusions. Unless death spares me them, I shall experience some
of them.

How shall I react? No man can know what his reaction will be in
affliction before he in fact undergoes it. I read moving accounts of
old people who say they are happy despite real sufferings; notably
the book by Father Leclercq, *Joie de vieillir*. I myself know such
old people, and admire them. But I see in it the grace of God. I
hope that it will be granted to me, but it will indeed be a gracious
favour. Other books leave me uneasy. They are the ones which
are determinedly optimistic. They are inspired by a good intention,
that of reassuring the old by underlining too heavily the benefits of
age.

That is not at any rate the road I can take here. My personal
experience is that those who have really helped me to accept
suffering have certainly not been those who minimized it, but
rather those who sympathized, who looked at it with me in all its

fullness, and bore it with me. My professional experience is similar. Throughout my career I have listened to the confidences of suffering people, people who have found it hard to accept suffering, to accept its reality. What has forged a bond between them and me, so that sometimes I have been able to help them, has been the fact that I have acknowledged and understood their suffering, instead of doubting its reality.

Has old age a meaning?

In reality, everyone fears old age. The vast majority try not to think about it or talk about it. Has not the expression 'third age' only recently been invented so that old age can be delicately referred to without the term actually being employed? It is right to use tact. People are extremely sensitive on the subject, and no one accepts easily the prospect of old age nor the signs of its onset. It is one thing to talk about it objectively, in the manner of the sociologists, as of the old age of other people, but quite a different matter to envisage it personally, as my old age which is approaching.

Whatever the favours which a man may be able to enjoy in old age, he knows very well that it will bring him ills. In the first place there will be physical suffering, sometimes very acute; and then, no doubt, infirmities. Even if he were to be spared both of these, he fears 'those successive failures, that decline of the intellect, the gradual, noiseless approach of inevitable dissolution', of which François Mauriac spoke when he was still quite alert.[11] Indeed, the thing that the strongest and healthiest people fear, sometimes a long time in advance, is mental decay. That original and sensitive psychiatrist Minkowski published at the age of eighty-two the second edition of his book *Vers une cosmologie*.[12] In his preface, he refers with a certain sly humour at his own expense to a remark he made in the first edition: 'I am approaching my fifties,' he had written, 'and I am aware of failures of memory.' Minkowski sees now that his gloomy forebodings have not been fulfilled, for more than thirty years have passed since then. And he concludes: 'The words quoted seem only to show that I have always been concerned with the question of growing old.'

It is the most clear-sighted and the most courageous people who dare to face all these problems squarely. There is one more problem, also serious, which preoccupies them, and which I must now tackle seriously: has old age a meaning? Man is always asking himself about the meaning of events. If an avalanche, an earthquake or a fire ravages a region and brings death to innumerable innocent victims, if the fortune of war upsets the course of history, if a scientific discovery transforms the economic and social order, bringing prosperity or facilitating catastrophic destruction, or if it heals innumerable sick people or brings new scourges, man always asks whether all this has a meaning, and what that meaning can be.

If he is struck by a cruel bereavement, or some disease, or failure, or if some unexpected good fortune comes his way, or again, if he has a terrible or a wonderful dream, man asks if that too has a meaning, and what meaning. But it goes further. Has life itself a meaning, or is it devoid of sense? The question has dominated the whole thought of Camus ever since his first book, *The Myth of Sisyphus*.[13] Sisyphus was the mythical hero whom Zeus condemned to pushing an enormous boulder eternally up a steep slope, only to have it roll back to the bottom whenever he got it nearly to the top. Does all the immense labour of men, of innumerable men each taking over from those before them in an indefinite series of relays, have any more meaning than the hopeless labour of Sisyphus?

This agonizing problem of the meaning of life is argued about passionately by young men of eighteen, just as they are about to engage personally in life, and when the example of the preceding generation seems to them to suggest the vanity of life rather than its meaningfulness. Work in order to live, and live in order to work! Then, the necessities of life, the relentless machine of career, family and society draws them in and submerges them. Objectives to make for are suggested to them, they enthuse, they struggle, they experience successes and failures, and it all seems to give a meaning to life. Who knows whether they are not engaging in all this activity in order to avoid the questions that have no answer?

Then with brutal suddenness retirement comes. Old age creeps on, a new generation takes their place, challenging the validity of the things they have believed in; bereavements bring loneliness and leave unfulfilled their dearest affections, and on the horizon death takes shape. If their career comes to an end before it is completed, taken over by other workers whose careers will, in turn, come to an end while still incomplete; if life comes to an end while still incomplete; if everything comes to an end while still incomplete; if everything flows ceaselessly on, as the Greek philosopher Empedocles said long ago, where is the sense in all that? I am interested to see how much this question of the meaning of life is occupying the attention of the young people of today. The same question haunts their hearts as haunts the hearts of the old. In the prime of life, it may become blurred. But it is only repressed beneath the noise and bustle of intense activity. In the evening of life, it is raised again, in a less theoretical form, more concretely and more personally than in adolescence. One may hear an old man say: I have lost everything that gave a meaning to my life.

The need to discover the meaning of things is impossible to eradicate from the human heart. It is even the feature that most clearly distinguishes man from the animals, according to the zoologist Professor Portmann, of Basle.[14] That is also the opinion of Dr Viktor Frankl, the leader of the new psychoanalytical school in Vienna. He does not challenge the work of his predecessors; he understands the importance of the sexual drives described by Freud and of Adler's will to power, and also Jung's view of man's aspiration towards integration. But he adds the need for a meaning: 'Deep within himself,' he writes, 'man seeks a meaning for his life, and tries to fulfil himself in accordance with that meaning.'

How is it to be found? According to Frankl, it is to be found through dialogue – non-directive dialogue. In order to discover the meaning of my life I need to express myself, to talk about it with someone else. But nobody can tell me what is the meaning of my life. Nor can anyone gainsay the meaning I myself discern without exerting an improper influence over me. True dialogue is not an intellectual discussion. Each of us can recognize the meaning of things only for himself. It is a rigorously subjective matter. One may argue about causal relationships, about the relationship of cause and effect which science studies. But as for the meaning of things, that is a matter not of the cause of a phenomenon, but of its purpose, and at that point all argument is vain.

Thus, the rationalists get out of the difficulty by simply excluding from the dialogue everything that is not objective, everything that relates to personal beliefs, every metaphysical question and every reference to transcendence. As if the world, life, the totality of phenomena, had causes indeed, but no meaning. Nevertheless, the rationalists cannot in so doing extirpate from the human mind its aspiration towards understanding the meaning of things. In that search they abandon man to his solitude.

Detachment from the world

To the aged person who suffers because he no longer sees any meaning in his life, I must now try to bring an answer. I must try in particular to answer this disturbing question: how can the person who has seen a meaning in life also see a meaning in old age, which seems to him to be a diminution, an amputation, a stifling of life? Nevertheless, as we have seen, I can only speak of that in a subjective and personal manner. I cannot claim to be laying down what is the meaning of old age, as if it were a doctrine I was formulating. All I can do is to open my heart to my reader on my own search for a meaning for my own old age.

I confess that that is not easy. For more than a month I have been arranging and rearranging my notes on this subject, without being able to decide how to express myself. The best thing, no doubt, is for me to say frankly what embarrasses me. What embarrasses me is that I cannot repeat what I hear so often, and what is perhaps expected of me, that the meaning of my old age is to prepare me for death and for meeting God, to detach me from the things of the world in order to attach me to those of heaven. I do not understand what that means, to prepare oneself for death. I doubt if I should ever be ready, especially if I concerned myself henceforth only with preparing myself for it. Death will come for me just as I am, and what happens to me will depend exclusively, as it will for all other men, my brethren, on God's mercy, and not on my preparation, however sincere it may be.

In my view it is the whole of life which is a preparation for death, and I do not see how I can prepare myself any differently today than at any other time. Death is not a project, and it is not my reality. What concerns me is my life now, and to seek the will of God for me today, for the meaning of life seems to me to be always the same, from one end to the other – to allow oneself to be led by God. Detach myself from the world? That would be to run away from my own reality. To empty this time that God still gives me in this world in order to fill it with meditation on death, would, for me, be to give up the belief that my life as it is today has a meaning. Other men may feel themselves called upon to meditate upon death, but they can do so without waiting until they have grown old. For my part, I do not think I understand what is meant by meditating on death. I understand what the philosopher Jankelevitch[15] means when he asserts that when we think we are talking about death we are still talking about life.

Other authors praise the denudation that old age brings, as if it had some virtue in itself, as if it constituted a useful training in patience, renunciation, purification and spiritualization. Such praise leaves me uneasy, because it seems to me to proceed from a false contrast against which I have always fought, between earth and heaven, as if it were necessary to turn one's back on the world in order to approach God. 'When we grow old,' says René Bazin, 'everything leaves us, but God comes.'[16] It is a fine testimony, and one which certainly expresses the personal experience of René Bazin. But for my part, I am very glad that God did not wait until I was old to come into my life to call me to him.

Many people thus make a contrast between the world and God, between the attraction of the world and attachment to God, as if it were necessary to lose interest in the world and in life in order to be interested in God. A popular proverb puts the point naïvely: 'When the devil grows old, he turns hermit.' Montaigne has an answer: 'I hate the accidental repentance that comes with age.' It is because of God that I am interested in the world, because he made it, and put me in it. I do not see why I should be any less interested in it now than when I was young. One can live for God from one's youth up, and that, I have no doubt, is the best preparation for old age. In his inaugural lecture, Dr Jean Delay, of Paris, quoted the remark of a philosopher: 'For the man who has lived for the body, old age is decay; for the man who has lived for the spirit it is an apotheosis.'[17] That is true, and yet the formula is an over-simplification; it still suggests an opposition between body and spirit.

A sentence from St Paul will help me to define my thought. It is well-known: 'Though this outer man of ours may be falling into decay, the inner man is renewed day by day' (II Cor. 4.16). That is indeed a message for us old folk. There is indeed something which is destroyed, and which must be accepted – our physical strength, our aptitude for action in the world outside. But St Paul's inner man is not at all a disembodied being which indulges in ecstasies and has no interest in the world. That would be to understand and interpret him quite wrongly. He experienced ecstasies all right, and when he was young! And they certainly did not turn him away from the world – they thrust him into it. That engagement in the world characterizes his 'inner man' which is renewed day by day. He does not disengage himself, he does not resign. His inner self is not withdrawn into indifference – on the contrary, it is a presence in the world. You know how he speaks of the care that he has for all the churches, and for every individual: 'If anyone is weak, do I not share his weakness? If anyone is made to stumble, does my heart not blaze with indignation?' (II Cor. 11.29).

Renouncing without resigning

In his excellent essay on the psychology of growing old, the Parisian psychiatrist Dr Jean Dublineau aptly sums up the problem I am dealing with here. It is, he says, a question 'of knowing how to renounce without having to resign'. It is true, there are renunciations, sometimes difficult ones, to be made; it is true, there is denudation, there are frustrations. I used to do many things a few years ago which I cannot or must not do now; and I do things now which I shall no longer be able to do in a few years' time. It is true, there is a diminution in old age, a 'minus'.

But this limitation of life does not in the least imply resignation. All the renunciations demanded by old age are in the field of action, not in that of the heart and mind. They belong to the order of 'doing', not that of 'being'. I live differently, but not less. Life is different, but it is still fully life – even fuller, if that were possible. My interest and participation in the world is not diminishing, but increasing. In a well-known declaration, General Macarthur said, in 1945: 'You don't get old from living a particular number of years: you get old because you have deserted your ideals. Years wrinkle your skin, renouncing your ideals wrinkles your soul. Worry, doubt, fear and despair are the enemies which slowly bring us down to the ground and turn us to dust before we die.'

You can still live intensely as you advance in years. If there is a 'minus' there is also a 'plus', and it is the 'plus' of my old age which gives it its meaning, and which I must now try to define. One loses something only in order to acquire something else. There is something to discover in old age, an aspect of life which could not be known before.

What is this 'something'? I said just now that I am afraid of it being confused with a sort of resignation, an indifference to the world, escape into religion, what the Americans call disengagement.

Sometimes one does see men of action who retire to a monastery after a brilliant career in politics or business. But in that case, for them, there is no question of resignation: they do not care less for the world; they are interested in it and serve it from then on in a new way, by meditation and prayer. In the history of Switzerland one man played a decisive part. This was Nicolas de Flüe, who, when he was advancing in years, resigned from his important political functions to go and build himself a little cabin in the remote Ranft valley. With our children my wife and I have visited that hermitage, and together we prayed and meditated there.

So little disinterested was Nicolas de Flüe as far as his country was concerned that he was instrumental in saving it, at the time of the Diet of Stans in 1481, from apparently inevitable civil war between the city and the mountain cantons. It is probable that he did not intervene in person. He had given up direct action. It was his thought, his appeal, his faith and his vision that touched the delegates at the Diet, and re-established peace among them. When I was eighteen years old, I wrote in collaboration with a friend an historical essay on Nicholas de Flüe, and he has remained ever since for me the incarnation of my ideal: the combination of faith with care for earthy realities.

But the influence of Nicolas de Flüe on my country was much more profound and more lasting. He was able to discern the cause of the dissensions between the confederate cantons: he saw it in the power and wealth that they had acquired by means of war, in the jealousy, greed and demoralization aroused by war. It is dangerous for men to be powerful and rich. In the Europe of those days the Swiss played the part of a great power, They had waged war in all the countries around them – in Burgundy, France, Germany and southward as far as Rome. They were a force to be reckoned with in the ceaseless game in which political and military alliances were for ever being made, unmade and overthrown. Nicolas de Flüe gave them a watchword: do not meddle any more in the quarrels of the great. That is the source of Switzerland's perpetual neutrality.

On that day, Switzerland entered into its old age! Yes, I think it can be put like that. It means to say that Switzerland went into retirement as a juvenile and conquering nation. Those of its citizens who yearned for military glory were able to engage themselves in the service of the King of France, the King of Prussia, or the Pope; they were able to let themselves be slaughtered to the last man, on 10 August 1792, heroically defending the king against the popular forces of the French Revolution. But Switzerland has remained a tiny country. However determined it may be to defend itself, it must count more on its moral strength than on its material power. The only manner in which it has grown larger has been by the free adhesion of new cantons, of which the last was Geneva – and that with extreme caution.

After the First World War, when the former Austro-Hungarian Empire was crumbling, the province nearest to Switzerland, the Vorarlberg, applied for admission as the twenty-third canton. In my youthful patriotic ardour I was enthusiastically in favour of the project. With two friends I went to the Vorarlberg. We saw the Landamann and attended big popular meetings in favour of joining. But the Swiss Government turned a deaf ear. When later Hitler took over in Germany and then annexed Austria, I had to recognize that my country had been wise to remain faithful to Nicolas de Flüe's advice.

Thus Switzerland accepted its old age. And it is a happy old age, like that of those old people whom everyone loves because they make no more claims for themselves, and take an interest in everybody. It is on this interest that I wish to insist. Switzerland has not as a result resigned from its position in the world. It plays another role now, no longer a war role, but a peace role. It has lost nothing of its attitude of attention to the world. The opposite is the case. I have often been struck, as I have travelled about the world, to find that people in other countries took less interest in world events than those in my own, except for those that affected their own national interest. It seems that countries engaged in international rivalries and conflicts are fascinated by them, so that people in such countries pay less attention to other world events. I see, therefore, a certain conflict between the private interests forced on people by the power struggle, and the ability to open the mind to universal matters. And so a philosopher who concerns himself with general concepts strikes us as being old, even if he is young. He has a serenity which benefits old age.

So too, the old man, freed from professional and social competition, can open his mind to wider horizons. This passage from the particular to the universal seems to me to be the great advantage of the passage from active life to old age, and it is in this contrast that I find a meaning in my old age. During the most active period of his life, a man must deal with pressing tasks. His career, his specialization, his professional, economic and social position, the success of his marriage, the upbringing of his children, and all sorts of conflicts, monopolize his attention and his energy. He does escape from time to time, to do a little reading, indulge in a hobby, listen to a sermon, or spend a little time in meditation. But he has not much time to spare, nor is his mind free enough for him to take much interest in problems extraneous to his immediate concerns. The meaning of old age seems to me to lie in liberation from these immediate interests, and the opportunity of enlarging the interests of the heart and mind.

A wider love

I think that one may even call it, somewhat paradoxically, a passage from interested interest to disinterested interest. When a man is young, it is above all the exigencies of action which arouse in him the interest he takes in things and in people. Even a schoolboy is interested in geography because he has obtained a good mark in geography, or because he likes his geography master. For others the same applies to mathematics or to literature. And throughout their active lives they will interest themselves in the disciplines in which they are successful, in people who show confidence in them, in the spheres that are most favourable to their affirmation of themselves. Thus the search for a certain personal advantage dictates, at least in part, the interest we take in things and in persons. It is this interest factor which becomes attenuated when retirement comes to put an end to the active phase of life.

Imagine two footballers, whom I am going to call Lucien and Charles – in the USA of course, they would be baseball champions, and would be called Bob and Will. They are both equally keen on their sport, and rightly so, because they are first-class players. Their names are in all the newspapers. They have countless admirers. Their success makes them keen, and their keenness ensures their success. Football occupies all their thoughts, it captivates their hearts. But a day will come – and very soon for such players – when they will no longer qualify to play in the big championships. All at once they will sink back into anonymity. Their personal reactions are going to be very different.

Lucien's interest in football is such that he still goes to watch all the matches, and often visits his club. He gives a warm welcome to the young members, lavishes advice and encouragement upon them, and is enthusiastic about their progress. His passion for the sport is freer, more disinterested, shorn of the feelings of jealousy which are inevitable so long as one is still engaged in competition. Naturally he is well-liked, appreciated by his new champions who tell each other stories about his triumphs in the past. He remains a leader. He will become a trainer, a referee, perhaps president of the club. He will be engaging in what I have called a second career.

Charles, on the other hand, is so upset by his removal from the big championships that he never sets foot again either on the football ground or in the club premises. 'It hurts too much,' he says, 'to go to a match and not be able to play. Obviously I was too fond of football, and I'm still too fond of it to be able to take being given the push.' So he sinks into bitterness. He talks cynically of the vanity of life and the ingratitude of men, who forget so quickly. Nothing interests him any more. His golden age is over. In order to help him to get over the crisis you are tempted to tell him he ought to follow the example of Lucien. He exclaims: 'Oh, he's adaptable and diplomatic. He'd do anything to get himself liked and appreciated. I've got my pride. And I say what I think – and nobody likes hearing the truth. Football isn't what it was. Young people today don't play it any more like we used to. I don't want to be an accomplice in a betrayal like that.'

There you have two ways of loving football, just as there are two ways of loving roses, or women, or life, or anything. There is love for one's own sake, for one's own pleasure and importance. And there is a love that has its eyes set less on what is to be gained; it is a spontaneous movement of the heart. Of course, for the sake of clarity I am exaggerating the contrast between the two. I am painting in black and white what in real life is in a thousand shades of grey. There is always a mixture of the two. In our interest in everything there is always at the same time the attraction that the thing exerts upon us, and the attractiveness of the part we play in it. There is a germ of disinterestedness in the most selfish love. And there is personal profit in the most disinterested love. But who will deny that man is called to grow in love, to pass from an over-possessive love to a more generous love, to pass, as the psycho-analysts say, from captative to oblative love?

Can we not see in this movement from the one to the other the meaning of the whole of life? At every moment that choice is before us. We can advance towards a wider horizon or withdraw towards a narrower love. Man must find a place for himself. He implants himself in the world by means of love. But the place he chooses may be narrow and limiting, or it can expand and lead him to universality. The choice is never so decisive as at the moment when retirement and old age come to deprive us of our old points of entry. When we are young we break into the world by means of action, but that is not the only means of entry. When our field of action is restricted, the heart can take over, and bring us a new dimension in our lives. That is where I see the meaning of my old age.

The man who clings to his position at work just as long as the rules and customs permit it, is standing out against the movement of life, against its call to go on evolving. His colleagues would very much like to see him depart, but dare not tell him so. He feels it, nevertheless, and becomes harsher in his authority, because real authority escapes him – the authority, that is, which flows from the person's being in accord with reality. Another old man, obliged by regulation to vacate his position, may turn in upon himself in resentment, regret, and bitterness, like Charles the footballer. He shuts up his heart and sinks into indifference instead of opening his mind to new and wider interests. You see, just to hold on to the interests of the past, or to withdraw into apathy, are two ways of spoiling one's old age, of emptying it of its true meaning.

A less possessive love

One might say of these two men that the first does not give up enough, and the second gives up too much. But that would only be a way of playing on the ambiguity of the idea of 'giving up'. This is not a question of compromise between incomplete resignation and too complete resignation. It is a question of going from a certain manner of being-in-the-world, as the philosophers say, which befits the age of action, to another manner of being-in-the-world which befits old age. What must be given up is the official function, the gold braid; the claim to obedience, to make decisions affecting others; and ambition. The difficult process of accepting the unfulfilled, of which we have spoken, is it anything other than the abandonment of the ambition to complete one's work?

I want to insist on one detail: we are too ready, I think, to evoke the legendary figure of Nestor, and say that the function of the old is to give advice. If old people give advice to young people who ask for it, that is fine. But it seems to me less than just that the old people should complain if the young people do not ask for it. Advice too, belongs to the sphere of action. To claim that it is one's proper function is still to claim hierarchical superiority. For some old people, to give advice, to tell other people what they ought to do, is a way of getting their revenge for being deprived of the opportunity of direct action. There are grandparents who spoil their relationship with their children and grandchildren by giving too much advice on the upbringing of young people, especially by criticizing their behaviour.

Many young folk avoid old people who give advice. Their task is to invent something new, not to copy the ancients. Old people complain that these young people are lacking in proper respect. That respect is one more hierarchical idea, valid in active life, but not in old age. We surround with respect those old people who do not ask for it. We ask advice of those old people who do not insist on giving it. The old have something better to do – to become confidants. We will open our hearts to those who will listen in order to understand us, and not in order to judge us or direct us. That is the function of the wide open heart. That is the manner of 'being-in-the-world' which befits old age.

A social worker dedicated to the service of the aged said to me the other day: 'Those who consider that they deserve to have everything done for them tend to put off those who would like to do something for them; for those who are grateful, one would do anything at all.' In fact, to claim respect, to claim the right to give advice, is to try still to exercise a certain power over others. The key to success in old age seems to me to be in the abandonment of the will to power. This is the more difficult, the more powerful one has been in active life. It is more difficult nowadays than it used to be, because man has become drunk with the power that technical progress gives him.

This abandonment is prepared for a long time in advance, well before retirement, by the manner in which we live our active lives, by the way in which we love our jobs, things, and people, enjoying them not so much on account of the sense of power that action gives, as on account of the satisfaction we derive from giving ourselves. Remember our two football players; both loved the game, but differently. I am not, therefore, setting the limited and concrete loves which fill our whole lives over against some sort of idealized universal love which is discovered all at once in old age, without our having previously learnt how to love properly. I have known people who professed a grandiose, universal love, but who did very little in the way of spreading love around them.

Life is a school of love, which is made up of successive stages, and it is the organic bond between the stages which I wish to underline here. The great pioneers of love, such as St Francis of Assisi, Father Foucault or Dr Albert Schweitzer, did not start from an abstract and universal love. Little by little, through successive acts of love in the world around them, they found the road towards a wider love. St Francis loved his little church of San Damiano, and set up its fallen stones before singing his hymns of love to the whole of creation.

So the love that is near is an apprenticeship for the widest love. Even that self-interested love of which I spoke, and which is the most natural for us at first, is an apprenticeship for disinterested love. Sexual love, for instance, is to start with a very possessive, very captative, very jealous, very exclusive love. It is very self-centred, as Freud has shown in relating it to the pleasure-principle. It seeks its own pleasure. In the same way, maternal love is at first very possessive. Nevertheless, it is through the blossoming of sexual love and maternal love that men and women discover a less egoistic dimension of love: the encounter with the other, acceptance of the other, respect for the other, self-forgetfulness for the other; they discover that the supreme pleasure is not to possess, but rather to give oneself. Thus in the crucible of a particular love is fashioned a less exclusive quality of love which can develop in old age, and give it its meaning.

Unmarried people make the same journey, travelling by different paths that are less easy to negotiate, but not less effective. By giving themselves wholeheartedly to limited tasks, they prepare themselves for an old age radiant with love. For all, it is this movement of widening which marks out the turning-point of old age. Freud called it sublimation. Is it not striking that it was the apostle of the pleasure-principle who spoke of sublimation? He saw, indeed, that sooner or later desire has its limitations, and that one cannot surmount those limitations except by setting one's desire upon a greater object. Freud's sublimation is not pleasure on the cheap, a consolation prize, an 'Ersatz', as the Germans say, but the source of the finest, the most valid and the most universal human achievements, as Freud himself showed in his studies on art, culture and religion.

Freud, of course, was speaking of the sublimation of the sex instinct; but the phenomenon he described, the displacement of the instinctual drives on to new, more universal objects, can be observed in the action of all the instincts. And so we shall use Adler's individual psychology in order to define more precisely this notion of sublimation, in order to apply it to the problem of old age.

The sublimation of the instinct of power

Everyone knows at least one expression of Adler's which has established itself and passed into everyday speech, the idea of the 'inferiority complex'. Without disregarding the importance of the sex instinct, Adler, like Jung, refused to see in it the sole motor of the human mind. He describes as an instinct the will to power which impels man to assert himself, to pit himself against others, to enter into competition, to struggle against obstacles, to triumph in social life through action. Naturally in this race for success he does not meet only external obstacles, but finds them in himself as well. He feels himself inferior to others in this or that sphere.

He then reacts either by the despotic exaltation of his power instinct, or by repressing it into his unconscious. It is this repression which Adler calls an inferiority complex. The individual does not feel himself only partially handicapped; he feels totally powerless, and sinks into a state of self-doubt. The task of the psychotherapist, according to Adler, is to aid that man consciously to accept his limitations, his inferiority in certain spheres, instead of compensating for them by means of a disagreeable vanity. At this price, he will also become aware once more of his real qualities, and will be freed to direct his instinct of power on to other subjects, where he will be able to use these qualities to achieve success: he will then have sublimated his will to power.

Let us look now, in the light of Adler's doctrine, at the different types of old people of whom I have just been speaking. The person who hangs on to his job, who refuses to retire, or the one who in family or social life still wants to be a leader, to be obeyed, to be respected as one whose advice, if not his orders, is sovereign, is the person who denies his limitations, who refuses to accept the inferiority which old age brings in the sphere of action and command. He takes refuge in unconscious compensations: he likes to recount his past successes; he hardens in his authoritarianism; he criticizes the young. He acts young, in order to hide his advancing years from himself. Professor Dürckheim tells of how he met a septuagenarian who was happy and proud of having successfuly completed the ascent of a mountain so perilous that many a young man would have hesitated to undertake it. 'It's stupid!,' Dürckheim had told him. 'What's the point of reassuring yourself with feats that age will soon prevent you from performing, instead of busying yourself with things that can really last?'

The second old person, the one who withdraws into apathy and indifference, is the one who has repressed his power instinct. For want of being able to apply it still to the immediate objects that have occupied his active life, his professional work and the education of his now grown-up children, he takes no further interest in anything, he is no longer conscious even of his will to power, of which he has nothing left but this looking-glass image which is regret, bitterness, and depression. For want of being able to continue the evolution of his personality, he is regressing: 'Hardening . . . bitterness . . . a withdrawn and uncommunicative character,' Dürckheim goes on, 'are the signs of human non-maturity.'

There is a third type of old person. It is the one who has successfully sublimated his power instinct, that is to say that he has managed to redirect his instinctive drive on to another object. The instinct of power, as we were saying, is an expression of the life-force. Life, however, is not only expansion, aggression and domination. It is also love, acceptance, exchange and communication. Just as one can be powerful in one's active life through professional, social, military, economic, political, intellectual or polemical success, so one can be successful on into old age through warm-heartedness, readiness to welcome all comers, kindness and disinterestedness.

Everyone senses at once the difference between such an old person as this and the previous type. Sitting quietly in their corners though each may be, the first is empty, the second full, the first empty of any interest in what is going on around him, the second full of interest. The one is absent, the other present. You old people, my brethren, come out from behind the doors you have shut upon yourselves and upon your empty inner selves! The world is an exciting place to live in, even when you are no longer playing a dominant part in it. Those are the old folk whom I like to see – their hearts are wide open, they are understanding, radiant with love that asks nothing in return, generous, genuine, not envious or jealous; without having to do or even say anything they impart life, consolation and courage to anyone who goes near them. For me, the meaning of old age is this sublimation of the instinct of power.

What is the significance of this in practical terms? It signifies a redirection of ambition. To renounce all ambition would not be sublimation but repression; it would be a sort of premature death, but ambition is one of the essential characteristics of life. Ambition, however, can be redirected from one object on to another. Instead of having an ambition to be powerful through the rank or office one occupies, through the right to give orders or make judgments which it confers, one may have an ambition to be powerful in oneself, through one's own person, through the spontaneous and infectious quality that emanates from what one is in oneself. This is no longer an ambition for hierarchical authority, but ambition for a quite personal moral authority, no longer constraining, but open-hearted and free.

There is one biblical character (I Kings 19.9-16) from whose experiences we can learn much in this respect. If ever there was a powerful prophet, it was Elijah. With his own hand he destroyed four hundred and fifty prophets of the false god Baal. For him the power of Yahweh burst forth in numerous miracles. At the height of his triumph, though threatened by Queen Jezebel, he goes off into the desert. Were all those wonders for nothing? He is depressed, he hopes to die! It is a veritable crisis of retirement. Then Yahweh comes to meet him. Yahweh places the prophet in a cave, and announces that he is about to reveal himself to him. A hurricane passes by, but Yahweh is not in it. An earthquake shakes the mountain, but Yahweh is not in it. Then a fire, but Yahweh is not in it. Finally Elijah hears the sound of a gentle breeze, and he recognizes his God, and veils his face.

Then God acts as a psychotherapist. He brings him out of his cave and helps him to confess his jealous zeal, his anger and his aggressiveness against his people. Yahweh does not reproach him for having fought like a hurricane, or like an earthquake or a fire. That was his vocation while he was still in the prime of life. But he invites him now to hand his sword over to Elisha, to designate him 'as prophet to succeed you'. And he reveals to Elijah that he may still serve his God in a quite different manner, with the softness of a 'gentle breeze'.

I spoke just now of the history of Switzerland, of the change of direction which it made under the influence of Nicolas de Flüe, when it renounced offensive wars and imposed perpetual neutrality upon itself. The foundation of the International Red Cross by five of my fellow-citizens strikes me as an exemplary illustration of this sublimation of the instinct of power, redirecting it from its aggressive expression to its generous expression.

There is a relationship between the two instincts of which we have just been talking, that of Freud and that of Adler. It is no accident that the sex instinct is decribed in terms of conquests: we say that a woman exercises her 'power' of seduction, that a man 'conquers' or 'possesses' a woman. But it is also true that there is something of love in the professional or social adventure in which the power instinct of a man is exalted. It is because he loves his work that he makes it his career, and that he derives pleasure from the authority and effectiveness it gives him. The quest for profit has the same character of self-interest that marks the amorous conquest. The sublimation in old age which I am describing here is a sublimation of both these instincts, the redirection of the energy of which they consist from a more particular and selfish object towards a more universal and disinterested object.

There is an odd paradox: the man who is incapable of sublimating his instinct of power, who clings to his post, who is unwilling to surrender anything of his prerogatives or his authority because he thinks in this way to prolong his youth – he is the one who ages morally. Because he remains fixed in his past, because he thus deprives himself of the renewal that he could find in a second career, a career befitting his age, less heavily laden with responsibilities, but richer in imagination.

Outside the hierarchy and money

A few days ago I gave a lecture in a small village in a neighbouring canton. The local doctor and his wife very kindly invited us to dinner. After the lecture my colleague said to me, by the way of a compliment: 'You must give me your secret for staying young.' I did not have the presence of mind to answer his request. I thought about it afterwards, as I drove homeward along the motorway. It seems to me that I ought to have said to him: my secret is that I have several times in my life negotiated one of those decisive turning-points which bring rejuvenation of the heart because they mark a new departure.

The Americans experience this sort of renewal more frequently than we do. They readily change their careers, or go from one enterprise to another, or again they move house more often, from New York to California, or from Florida to Chicago. In Europe when a man has got a job he seems concerned most of all to keep it. What nails him to the spot is his fear of losing his right to a retirement pension. Firms and organizations which are interested in keeping the personnel they have trained, bind them to them by means of the regulations governing their pension funds. This is a new form of alienation of personal rights, quite different from that denounced by Karl Marx, one that arises, not from a lack of social legislation, but from social progress itself. That is why people are now campaigning for the right of free transfer from one pension scheme to another.

The instinct of power drives man to love and to work; and it is in his sexual, professional and social successes that man first shows his power. But in this possessive phase the instinct of power imprisons him as well. He has won a wife and a position in the professional hierarchy. He is condemned to fight to maintain his conquests: his position, his customers, his prestige. I might have added his wife, were I not afraid that it might appear to be in bad taste; and yet, it is very true. For to this possessive phase jealousy also inevitably belongs: jealousy in love as well as professional jealousy.

The positive aspect of retirement and old age is that it liberates the instinct of power from these immediate and limited objects. Man can then see the door opening to a more generous love, to an activity which is no longer so dependent upon the social hierarchy or on profit.

Hierarchical authority, and money, are in fact the two attributes of the elemental will to power. At this first stage, man's authority and his value are measured exactly by the position he occupies in the social hierarchy and by his income. The sublimation of the instinct of power brings about a radical change in the scale of human values. From then on a man's value is judged not by what he does, but by what he is, not by the position he occupies or by his titles, but by his personal maturity, by his breadth of mind, by his inner life, by the quality of his love for others, and by the intrinsic, and not the market, value of what he brings into the world.

The following anecdote will make the point clear. My son has just made me a present of Bertrand de Jouvenel's excellent book, *Arcadie, essais sur le mieux vivre*. At the beginning the author quotes the dialogue between Socrates and Antiphon, as reported by Xenophon. Antiphon says to Socrates: 'If an article of clothing, a house, or any other thing in your possession has a value, you do not give it away for nothing, and you do not let it go for a price less than its value. It is therefore evident that if you attributed any value to your words, you would ask those who listen to them to pay you according to their proper value.' Antiphon, Jouvenel points out, was a sophist by profession: he sold lessons in wisdom; in his eyes the fact that his lessons were sold was proof that they had value in the eyes of his pupils, whereas Socrates must consider his own lessons to be without value since he did not ask for them to be paid for.

In the perspective of history, who would dare to claim that Socrates' value was inferior to that of the merchant Antiphon? His prestige and his power were of another order, less self-interested and more universal. However, says Jouvenel, our modern Western society comes down on the side of Antiphon against Socrates, because the economists who are its wise men cannot evaluate in their statistics what is not paid for. 'Services that are sold are included under "production", but services that are given are not.' The author quotes a number of examples, beginning with this one: 'The existence of society depends on the care devoted to children by mothers. Since, however, there is no remuneration made for these activities, they do not figure in the evaluation of the national product.'

The same may be said of the activity of retired people, useful and valid though it may be. With their working job they have lost their social power, since that is expressed only in terms of accountancy. They do not even have, like the young, a place of honour in the statistics of consumption. 'If old age has so lost its stake in society,' writes Jean-Marie Domenach,[18] 'it is essentially because it is the age of life which it is most difficult to force into consumption.'

The Prior of Taizé, Brother Roger Schutz, also speaks of this

consumer society founded on money.[19] He does not oppose it
entirely, but he suggests that it should be complemented with a
'sharing society', in which people would rediscover the desire for
service for the pleasure of giving, and not for profit. The development of voluntary activity by retired people could make this
'sharing society' a reality. The sociologists have observed that the
majority of retired people turn down every opportunity for voluntary work. They seem to prefer boredom to the performance of any
non-remunerative activity, such is the social prejudice which
measures a man's value not by the service he renders but by the
income he receives.

This is the more absurd, in so far as it is often through voluntary
activity that a retired person makes a place for himself once more in
society, and this can develop into a second career and even bring him
in, eventually, some return. But it is clear that for this he must first
honestly renounce, in his own heart, a purely commercial estimate
of human value. The sublimation of his instinct of power means the
application of it to an object quite different from titles, profit and
expenditure – to his personal development, his culture, and most
particularly to his growth in love.

Thus individuals and nations pass through successive stages. They
do their apprenticeship in love, first of all in limited, rather selfish
loves, before being able eventually to discover a more general and
universal love. They also do an apprenticeship in self-expression,
first in the aggresive form of the instinct of power, to sublimate it
thereafter in a less selfish flowering of self.

Each stage has its meaning

I can now describe all this from another point of view, that of the
meaning of life. Men make plans and strive with all their might to
realize them. One is intensely interested in the adventure of his
professional life. For years he devotes all his evenings to the com-
pletion of his education, he takes correspondence courses, learns
foreign languages from gramophone records. His whole behaviour,
all his friendships, all kinds of manoeuvres, are aimed at promotion
up the rungs of the ladder – to office manager, general manager and
finally managing director. Another is a revolutionary. While still
quite young he has read Karl Marx or Lenin. He wants to build a
better world, rescue the exploited masses from their condition of

slavery. He devotes his whole time to political agitation, he turns down a chance of marriage because the connection would be too bourgeois.

Yet another loves a woman who refuses to marry him. He perseveres ardently, goes from hope to despair, but will not give up. A woman wants to get married, but has been courted only by insignificant, selfish or vulgar men whom she despised. The only reason why she frequents lectures, concerts, church, clubs, or goes on holidays is that she thus hopes to meet some man worthy of her, who will ask her to marry him. Another woman longs for a baby that does not come. She consults the most renowned gynaecologists, she searches through medical dictionaries. Yet another simply cooks and does the housework as well as following a career that is hard work in itself, to keep her husband and children happy.

A sick man imposes upon himself every privation, submits without complaint to the most painful treatment, and fights to keep hoping; a handicapped person applies himself with admirable perseverance to his rehabilitation exercises; a neurotic perseveres with his course of psychoanalysis despite dramatic crises, then he undertakes a second course, and a third. War calls a man to take up arms. Thereafter, nothing counts for him other than the defence of his country, repelling the invader; if the latter triumphs temporarily, he escapes overseas, braving the gravest dangers, in order to enroll in the allied armies. A skier trains rigorously, leads an ascetic's life and thinks only of the Olympic gold medal which he hopes one day to win. A philosopher reads from morning till evening. He works for years on a treatise with which he hopes to make a name for himself. He has his eye on a university chair, but the opportunities are few. He turns down various nominations which would rescue him from his life of poverty, but which would be deviations from the line he has mapped out for himself.

Obviously I could go on endlessly giving examples, mentioning the musician who leaves the orchestra to take up a career as a soloist in which he does not yet know if he will be a success; the doctor who gives up a good practice to go and work in the African bush; the detective who wants to arrest the criminal, and the criminal who wants to escape the detective; the specialist who is looking for a cure for cancer, and the grandmother who would like to live long enough to see her mathematically gifted grandson get his doctorate; and so many, many more! Each of these men and women has a concrete project, immediate or long-term, on which their heart is set, and they devote all their energies to its realization. They hardly ever wonder about the meaning of life.

If you question them on this subject, they will tell you that they have no time to waste on idle argument. The hard fight they are engaged in gives a meaning to their lives! They will say, perhaps, even more sharply: 'I know what you are trying to do; you're trying to convert me, to convince me of the vanity of earthly ambitions and get me to turn my eyes to God, towards the gospel, towards his promises, and towards eternity.' There again we have that false distinction between earth and heaven against which I was protesting a while back. It is quite true that all those demanding and often very difficult earthly enterprises give a meaning to the lives of all those men and women.

Nevertheless it is a provisional meaning, since it cannot last. So often people cling desperately to the thing that has for a time given a meaning to their lives, because they have not found a goal in life that is more in conformity with their age. Suzanne Pacaud and M. O. Lahalle have conducted an enquiry into the behaviour of grandparents living with their married children.[20] The authors observe that 'the majority of aged women have persevered with housework at the cost of serious fatigue, in order to persuade themselves, and to show others, that they still had a purpose in life. Their children still allow them that pleasure.'

The striking thing to an observer like me is that misfortunes and trials give a meaning to life just as much as good fortune. This is clearly seen in the case of a mother whose child is suffering from some chronic disability, and who devotes herself to him without respite. It is clear in the case of a man who at last wins a case that he has fought tenaciously for more than twenty years, in spite of all kinds of insult and injustice. Suddenly he finds himself in a painful void. If he had lost his case, his dismay would be understandable. But in winning it he has also lost what had become the meaning of his life.

Our life, then, has a meaning for us when we have a definite goal, when we struggle to attain it, when we concentrate on the effort it calls for, when we face obstacles and accept sacrifices. Of course, it is not yet the total meaning of life, it is a provisional meaning, but a valid one. It is only a stage, but a necessary stage.

To illustrate this truth, let us imagine that I am on a journey: I am in another country, in Amsterdam, for example, and I wish to come back to Geneva. I am too far away for any signpost to carry the name of Geneva. I must take the road to Arnhem, then, as I go from stage to stage, I shall find signs pointing to Cologne, to Frankfurt, to Basle, and it is not until I am approaching Geneva that I shall find a signpost carrying the name of my home town. During the Dutch part of my journey, the direction of Arnhem was in a sense provisional, but it was necessary for me to take it. What gave its full meaning to my taking that direction was that in the end my journey would take me to Geneva. So the total meaning of life transcends all the partial meanings, but it is realized also through them, and not without them.

The idea of a general meaning of life seems to me to be inconceivable without some reference to transcendence, some reference to God, the creator of the world and of life. But if there is a global meaning of life, it is to be discovered and fulfilled only step by step, and each step has its meaning. Life is a journey, and there are not two journeys, but one only. As I drove towards Arnhem, I was driving towards Geneva. For me the meaning of life is what Jesus variously calls the Kingdom of God, the Kingdom of Heaven, and eternal life. He does not situate it in the distant future, but in the immediate present. The Kingdom of God, he says, is very near you (Luke 10.9). And elsewhere: It is among you (Luke 17.21). He has taught us to ask for its coming every day in the Lord's Prayer. And afterwards he explicitly says 'on earth as in heaven' (Matt. 6.10). Thus he joins together what many people separate: the immediate earthly reality and the transcendent and eternal reality which in biblical language is called 'heaven'. There is something of eternal life in every authentic personal act, and every genuine personal contact.

Towards a more universal meaning

Living with Jesus means living every detail of my daily life in that light. It does not mean detaching myself from the world and from those immediate concerns which give a meaning to my life. I do not have to deny or oppose these provisional meanings of my life, but I shall be able to distinguish the transcendent meaning in every provisional meaning. Where is God leading me in these daily events, in this ardour to achieve a goal that he has implanted in my heart, in this success, in this failure, in this joy or this sorrow, in this affliction or this healing, this friendship or this rebellion, this light or this darkness? Meditation is just that – seeking the divine meaning in everything that happens to me, a familiarity with God which brings him into my life at every moment. It asks what is God expecting of me, here and now.

Then the 'coming of God' which René Bazin said, in the remark I quoted, takes place in old age, is in fact the experience of the whole of life, from birth to death, from the present moment to eternity. There is no gap between the stages, between active life and old age: life is a unity. Everything becomes a movement towards God, a commitment to the Kingdom of God. It is easier, however, for this commitment to be made in action, for it is action which grips us, even more than our committing ourselves to action. And so action is our first lesson in this course in commitment which we call life. The first lesson is always easy! We learn to give ourselves in the fire of action in those provisional meanings which suggest themselves to us, and which all belong to the realm of action. It is, in fact, these provisional meanings that begin to fade when old age comes, and our capacity for action is restricted. What is left is the spirit of commitment.

We are back with that realignment on a different object of which I have spoken, the passage from the particular to the universal: from the particular commitment of 'doing' to the much more profound commitment of 'being'. This is what the Russian surgeon Nicolas Amossov means when he says: 'Now that my life is in decline, I desire one thing only: to understand what man is.' If there ever was a vocation to direct, concrete, particular action, it is certainly that of the surgeon! And here we have Dr Amossov, in the midst of his active life, prompted by the very fact of his intense engagement in his profession, witnessed to by his book, opening his heart to a more universal preoccupation – the understanding of the nature of man. That is a concern which he will still be able to follow up when he has laid aside his scalpel. This is no disengagement: his commitment is widening. He is not becoming less interested in the world – his interest is changing its object, from 'doing' to 'being'.

A man asks me: 'Who are you?' I reply: 'I am a doctor.' – 'Yes,' he says, 'I know, but who are *you*?' At the age of action, I am defined by my function, by what I do. As old age comes, this function, this 'doing', gradually ceases to define me. I have to define myself in terms of what I am. Then the temporary meanings that I have seen previously in my life may seem rather naïve. Nevertheless it is first of all through action that I have become what I am, that I have learnt commitment. Only he who commits himself completely to all he does, to all the successive tasks which have given meaning to his life, only he can develop, grow, become fully man – become what he is, in Pindar's apt phrase.

There is a third way of describing this pilgrimage from the particular to the universal, from the provisional meanings to the global meaning, from the selfish loves to disinterested love. I borrow it from the language of the Pavlovians: it is a movement first of conditioning, and then of deconditioning. Active professional life demands strict conditioning. The whole of our upbringing and schooling act like a long assembly line for the manufacture of perfectly adjusted workers. Within the family we acquire the conditioned reflexes of social convention. 'Wash your hands – hold yourself straight – eat properly – say thank you – tidy your things – look at people when you're talking to them!'

At school we acquire the intellectual conditioned reflexes necessary for correct reasoning and the solving of problems. At college, at technical school or in apprenticeship we acquire the conditioned reflexes of our profession or trade. All this is necessary to the proper functioning of the great machine we now call the consumer society, which is just beginning to rescue mankind from his age-old poverty. It is necessary that it should function correctly. Anyone who cannot be adjusted down to the last tenth of a millimetre is pitilessly thrown on the scrapheap. Even at university, despite its much-vaunted liberty, we must espouse the doctrines of the grand-masters in order to obtain our doctorate. The current philosophy, legislation, customs, the church, all add their conditioning. The consumer is conditioned by advertising. And the great efficiency of America derives in part from that perfect conditioning which is called the American Way of Life.

To this must still be added the individual conditioning which we receive from our daily routine. The whole process is an economic and social necessity. If everyone could do what he liked, when he liked and as he liked, humanity would slip back into chaos and poverty. But, as we have seen, it is men who are too well conditioned who find themselves disoriented on retirement, who may undergo a serious crisis, sink into disease, apathy, or depression. Conditioning turns man into a thing, a robot, an automaton, good only for fulfilling a narrow specialized function. It takes away what is most human in him, his imagination, his spontaneity, his creativeness. Mme Lévy-Valensi and Dr Claude Veil write: 'Many workers are dehumanized, brutalized (in the etymological sense of the term), by work that is stereotyped and devoid of interest, so that they are no longer capable of using their leisure time intelligently.'[21]

I emphasized just now the developmental value of any commitment to a precise task which gives a meaning to life. At the same time any commitment is a restrictive choice. In order to devote oneself to one thing, one has to leave behind a host of others. While the particular is a necessary road towards the universal, it is also an obstacle. It narrows life, even if it intensifies it. It is necessary, therefore, for two great opposing currents to flow together – that of conditioning and that of deconditioning, specialization and universalization. Conditioning is indispensable to what is called success in life, but deconditioning is also necessary to success in life, in terms of its expanding development. A day comes, as Patrick Lecomte writes, when what is needed is 'to reawaken the faculties put to sleep by specialization'. In youth we must interest ourselves in what we do, in order to become competent; in old age, we can interest ourselves in everything, in order to become more human. We rediscover the particular flavour of all those things we have tended to forget, even the flavour of existing, of living, different from the taste of action.

Surrender

I can sum up all that I have just been saying about love, about the meaning of life, and about conditioning, as a sort of cleavage – a cleavage between action and being, between the professional and the personal attitude, between the technical role and the community role of the individual in society, between utilitarian interest and cultural interest, between a profit motivation and a disinterested motivation, between a conditioned and a free behaviour, between the limited and the universal. This cleavage is imposed, in the literal sense of the words, in sudden retirement, and the turning-point is then very difficult to negotiate because of its abruptness. But old age also imposes it upon us, little by little, and the danger is that we may spoil our lives in old age, through not having learnt how to replace the old substance of our lives with something new.

We have indeed something important at stake in this – the very success of our old age. As Fr Leclercq puts it: 'I know that old age is beautiful, but only on certain conditions.' Lévy-Valensi and Veil speak of the need for a sort of conversion. The word may be taken in a secular sense, in the way the sociologists mean when they talk of the conversion of the individual from one form of activity to another. But the word always has also religious overtones, in the sense of an inner change in man himself, in his fundamental attitude to others, to the world, and to God. This change of attitude, this decisive step, is necessary if old age is to be, as Dürckheim puts it, 'the veritable apogee of life, the period in which man fulfils himself'.

Experience teaches us, in fact, that true sublimation is rare, whether it be of the sex instinct or of the instinct of power. The Freudians have little to say on the subject of sublimation, even though it was their master who defined the concept. It seems that they are not really at ease in face of a phenomenon which they intuitively feel has two aspects: a natural aspect – the psychological process described by Freud; and a supernatural aspect – grace; whereas they are anxious to remain pure naturalists. But I am in agreement with them when they say that it is unconscious. It arises without the subject himself being aware of it, without his willing it. It is even the opposite of an act of will. What he is aware of is the irruption into his mind of a force which does not come from himself and which destroys his claim to lead his life according to his own will.

This experience may be expressed in various ways, some of the words used being only designations and not descriptions, for it is lived, rather than thought. In the East it is called wu-wei, that is to say 'non-acting'. The German mystic called it 'leaving oneself'. The American minister Frank Buchman called it a 'change of life' or 'surrender'. It is often compared to a leap into the void. It is, in fact, in a study of this idea of a void that Professor Karlfried von Dürckheim speaks of 'the grace granted to the man who, when he "lets go" of everything, finds Everything'. Again, he speaks of a 'threshold which only allows him who accepts to pass over it'. Here again we have this idea of acceptance which I have discussed previously. Through acceptance the old person finds, says Dürckheim, 'a basis, a meaning, and a deep secure peace which are not of this world'.

That is the detachment necessary to a happy old age. It means the liberation of one's will, of the will to power. Of course it is an event which can take place outside of old age. I experienced it, very naïvely, in my childhood. I experienced it again, more decisively, at the age of thirty-five. And I have known it often since then, for we are always going back to our old ways; but God seizes us anew in his powerful hand, and constrains us to surrender. This surrender, incomplete though it may be, prepares us for old age, in which our capacity for action declines.

For me, this surrender of my life to God has never meant that I was turning my back on the world – rather that I was interesting myself in it in a wider and deeper way. Nor did it mean, at that time, that I gave up action. What I was giving up was my claim to act in accordance with my own will, in order to allow myself to be led as much as possible by God. This decision brings considerable relaxation of tension, especially in the case of anyone as anxious by nature as I am. And this relaxation is greater still when God, through old age, relieves me of various responsibilities which he had laid upon me. It is also the answer to the problem of the 'unfulfilled' which I have already discussed at length: we can surrender to God all the worry about the things we have left uncompleted.

So, it was God who made me grow up even before I knew him. It was he who called me to become a doctor. It was he who impelled me into action. It was in action that he revealed himself to me in his sovereign authority, and that authority has guided my life ever since, despite all my backslidings. And now it is he who is leading me along the new paths of old age. It is he who has made the unity of my life.

VI

FAITH

Old age foreshadows death

You can be a sincere, fervent, orthodox Christian without having the experience of surrender. You can also experience it without being aware that it comes from God. This observation leads me to the question that we ought to face now: do believers accept old age more readily than unbelievers? Do they accept death more readily than unbelievers, and the prospect of approaching death?

Many of my readers will perhaps be astonished, on reading these last few lines, not that I should mention the place of faith in these problems, for that is in everybody's mind, but that I should thus, all at once, put together as if they were one, two questions which they have thought of as quite distinct – the question of old age and that of death, the acceptance of old age and the acceptance of death. Would it not be more logical to keep the two questions apart? Old age is a concrete, lasting problem, which raises practical problems that are susceptible of objective discussion. Death is still an impenetrable mystery which is not amenable to rational argument. Death, says Roger Mehl, 'is at one and the same time necessary (and therefore explicable) and incomprehensible'.

Well! It seems to me that at the point I have reached in this book, the frontier between the problems of old age and of death disappears. When my publishers asked me to write it, they spoke only of retirement. I very soon realized that I could not write about retirement without writing about old age, which is bound up with it. I have tried so far to examine these problems of retirement and old age on their own account, on the basis of objective experience and thought, with the least possible allusion to their metaphysical aspect. This is because positivist readers – notably the majority of doctors, as Georges Gusdorf has pointed out[1] – see any reference to religion as a sort of trick, a means of avoiding having to face the practical problems.

But it is clear that if we stopped there we should be cutting out of the argument a considerable part of what ought to be included, namely the consciousness of death which every man carries about within him all his life long, and which becomes more threatening as he grows old. If retirement speaks of old age, old age in its turn speaks of death. If old age is only a passing, a moment of no duration in our eyes, which is not susceptible of rational discussion, what does last, what cannot be put on one side, what is objective, is the preoccupation with death which haunts every human mind. On this subject the experience of all the psychologists is in agreement. Even Freud, who desired to be purely rationalist, never stopped discussing religion and thinking about death. He ended up by postulating a 'death instinct', and this instinct of death is oddly reminiscent, as Dr Affemann[2] points out, of what St Paul writes about death: 'Sin entered the world . . . and through sin death' (Rom. 5.12).

All the psychologists see how the mystery of death obsesses man. The sociologists cannot take it into account in their surveys, because their contact with those they interrogate is not sufficiently intimate; and also because people are not themselves thoroughly conscious of the terrible anxieties that inhabit their minds. But one only needs to hear the accounts of a few dreams, with their familiar tale of imminent dangers, implacable monsters and hopeless situations, to become aware of how much mortal anxiety lies deep within the human mind. Even splendid dreams in which the dreamer comes suddenly on to a mountain-top, in blinding light, reveal once more this poignant questioning about the meaning of death, from which none escapes.

In the last analysis all anxiety is reduced to anxiety about death. Proof of this is the large number of stories in which a man freed from the fear of death is seen to be freed from all other fears: he has no more fear of anything or anyone; no one can overcome him, even by killing him. Nevertheless the sociologists are right: men do not talk much about this anxiety concerning the threat of death. That is because all men attempt to repress it.

A friend of mine, an old retired doctor, often used to visit a neighbour, a clergyman who was suffering from an incurable disease, and who was gradually approaching death. Their conversations were cordial and friendly, but always superficial. My friend was on the look-out for a more profound opening of the heart. One day, after a long silence, the patient murmured: 'There's something I want to tell you.' My friend pricked up his ears – were they at last going to talk about what really mattered? No! 'I've got a dozen bottles of sherry: would you like to have them?' asked the patient. It was kind, but it was a disappointment. Many subjects of conversation are no more than reassuring diversions to avoid the problem of death – death which will swallow up everything that we talk about. Talking to such old people in a tone of forced gaiety, being careful ourselves to avoid any allusion to death, may make us accomplices in this naïve artifice, and that would be to leave them in solitude with their anxiety.

Moreover, soothing talk is not only a diversion. It represents an ineffective attempt to get rid of a latent, blind anxiety. By means of a well-known mechanism, this anxiety is directed on to other less serious objects, which become imbued with its emotional content. Old people thus grumble incessantly about their rheumatism, their failing hearing, the ingratitude of their friends, the immorality of the young or the injustice of the government. In order to rediscover their inner truth they must be made aware of their repressed anxiety and of its true object. For this they must be able to talk about it, for one is only really conscious of a thing when one can express it. I am not suggesting that you should go up to them and ask them if they are afraid of death. They would probably reply that they were not, and would shut up all the more. People do not open their hearts when one interrogates them, but when one listens to them with attention. That is what a true dialogue consists of.

People are reluctant to talk about old age and death because they are afraid of emotion, and they willingly avoid the things they feel most emotional about, though these are the very things they most need to talk about. Mme Simone de Beauvoir wants to destroy the taboo on old age. That is why she wrote her lengthy book; we must put an end to our cowardly silence! We must talk simply and realistically about old age in order to exorcize it. But in her book the author hardly ever mentions death, which she had nevertheless written about elsewhere. Can one really abolish the taboo on old age without also abolishing the taboo on death? This seems to me to be one of the requirements of our time. We aspire to looking everything in the face, bringing everything out into the open. The sex taboo has been overthrown. It is desired to abolish the taboo on old age. But the taboo on death is in the same basket.

When a man looks for a meaning for his life, when an old person looks for the meaning of his old age, they are really, underneath, asking about the meaning of death. The word 'meaning' contains two aspects: on the one hand it speaks of the significance of things, but it also involves the idea of destination. This will be clear if you remember my imaginary journey from Amsterdam to Geneva: the significance of my journey, which already gave meaning to the first stage, was that my final destination was Geneva. Who can deny that the meaning of life is death, since it is a journey whose final destination is death?

Now the meaning of death is the religious question *par excellence*. Does there exist something other than the visible world in which we are enclosed from birth to death? Something which transcends death, which sets beyond death the destination of the journey of life? My old age has meaning, I can live through it with my gaze still fixed before me, and not behind me, because I am on my way to a destination beyond death. There is no need for great sermons to help people to grasp that. Dürckheim tells of a visit he made to the bedside of an old friend on the point of death. The friend talked to him at great length, as if to delude himself, of a project which he certainly could not carry out. 'You would do better,' Dürckheim said to him simply, 'to fix your eyes beyond death.' There was a long silence, and then his friend said, quietly, the two words, 'Thank you!'

Is it easier for believers to accept?

That is why, just now, when I had come to the point of asking myself what was the part played by faith in acceptance, I could not dissociate acceptance of old age from that of death. The two problems are so intimately bound up together that we may say that acceptance of old age is the best preparation for death, but also, conversely, that the acceptance of death is the best preparation for old age. Let us come back, then, to my question, which lends itself quite well to objective discussion: is acceptance of old age and death easier for believers than for unbelievers?

I do not think that one can honestly reply 'Yes' to this question. It is not as simple as that. In the first place, faith appears in two quite distinct aspects: an intellectual, dogmatic aspect, involving assent to a creed and a gospel; and an aspect involving experience, encounter and friendship with God. This corresponds with the distinction I have made between an exterior and an inner truth. The creed does not of itself involve what we have called surrender. It may even seem like a fortress protecting the believer against his inner truth, against his repressed anxieties. It is then rather a stiffening of the defences than a surrender.

But the question is still more subtle. American Christianity, for instance, is much less dogmatic than European Christianity. And America is also more religious than Europe. And yet Americans suffer more than do Europeans from a complex about death. I remember an evening spent at Chapel Hill, North Carolina, with a few colleagues and other friends. They talked at great length about the blackout cast over the brutal reality of death, which the flourishing funeral industry of their country knows so well how to exploit. One can indeed say that there is a taboo on this subject, with all the ambivalence of fascination and dissimulation that is so characteristic of the taboo.

My impression is that psychological determinism, both individual and collective, plays a much more important role than faith in the acceptance or non-acceptance of death. In other words, this is a psychological problem much more than a religious one, in spite of appearances. I have seen believers who were very much afraid of death, and others who contemplated it with equanimity. And I have also seen unbelievers full of anxiety at the prospect of death, and others who viewed its approach with scarcely a qualm.

Extreme cases are instructive in this matter. I have never met a worse case of fear of death than that of an old colleague whom I treated over a number of years. I never succeeded in bringing him peace; nor were the good dozen psychotherapists who followed one another in succession at his bedside any more successful – to say nothing of several eminent priests. Some of them talked to me about him, and told me that they too had never known a man more obsessed by the idea of death. They had given up, whereas I persevered, perhaps because I find failure easier to bear.

My patient had faith – he even had that extra fervour which the convert shows, for he had lost his faith for several years and miraculously found it again. He even believed in the salvation, not just of a little band of the elect, but of all men, and he often told me that it was in his view an insult to God to suggest that he had the intention of inflicting eternal torment on anyone. In order to understand him we must go further back into the history of his life. Long before his obsession about death had reached the point of being a veritable disease, right back in his childhood, it was showing itself. He used to spend whole days in the cemetery. Or else he used to hide near by, anxiously watching the funeral processions, which inspired in him both fascination and revulsion.

You can imagine the effect of the religious teaching he received. He had been a boarder in a denominational school, in which the custom was to have a week's retreat each year. All the pupils knew in advance that the last day of this retreat was entirely devoted to Dantesque descriptions of the pains of Hell. His comrades, who were less emotionally disturbed than he was, took the whole thing somewhat philosophically. They enjoyed making the macabre jokes which serve so many people as a protection against anxiety. But in the case of my future patient it was a catastrophe.

It must be recognized that all our Christian churches have for centuries exploited the fear that men naturally feel when confronted by death, in order to maintain their ascendancy over them. They have made great progress in this respect in the last few years, and this is due, I believe, to the psychologists. Nowadays one hears more sermons about God's mercy and forgiveness than about his anger. But I do not think that one can say that the problem has been solved. There still persist many unconscious echoes of the old terror, even in the minds of those who are detached from the church or who are hostile to it.

It is clear from the case I have just quoted, and from many more, that the primordial and decisive factor in anxiety is psychological and emotional. That is the great truth revealed by modern psychology after so many philosophers and moralists have described human behaviour as if it were determined only by ideas, by reason and the will. But as we have seen also from this case, religious controversies come in their turn to add their poison to the emotional drama by means of the mechanism of a vicious circle: anguished minds tend to retain from the Bible and the preaching of the church the implacable threats, while untroubled minds only retain the reassuring promises of divine grace. It is for this reason, I think, that close collaboration between psychologists and theologians is of such importance.

While too many theologians still ignore the primacy of the emotional factor, it seems to me that too many psychologists also ignore the part played by the choices of faith which are grafted on to that factor. I think the analogy of the graft is a good one; after all, the apples we pick from the tree and eat are determined by the scion. The stock gives it its vital energy, but what is made of that power is determined by the grafted scion. On the one hand, it is true, we must admit that Christianity has done little to lessen the anxiety of the faithful in face of death, despite its triumphant message about the resurrection of Jesus. But on the other hand, we must also recognize that great victims of anxiety such as St Francis of Assisi, Pascal, Luther and Kierkegaard won a victory of a quite different kind, through the faith that was grafted on to their anxiety.

Faith does not exclude anxiety

I must explain what I mean by this quite different kind of victory. It means accepting anxiety as an inescapable constituent element in our human nature, instead of imagining that we can ever free ourselves from it. Idealist philosophies such as that of Plato, or cynical philosophies like that of the Stoics, or again, naturalist philosophies like that of the Epicureans and that of the Freudians, are all to some extent a response to this utopian desire to eliminate anxiety. Christianity is much more realistic. Christ himself experienced the anxiety of death, so that he sweated blood and cried out from the Cross: 'My God, my God, why have you deserted me?' (Matt. 27.46). So far did he share our human nature.

On the very eve of her death I talked at length about these things with my sister. She was a courageous soul, who had been converted to a deeply pious faith, and she was also anxious, sensitive, as scrupulous as I am – even more so. She had suffered more than I from the death of our father, because she was then four years old and during those few years had been the apple of his eye; no doubt also because during the few years during which our mother had survived him, she had naturally shown preference towards me.

At Christmas, 1948, my sister caught a chill while taking part in a street collection in aid of the Salvation Army. She became seriously ill, and I remember one visit I made to her in hospital. A week earlier she had had a cardiac failure, from which she had been brought round only with difficulty. We were talking about it quite naturally now that she was better. She had really believed, she said, that she was going to die. She had experienced terrible anxiety. And now she was questioning me because she felt ashamed of her anxiety, which she looked upon as a lack of faith. Should a Christian believer like her not have faced death with serenity?

'I do not think so,' I said, and talked to her about the anxiety which Jesus experienced, as I have just pointed out. The ideal of indifference in the face of death is not Christian. It was the ideal of the Epicureans, of whom I shall have more to say later, and the Stoics, who called it *ataraxia*. This latter ought to be looked upon as a repression of emotion, a stubborn bracing of the mind against the drives of the unconscious. It is just the opposite of the surrender of which I spoke above. It may have worked in the case of strong-willed personalities like Epictetus, Cicero or Marcus Aurelius. But it lacks the tenderness which is an inseparable element in the Christian gospel.

Christian faith, I said to her, does not involve repressing one's anxiety in order to appear strong. On the contrary, it means recognizing one's weakness, accepting the inward truth about oneself, confessing one's anxiety, as my sister had so movingly done, and still to believe; that is to say that the Christian puts his trust not in his own strength, but in the grace of God. The next day my sister suffered a second heart attack. When I arrived in haste at her bedside I felt at once that this was the end. She could no longer speak – and I had no more to say. We looked at each other face to face for nearly an hour, and in that silent exchange there was all our conversation of the previous day about anxiety and faith.

I am not writing this book, therefore, to offer you unreal and utopian comfort. Of course I try with affection, and with the help of faith and of psychology, to lighten the load of anxiety which weighs upon all those who come to see me. But I know that some anxiety will still remain, conscious or not, especially in face of death. And I believe that there is more peace to be found in the acceptance of human anxiety than in the hope for a life or an old age freed from anxiety. Death remains a fearful and cruel monster. The Bible says that it will be the last enemy to be overcome (I Cor. 15.26). Jesus himself overcame it only by accepting it and accepting its anxiety.

Old age is often spoken of as a school of detachment which ought to prepare us for death. For all that, we must distinguish between detachment from things and detachment from persons. True, detachment from things prepares us for death, and it is bound up with the turning-point of old age of which I have spoken, when we gradually give up action – at any rate, in so far as action belongs to the world of things. But I have been at pains to point out that this turning-point means a detachment from things only in favour of a wider, deeper, and more welcoming opening of the heart to people. However detached we may be from things, death remains a harsh wrench because it brutally ruptures the bonds that attach us to people, bonds which become even stronger in old age.

My sister's death recalls a passage in the *Dialogue des Carmélites*, by Georges Bernanos.³ Sister Blanche is dead. A young nun who has greatly admired her for her exemplary piety is overcome with grief, and is wondering about her: 'Who would have thought that she would have found it so hard to die!'

The thing that strikes me as being so great, and salutary, about death, is the way it makes real the equality of all men which we claim to believe in, and which we constantly deny through our prejudices. Not only equality between rich and poor, between the strong and the weak, between black and white, but also between believers and unbelievers. Nevertheless, which of us, believer or not, has not dreamed with a sort of supreme vanity of 'making a good death' for the edification of those around us?

Death is indeed the moment of truth which upsets all our vain categories. It is only our preconceived notions which are surprised by unexpected, but quite natural reactions. There is a physical factor in our anxiety over death which reminds us that we are not pure spirits, despite all our high-soaring doctrines. It is this animal weakness, and not our spiritual virtues, which wins us the compassion of God. This needs to be understood well before death.

Nevertheless, at the moment of death, anxiety is much more rare than most people think or fear. The excellent French magazine *Présences*, a magazine of the sick, has published an article by an Italian doctor, Paolo Rovasio,⁴ which gives a pathetic description of the terror of the dying, and especially religious people, as if it

were general. The editors received in response a flood of letters
from those who are daily at the bedsides of dying people – almoners,
Sisters of Charity, nurses, and doctors. 'Death,' writes Dr René
Ducret,[5] for instance, 'only exceptionally presents the appearance
of tragic despair' of which the Italian writer speaks. They all voice
doubts as to whether Dr Rovasio has in fact much experience of
people dying.

What man needs most is not to be alone when he faces death, as
if a human presence, even that of an unbeliever, were a pledge of
the divine presence. A silent, discreet, respectful, but real presence –
a presence of the heart, true participation. The American doctor
K. R. Eissler puts it admirably in an article on the role of the psychiatrist with a person who is dying, quoted by Dr Sebillotte: 'What
you can really do for a person who is dying, is to die with him.'

Philosophical positions

My subject in this book, however, is not the dying, but the living,
as they grow older, and their problems, that is to say, their worries.
The question of death deserves much more extensive treatment. I
have touched on it here only because its approach is one – and not
the least – of the preoccupations of the aged. All doctors are aware
of this. Their patients express it so often, in veiled terms. Even a
patient with the most ordinary of illnesses, will venture a timid 'Is it
serious, doctor?' – which means 'Is it something I'm in danger of
dying of?'

He is thinking of death already. And which of us does not think
of it, as soon as some illness comes along to remind us that we
are mortal beings? Do not the patient's wife and his children and
his friends also think of it at once? Even in good health, is there
anyone who does not think of death as he feels time passing, old
age coming on, and sees his contemporaries pass away? 'One day
is dead, long live the next! Midnight strikes. One more step towards
the grave!' These are the last lines of the diary which my illustrious
fellow-citizen Henri-Frédéric Amiel wrote, day after day, throughout his life.

Let us go back once more to the ancients. I spoke just now of
the Stoics, and of the way they braced themselves against anxiety
concerning death. I must now quote Epicurus, and the celebrated
argument by which he sought to vanquish the fear of death: 'How

should I fear death? When I am, death is not; and when death is, I am not.' The logic is impeccable, and no philosopher has ever been able rationally to refute it. True enough, so long as I live, death is not there. But what *is* there, in my heart, is the consciousness of death, the certain prospect of death, and its inescapable emotion.

We see here the profound influence that psychology has had on thought. The ancient maxim of Epicurus seems just a sort of verbal trick, an almost childish playing with words, to a psychologist accustomed to another truth, the truth lived in every human mind, a very real truth, which no words can efface. Already St Augustine had opposed Epicurus, whom he had loved in his frivolous youth, by pointing out the constant relationship between life and death. The great answer of our own day was given by the German philosopher Heidegger.[6]

He described in striking terms our human condition: 'Death is not an event which happens to man, but an event which he lives through from birth onwards.' Thus from the moment he appears, man is on the point of dying. 'He is born and lives in the mortal mode. As soon as a man lives, he is old enough to die . . . Death is a constituent of our being. Day after day we live through our death. Man is, in his essence, a being-for-death (*Sein-zum-Ende*).' 'What is the meaning of this death for the individual consciousness?,' Heidegger asks. 'That by interrupting life it makes it incomplete. Incompletion is a constituent of my being . . . Death teaches us that life is a value, but an incomplete value.'

The permanent presence of death dominates Heidegger's philosophy, and gives it its depth. The poet Rilke also spoke of it when he evoked 'that great death which each of us carries within himself', or when he wrote: 'We always act like men who are going away.' For my part, it is also by intuition more than by reflection that I have always lived in this sort of familiarity with death – perhaps because I was an orphan. This view is also close to the wisdom of the Hindus, for whom, Eliade tells us, 'we are – not mortal – . . . but dying'.

On the other hand Sartre, despite his debt to Heidegger, has radically opposed him on this point. Death, he says, 'escapes me on principle . . . Death is a pure fact, like birth . . . It is absurd that we should be born, it is absurd that we should die . . . We always die into the bargain.' For Sartre, then, 'Life, so long as it lasts, is pure and free of any death. For I can conceive of myself only as alive. Man is a being for life, not for death.'[7] It is rather odd, I feel, that Sartre, who sees himself as a realist, who has debunked so many of our idealistic myths, should have convicted himself of lack of realism in denying the reality of finiteness and death.

There are, therefore, two fundamental attitudes possible in face of death: Heidegger looks it in the face and Sartre runs away from it. I find one or the other of these two attitudes in all the people with whom I enter into personal dialogue, and particularly in the old: some are acutely conscious of the reality of death and of its importance to an understanding of life; others repress the fact of death into their unconscious. The latter hope to achieve security by not thinking about death. For my part, I doubt if it is possible to achieve true serenity in this way. At most a tense, rigid and rather anxious impassiveness. For when a thing is repressed there is always a threat that it will come back to the surface – and suddenly one will become brutally aware of the inescapable reality of death.

These two contrary attitudes are also found among those who visit old people – or those who visit the sick, for disease, like old age, is a proclamation of death. There are some, even among doctors, who in order to maintain the morale of the old and the sick, seek to distract them from their worries with a flood of stories, gossip and banal chit-chat, taking care to avoid any illusion, however remote, to death. The people they are talking to intuitively feel that a barrier is being set up, like a closed door through which it is forbidden to pass; as if someone were saying to them: 'Above all, do not talk to me about your most private worries.' They willingly become accomplices in this flight into banality. The witty remark or the playful pleasantry serve, on both sides, to avoid a true dialogue. But the old person may feel a certain malaise after the departure of his visitor: what the latter has really done is to leave him alone with his anxiety.

I know very well that one can make the opposite mistake. There are in fact zealous and idealistic people who with best of intentions enter too easily and indiscreetly upon the delicate questions of life and death, or of religious faith. One might say that on such subjects some do not say enough and others say too much. In any case I would suggest that visitors should not so much talk as listen. An open, attentive and serious attitude puts the person at ease, so that he can say with confidence all he needs to say, without being afraid that he will be stopped either by an embarrassed silence or hasty and peremptory replies. There always takes place a very subtle psychological process when one tackles these problems which are highly charged with emotion: the emotion can be discharged only if it is expressed, but fear of the emotion often prevents its expression.

So there are two attitudes, which are represented more or less by the two existentialists, Heidegger and Sartre. But to take up a position as resolutely as that one needs to be a philosopher. In practice we, whether we are Christians or not, constantly mix up or alternate the two reactions, because the problem of death is so far beyond us. We share to some extent in both – we feel the full seriousness of death, or else we hide it from ourselves.

The Christian position

In some respects Christian thought is nearer to that of Heidegger. 'For the whole of the Bible,' writes the philosopher Roger Mehl, 'in fact shows us man as journeying in the shadow of death, as suffering from a disease, or, as the New Testament prefers to put it, suffering from a weakness which is already an anticipation of death . . . Death does not come upon man like a natural disaster. It is bound up with his most intimate existence, his existence before God.' Again he says: 'It remains so, in a certain sense, even after his justification, for though by faith in Christ, a new being – the subject of faith – is born in him and escapes from death (John 11.25), the old man . . . continues to lead its mortal existence, to be, in St Paul's words, a "body of death" (Rom. 7.24). There is, then, on essential points, a certain harmony between Christian thought and that of Heidegger. For both, death is interior and immanent in human existence.'

I have been keenly aware of this since my youth, but that has not disengaged me from the world and its struggles. On the contrary, I have thrown myself into them with passionate enthusiasm. But it is as it were a provisional world in which God has placed me for the sake of my personal training. My home is in heaven. And the more I have advanced in age, the more has earthly life seemed to me like an apprenticeship in the love and the knowledge of God. What is peculiar to Christianity, and seems to be lacking in Heidegger, is love, faith and hope. That is not a criticism of him, for that is no longer a matter of philosophy, but of a concrete experience which we can have in this life – the experience of fellowship with other people and with God.

So the Christian answer to death is not philosophical, and intellectually it seems to me to retain a certain ambiguity. If I am asked, 'Can you, in faith, accept death?' I cannot honestly reply anything other than 'Yes and no'. What a contradiction! I am very much afraid that will disappoint many of my readers, who expect solid affirmations from a Christian. But the contradiction lies at the heart of our human nature.

Can one accept anything without repressing some rebellion? Can one rebel without repressing some longing to accept? Can one never utter a yes without repressing a no, or a no without repressing a yes? Can one say 'I have faith' without repressing doubts, or can one talk of one's doubt's without by that very fact expressing one's faith? Does not faith consist most of all in recognizing that one lacks it? I am very sensitive to these awkward questions. I am as certain of what comes from God as I am uncertain of what comes from man. I have sometimes got to the point of admitting my perplexity and my incapacity to say clearly whether I have faith or not. And it has happened that readers as sensitive as I am have told me that they are grateful, because they felt less lonely as a result. And yet we all long for a clear and indubitable answer! But is it possible?

Lately my wife has sensed my perplexity. She asks me:

'Are you getting on all right with your book? Where have you got up to?'

'I'm still at death,' I reply.

'Aren't you going to get to resurrection soon?'

I know what she means! But resurrection does not do away with death. It follows it. I cannot minimize death because I believe in resurrection. Even the tragedy of Good Friday only had the intensity it had because Christ was really and exclusively experiencing death, and not, in anticipation, his resurrection, the mystery of which was still in God. We fully grasp the tragedy only by forgetting, so to speak, the resurrection which followed it. And when we sing our joy on Easter Day, we inevitably tend to forget Good Friday.

Christianity, then, does not minimize death. It has not simplified the problem, since it has affirmed, as Roger Mehl further remarks, that death can even assail God himself, in the person of Jesus

Christ. Yes, we can, from afar and in thought, anticipate the turning of the page, we can rejoice in heaven as I rejoice in it. But in the
reality of life the pages are turned only one at a time, each at its
proper time, and not before. My page of death is not yet turned;
I cannot turn it until I experience it.

The victory of faith

And yet, just now, when we were asking if faith makes it easier to
accept death, I was careful not to reply simply 'No', but rather
'Yes and no', for there is also a 'Yes'. All the martyrs are there,
and their witness is irrefutable: martyrs of the early centuries, and
those of all ages up to our own day. People may object, and say that
Japanese and even Western non-believers are also capable of facing
death, without fear and without rebellion, in heroic situations. For
my part, and from a psychological point of view, I can see their
victory as a victory of faith, a kind of faith, the faith that they have
in the cause for which they die.

But it is a fine point. The question we were asking concerned
faith in Jesus Christ. That is why, without neglecting the testimony
of the martyrs, it seems to me to be more convincing still to listen
to the witness of humble Christians who can say, quite apart from
the exceptional circumstance of persecution, and with assurance:
'God has laid hold upon me, he has revealed himself to me, I have
surrendered my life to him, I believe in him and in his promises,
I fear nothing, not even death.' Who would not agree that a certainty of that sort would provide an incomparable atmosphere for
old age? But it is the atmosphere of the heart that one perceives.
What always moves me most is not this or that declaration of fervent belief, however impressive, but the feeling that a person is
living his personal experience of Jesus Christ. Thus, for instance,
everything that Marie Fargues says with such insight in her book
La paix de l'automme, is beautiful.[8] But what counts most with me
is what lies behind what she writes – her person, and the presence
of God which inspires her and which she communicates.

A Zurich medical student, David Kurzen, has written an essay
on 'Old Age in the Bible'.[9] He shows that the Bible is realistic in
it treatment of old age, and does not try to hide its sufferings. But
the Bible also shows the total contrast between old age without

God and old age with God. It is the personal bond with God established by faith which transfigures old age.

Then the aged person can look upon death as a deliverance, as the end of his afflictions, as repose in God, like a haven in which he can take shelter from all the vicissitudes of life. This was expressed by the Huguenot poet Agrippa d'Aubigné in the evening of his life:

> Voici moins de plaisirs, mais voici moins de peines;
> Le rossignol se tait, se taisent les Sirènes;
> Nous ne voyons cueillir ni les fruits ni les fleurs;
> L'espérance n'est plus, bien souvent tromperesse;
> L'hiver jouit de tout; bienheureuse vieillesse,
> La saison de l'usage, et non des labeurs.
> Mais la mort n'est pas loin; cette mort est suivie
> D'un vivre sans mourir, fin d'une fausse vie,
> Vie de notre vie, et mort de notre mort.
> Qui hait la sûreté pour aimer le naufrage,
> Qui a jamais été si friand de voyage,
> Que la longueur en soit plus doux que le port?
>
> (Here are less pleasures, but also less pains;
> The nightingale is silent, so are the Sirens;
> We see plucked neither the fruit nor the flowers;
> Hope is no more – so often deceiving;
> Winter enjoys everything; blessed old age,
> The season of use, and not of toil.
> But death is at hand; death which is followed
> By living without dying, the end of false life,
> Life of our life, and death of our death.
> Who hates safety, and loves shipwreck?
> Who has ever been so fond of travel,
> That the length of it is sweeter than the haven?)

Of such an old man, one may say with Charles Péguy that 'he is on the edge of the eternal' – even nearer than the edge. I have just received a letter from my old friend Dr Théo Bovet, whom I have mentioned several times in this book, and who has just lost his wife after fifty-one years of happy married life. 'My present experience,' he writes, 'is that Eternal Life does not begin after death, but that we start living it now; only it is masked by our daily cares, and it is only on contact with death, perhaps, that we discover it. God is not a God of the dead, but of the living, since for him they are all living. Which, to my very great astonishment, fills me with joy, despite the sadness.'

Eternal life does indeed begin on this earth. To live with God is to share already in his everlastingness. He who has one foot in the infinite can accept his finiteness. And this decisive step, this birth into eternal life, can be made well before old age and the approach of death. But it is often, as Dr Bovet says, the death of a dear one that can lead us to it.

This very day I have received yet another letter, from one of my former patients from abroad, who has recently lost her father, to whom she was very much attached, and who had reached a great age. She writes: 'An element of balance is coming into being within me, on another level, bringing me a valuable inner enlightenment. It is the lesson of death, opening the door to the true realities, giving to life its true meaning and its true light ... There! My father, on leaving us, has opened a door towards which I look more often, happy to think that there is a bright goal there, and a meaning for the adventure of our life.' You will see that the image of light appears three times in these few lines, written as they are out of deep mourning.

Max Scheller has wonderfully described this effect of the death of a loved one – a sort of participation or interiorization. 'My death,' says Paul Ricoeur, 'is still floating out there somewhere, sharpened against me by I don't know what or whom.'[10] In the perspective of Christian thought, and of that of Heidegger, that death has also been floating in me since my birth, and it is the experience of the death of someone else which really makes me aware of it.

Another psychiatrist, one of my close friends, and one from whom I have learnt much, said to me recently: 'I think more and more about death, not death in general, in the abstract, but my own death.' And yet he is quite a lot younger than I! He continued: 'I talk about it more and more with my patients as well, and I am surprised to see what new depth, what new efficacy, it gives to my psychotherapeutic action on their behalf.' Doctors think much more about death than they usually care to admit, and they are wrong to keep silent. By talking about our own attitude to death we help our patients to talk about theirs.

Thoughts of a priest-doctor

I am reminded of another of my friends, the Abbé Oraison. I understood his life when he told us, at a conference on the medicine of the person, that before he was born his parents had lost several children. And so, rather like me, he had made his discovery of the world and of life against the background of a family in mourning. This explains why the problem of death has always occupied his mind, as it has mine. In order to fight against death he chose, as his father had, the career of surgeon. I have always noticed how sensitive surgeons are about death.

But the surgeon Marc Oraison soon realized that while medicine can postpone death – what unspeakable joy we can experience when a patient is healed! – it cannot solve its problem. Therefore he became a priest. The priesthood then confronted him with the discoveries of psychology, and he went on to become a psychoanalyst. So he is a real doctor of the person, who has learnt how to know man through his body, as a surgeon, through his mind as a psycho-analyst, and through his soul, as a priest.

To his three careers he has added a fourth, that of writer. After several books on sex, marriage, celibacy, the search for a new morality of love, and on his own life, he has come back to his main preoccupation – death.[11] He has tried to set down what a modern man, cultured, clear-headed, scientifically-minded, may think about death. He insists in the first place on the necessity of death, on the need to look upon it as a perfectly natural phenomenon. Perhaps that seems naïve to many of my readers, but is it not true that we need to get back to a certain simplicity?

Some years ago now my grandson Nicolas said to me:

'You know, grandad, you're going to die soon.'

'Why?' I asked.

'Because you are very, very old.'

'Yes, you are right,' I replied with the same simplicity. 'I am very old, and I'm going to die soon.'

How good children are at helping us to be simple and sincere. How soothing it is to talk about death, instead of having to be careful to say nothing about it because it is taboo. Old people do not so much need a neat intellectual reply as to express their own thoughts and to feel that they are understood. Man's perennial dream is to spread out the narrow limits within which Nature confines him. This dream is encouraged by the success of his great modern scientific and technical adventure. This is why primitive peoples and children can look upon death with much greater simplicity than we. As you see, we have come back to the fundamental respect for Nature which I mentioned in connection with the acceptance of old age.

'Everything that is born must die.' That is the remark we called attention to earlier, from the pen of Professor Jores. It is an elementary truth, which we find it terribly difficult to recognize. Anyone who wishes to reflect upon man and his destiny must be prepared to bring birth and death together in this way. For after all, birth is no easier to understand than death. Like death, it is both a natural phenomenon and a mystery. Every young couple awaiting the birth of their first child feels this intensely, as is proved by the fact that well before the baby arrives they have already thought of a name for it – the symbol of the person. Some parents already call it by its name, and talk to it as if it were able to take part in a real dialogue. Birth is not just a biological phenomenon, the development to full term of a fertilized egg in accordance with the laws of Nature; it is also the creation of a person, with all the metaphysical overtones that that word inevitably evokes.

'Death figures, in the destiny of the person, as the second and final stage of birth,' writes the Abbé Oraison.[12] I feel very strongly that this way of looking at birth and death together helps us to see them both, but especially death, in a new light. This wider vista liberates us from too narrow a vision of death. The person is a mysterious reality which goes beyond existence at both ends, transcending both birth and death. Between these two it remains always to some extent veiled by its earthly limitations. Death is but the end of the earthly adventure, and we know that no adventure lasts for ever. It must die before it starts again beyond its limits.[13] To accept death is to accept this law of transcendence of limits, to fix one's gaze on what lies beyond. Then one can understand Landsberg's remark: 'The acceptance of death transforms death.'[14]

Resurrection

The Abbé Oraison, too, entitled his book *Death . . . and then afterwards?* In fact the question which death puts to us is that of this 'afterwards'. An essential and unavoidable question for man as he grows old, as he wishes to go on looking forward, like all living creatures, and not backward. Goethe wrote: 'I will say with Lorenzo de Medici that those who do not hope for another life are always dead to this one.' And Jean Lescure remarks: 'The anxiety of death is not about going to sleep; it is rather about not waking up again.'[15] On this point the gospel is clear and categorical. Our resurrection is promised, and the resurrection of Jesus Christ is the pledge of it. St Paul made no mistake about it when he exclaimed in the face of his contradictors: 'If Christ has not been raised then our preaching is useless and your believing it is useless' (I Cor. 15.14).

Consequently, 'for believers,' as Professor Menoud writes, 'death is no longer a curse or a punishment; it is the event that is preparatory and necessary to resurrection.'[16] He quotes, in this connection, Cardinal Daniélou: death is 'a crisis of growth'. A new life is announced, a new life awaits us, and we can already have some partial experience of it in this life, in moments of true communications with other people and with God. A life of fulfilment which will at last answer that need for fulfilment which torments us all through our limited earthly existence. But what sort of life will it be? Can we honestly say?

His readers' questions on this subject have been so numerous, their reactions so pressing, that the Abbé Oraison has had to hasten to write a second book, this time in collaboration with a famous journalist, Bruno Lagrange: *There exists elsewhere . . .* [17] That there is something else elsewhere is something which man has intuitively felt in all ages: something other than this visible world in which he is enclosed, the extreme complexity of which he never ceases to explore, and which he will never finish exploring with excitement and wonder. But between intuition and knowledge there is a distance which every poet knows the pain of. And also the popular imagination has given us very naïve mental pictures.

These pictures, or archetypes, are inscribed in the collective unconscious which constitutes the deep common layers in the minds of all men. We uncover them in our patients' dreams. Often I have heard the same story with the slightest of variations. The dreamer is mysteriously transported into an absolutely square room, a disposition which Jung has called 'numinous',[18] a symbol of perfection. There he finds himself a member of a choir, all the members of which are dressed, as he is, in long white robes, and are

standing in a regular semi-circle. He has found his place without
difficulty. Without actually knowing the choristers, he feels himself
to be neither a stranger, nor a guest, nor a person of no importance
among them. He is really part of the choir, and in unison with all
the others, without any conductor being present or necessary, he
sings heavenly melodies without having learnt them.

Of course the whole scene is only symbolic. The prospect of
singing hymns – however beautiful – forever in heaven is unlikely
to be a very attractive one for the majority of men, even the most
religious. My wife's grandmother, who was very active, was in the
habit of saying that she hoped there would be work to do in
heaven, for she was afraid that she would get bored with eternal
rest. These archetypes printed on our minds symbolize perfection,
joy, fellowship, harmony, unadulterated fervour and peace.

Here, for instance, is one of my patients who is well on the way
to recovery from an affliction which has been a great trouble to her
for twenty or thirty years, to say nothing of other tragic circumstances which had engulfed her. The dream begins in a consulting-
room, where a clever surgeon is fascinating her. This symbolizes
active life, the seductive power of technology and of man who has
the skill to control it. Then she finds herself in a huge ruined
château, and she is feverishly rushing up and down innumerable
staircases and along dark corridors. She is looking for something, without knowing what it is, and without finding it, with
growing anxiety. This part of the dream is a symbol of the difficult
self-investigation which she undergoes in her psychotherapeutic
treatment.

Then suddenly the dream concludes with the numinous choir
sequence. I choose this dream because of a remark which the
dreamer made, and which stuck in my mind. The moment she
found herself in her white robe, singing at the top of her voice, she
felt, she said, as if she had been relieved of an enormous weight
from off her shoulders. That, no doubt, was the weight of the illness; and also the weight of all her regrets, all her vain searches,
all her temptations. But it was also the weight of life, which lies
heavy on all men, however strong and valiant they are. And there
are many old people who long to lay down the burden, to receive at
last in François Mauriac's words, 'the last of God's mercies . . . to
die'.

To die, to come to a quite new life, exempt from all that weighs down our earthly existence, even for the most privileged among us, is the ineffaceable aspiration of the human heart. The naïve quality of the mental pictures I have referred to demonstrates that our minds are totally incapable of conceiving what that other life will be like, of conceiving a world radically different from this present world, as it is presented to our senses, to our experience, and to our intellect. It is for this reason that the Abbé Oraison, while proclaiming our faith in resurrection, is honest enough to avoid all the descriptions of heaven and hell that men have imagined in poetry or piety, and which do nothing but make the problem more obscure.

What do we know of the beyond?

Really, we know nothing of what our resurrection life will be like. It is better to recognize this. Probably it is better that we should know nothing. We are back at the comparison that our priest-doctor made between death and birth: 'The child comes to his term in his mother's womb, not knowing anything more about what he will find when he is outside and opens his eyes on life.' And again: 'Before my birth, I was in a Protean situation, but in a sense comparable to my situation in my conscious existence in time: desirous of "seeing" something else, but incapable of having *the least idea* (his italics) of what it might be.'

It is true that we know nothing about it. But how nice it would be to know! This did not escape St Paul, who wrote: 'Someone may ask, "How are dead people raised, and what sort of body do they have when they come back?" They are stupid questions. Whatever you sow in the ground has to die before it is given new life, and the thing that you sow is not what is going to come; you sow a bare grain, say of wheat or something like that, and then God gives it the sort of body that he has chosen . . . It is the same with the resurrection of the dead: the thing that is sown is perishable but what is raised is imperishable; the thing that is sown is contemptible but what is raised is glorious; the thing that is sown is weak but what is raised is powerful; when it is sown it embodies the mind, when it is raised it embodies the spirit.' (I Cor. 15.35-44).

St Paul speaks again in other passages of his spiritual, incorruptible, glorious body (Phil. 3.21). His insistence on using the word 'body', while making clear that it is no longer the body of the anatomists, is evident. It signifies that the resurrection promised by the gospel is a personal resurrection, a resurrection of the person. When I say that I have met so-and-so 'in the flesh' I am asserting that I have met him personally, that I have identified his person. In the resurrection, we shall once more have this personal identity.

We are a long way, therefore, from the immorality of the soul, as taught by Plato, who saw the soul liberated at last from the body in which it had been imprisoned, and returning to the realm of pure ideas. We are a long way, too, from those Oriental concepts according to which the individual, losing his personal identity, is lost in the Infinite. I know nothing about what form life will take in the beyond, but I know that it will not be an unincarnate, abstract, impersonal world of ideas, of pure anonymous spirits or of phantoms. I know that I shall retain my personal identity; and it is a fact here below, in personal fellowship, in the person-to-person relationship when it is true, that I find a foretaste of heaven.

The resurrection of Jesus Christ

We see this clearly in the accounts of the historical resurrection of Jesus, the sole foundation of our faith, the only light that lightens this dark problem. I leave on one side the other resurrections of which the Bible speaks, that for instance of a child brought back to life by Elijah (I Kings 17.22), Jairus' daughter (Luke 8.55), or even Lazarus (John 11.44). All of these seem to be miraculous and temporary returns to earthly life, quite different from resurrections to a quite different life. The evident intention of all these accounts – even the intention of Jesus himself, as he expressed it – was to show forth the glory and power of God, rather as cases of resuscitation in our hospitals bear witness to the power of medicine.

The case of the resurrection of Jesus is quite different. Jesus himself in person surprises his disciples in the upper room where they sat in despair (John 20.19). But he was no longer an earthly being, since he came to them 'all the doors being closed'. Furthermore, the disciples had great difficulty in recognizing him. All the accounts are marked by these contradictions. Mary of Magdala mistook him for the gardener (John 20.15) and recognized him only when he called her by her name. The travellers on the road to Emmaus (Luke 24.13-35) conversed at great length with him, and recognized him only by a familiar gesture. They were astonished then at not having recognized him, but at once he mysteriously disappeared. Later, on the shore of the Sea of Tiberias, Peter and John, the closest of his disciples, were to be slow to recognize him (John 21).

The resurrection of Jesus Christ raises, therefore, as many difficulties for our intellects as it solves for our hearts. We are beyond the limits of intelligibility, conditioned as it is by our nature. Human eyes, even those of the disciples, are powerless to identify a being who is no longer of this world. An enlightenment of the mind is needed then. But in spite of everything it is still by corporeal reality that the mind will be convinced. In order to make himself known, Jesus shows his body, that mysterious body which passes through the closed door. He shows his hands and his feet: 'It is I indeed,' he says, 'a ghost has no flesh and bones as you can see I have' (Luke 24.39). And in order to convince them he eats in front of them – the corporeal action *par excellence*. Later, Thomas is invited to put his finger in the mark of the nails that had pierced the hands of Jesus (John 20.27).

There could be no clearer expression of the great truth that the person is identified through the body. Whether it is our face, our expression, the way we smile, our gestures, our walk, or our voice, it is by our bodies that we are recognized. The law recognizes this, in admitting no other proof of identification than finger-prints. And yet, that body of the Resurrected Lord is still radically different from the body which the doctor studies in the anatomy laboratory. You might say that all it retains is its function as a means of identification. It addresses itself to others. It is a proof of resurrection only in so far as it is recognized by others. There is no material scientific proof of the resurrection.

Personal experience

But there is another, non-material proof which is none the less scientific. For science is no longer only the science of matter, since psychology and sociology have won their scientific spurs, and since the physicists are no longer quite sure what matter is. The Abbé Oraison insists on this other proof. He calls it the 'Christian fact'. It is the 'quite new and specific view of death' which Christianity has introduced into human history. It is the experience of Christians themselves, the personal transformation of the disciples which turns them into the messengers of an invincible hope as soon as they are sure that their master is alive again.

I recognize a colleague in that argument! The theologian starts from doctrine; the doctor, from experience. They are often thought of as being in opposition to one another, especially by theologians who are afraid that a theology of experience may open the door to the abuses of illuminism; and I recognize that that does sometimes happen. For this reason it seems to me to be essential to join these two approaches together, instead of separating them. What convinces me of this is the exact concordance that exists between experience and doctrine. The case of St Paul is conclusive: he preaches the resurrection of Jesus Christ with so much assurance because he has himself met the Resurrected Christ on the Damascus road. He says so, expressly, as the supreme argument in support of the authority of his preaching (II Cor. 12.2).

There is, then, no conflict between experience and doctrine, but rather concordance. Nevertheless there is an order of succession between them: experience does not have primacy, but it does have priority. I first experience the encounter with Jesus: afterwards, I open my Bible, and I observe that my experience is in conformity with the gospel. I believe in the resurrection of the body, but I realize perfectly well that as death approaches my supreme security lies not so much in which doctrine, as in the close bond which attaches me to the person of Jesus. I am not alone as I face death. I am with Jesus who has faced it himself.

Like the Abbé Oraison, I too am a doctor, and my thinking proceeds from experience rather than from doctrine. I cannot end this book with theological arguments which will never come to any definitive conclusion, however important they are. The trouble with doctrines is that they separate men, whereas experience brings them together. I cannot say 'I believe in the resurrection', without those of my readers who cannot say it with me feeling separated from me. They place me in the camp of the believers, and they put themselves in the other. There are no camps; there are only people. People who stand together because they have the same destiny: birth, maturity, old age, and death; asking themselves questions, experiencing joys and sorrows, making mistakes, picking themselves up again, doubting and hoping.

And then, there is Jesus Christ, who came for the sake of all men, who understands them all and envelops them all in one and

the same love, but who said himself that he has more solicitude for
the unfortunate than for the fortunate, for those who suffer than
for those who are well, for the humble than those who are proud of
their behaviour and their beliefs, who died and rose again from
the dead for them all, who goes before them, as the Gospel says, and
prepares a place for them (John 14.2). And it happens that men meet
him and recognize him, at any age, and almost always in some unexpected and surprising fashion. Then he awakens in them a faith,
which is not so much a belief in a set doctrine as an attachment to
his person.

This personal bond with Jesus makes me one with all those who
are surrounded, as I am, with so many uncertainties. It allows me
to accept that many of the questions raised by life remain unanswered. Job received no answer to the problem of undeserved
evil that overwhelmed him. But he experienced a personal encounter with God (Job 42.5). I do not claim to answer anyone in
this book. As in life, I listen much more than I try to reply. The
answers do not come from men, but from God.

I have just received a letter from an American lady, which
touches me deeply. She tells me that she has been a widow for
fifteen years. Her husband's death was a catastrophe for her. She
felt as if the ground was giving way beneath her feet. Her life had
no more meaning for her. Then there came a day when she realized
that God needed her, that she could be an instrument in his hand
for his work. 'God,' she writes, 'is now really the mainstay, the
shield, and the strength of my life. He is my reason for living.'

It is he also who then becomes our reason for hoping. 'I remember,' writes Dr Sebillotte, 'an old woman whose faith in Jesus as
Saviour was quite solid. She suffered a cerebral haemorrhage, and
realized that she could not recover. Almost her last words were:
"At last, I'm going to know."' The doctor goes on: 'Those who
saw her there lying dead that Easter morning, as she had wished,
also wait to know.'

That same remark, 'I'm going to know,' was said to me, word for
word, during a recent visit. It was to one of my former patients, an
old lady of more than ninety now, more or less housebound. She
had written to say that she wished to see me again. It was a wonderful conversation, for there is a strong spiritual bond between us.
We talked about death. I had known her as a scrupulous soul, in-
clined to worry. I found her at peace, and serene. She said: 'I am

ready to go on living, and I am ready to die. At last, I am going to know.' The next day she wrote me a letter, as if to prolong our meeting: 'For myself,' she wrote, 'I shall be very happy to see the beyond, and perhaps to hear Christ himself talking about the mysteries of the grace of God.'

NOTES

PART ONE

1. Paul Paillat, *Sociologie de la vieillesse*, Presses Universitaires de France, Paris.

2. Henri Bour, 'L'homme et le vieillissement', in *Vieillesse et longévité dans la société de demain*, Presses Universitaires de France, Paris, 1968.

3. Alfred Sauvy, 'Le vieillissement démographique', in *Revue internationale des sciences sociales*, Vol. XV, No. 3, 1963, Unesco, Paris.

4. J. Cipra, *Étude des conditions de vie des retraités de la Caisse interprofessionnelle paritaire des Alpes*, 1965.

5. Joffre Dumazedier and Aline Ripert, 'Troisième âge et loisirs', in *Revue internationale des sciences sociales*, Vol. XV, No. 3, 1963.

6. Joffre Dumazedier, *Vers une civilisation du loisir*, Le Seuil, Paris, 1962.

7. Denis de Rougemont, *Man's Western Quest*, Allen and Unwin, London, 1958.

8. Denis de Rougemont, op. cit.

9. Aline Ripert, 'Quelques problèmes américains', in *Esprit*, Paris, June, 1959.

10. Denis de Rougemont, *Penser avec les mains*, Albin Michel, Paris, 1936.

11. Denis de Rougemont, *Man's Western Quest*.

12. Adolf Portmann, 'Mensch und Natur', in *Die Bedrohung unserer Zeit*, Friedrich Reinhardt, Basle.

13. Hogarth Press, London, 1961.

14. Roland Cahen-Salabelle, *La psychothérapie dans la deuxième moitié de la vie d'après C. G. Jung*, Paris, Semaine Medicale des Hôpitaux, 26 mai 1950.

15. C. G. Jung, *Psychology of the Spirit*, Guild of Pastoral Psychology, London.

16. C. G. Jung, *Modern Man in Search of a Soul*, Routledge, London, 1933.

17. C. G. Jung, *Structure and Dynamics of the Psyche*, Routledge, London, 1960.

18. C. G. Jung, *Modern Man in Search of a Soul*.

19. C. G. Jung, *The Practice of Psychotherapy*, Routledge, London, 1954.

20. C. G. Jung, *Psychology of the Spirit*.

21. C. G. Jung, *Modern Man in Search of a Soul*.

22. Patrick Lecomte, *Une expérience de gérontologie sociale: le Centre de préparation à la retraite de Grenoble*, Institut d'Études politiques.

23. Robert Hugonot, 'Gériatrie et gérontologie grenobloises', in *Grenoble médico-chirurgical*, Vol. VI, 1968.

24. Michel Philibert, 'Le Centre de préparation à la retraite', in *Du Grenoble olympique au Grenoble social*, Aged Persons Office, Grenoble.

25. Jean Lacroix, *L'échec*. '*Initiation philosophique*', Presses Universitaires de France, Paris, 1965.

26. In *La Suisse*, Geneva, 20 November 1969.

27. Paul Ricoeur, *De l'interprétation*. *Essai sur Freud*, Le Seuil, Paris, 1956.

28. Aline Ripert, 'Quelques problèmes américains', in *Esprit*, Paris, June 1959.

29. Arthur Jores and H. G. Puchta, 'Der Pensionierungstod', *Medizinische Klinik*, Munich-Berlin, No. 25, 19 June 1959, p.1158.

30. J.-M. Domenach, 'Loisir et travail', in *Esprit*, Special No., June 1959.

31. Quoted by Alessandro Pizzorno, 'Accumulation, loisirs et rapports de classe', in *Esprit*, Paris, June 1959.

32. A. Gros, in *Vieillesse et longévité dans la société de demain*, Presses Universitaires de France, Paris, 1968.

33. Aline Ripert, 'Loisirs', in *Esprit*, May 1963.

34. Georges Gusdorf, *La découverte de soi*, Presses Universitaires de France, Paris, 1948.

35. Alessandro Pizzorno, 'Accumulation, loisirs et rapports de classes', in *Esprit*, June 1959.

36. Paul Tournier, *A Place for You*, Harper & Row, New York, 1968.

PART TWO

1. Henri Bour, 'L'homme et le vieillissement', in *Vieillesse et longévité dans la société de demain*, Presses Universitaires de France, Paris, 1968.

2. Paul Miraillet, 'L'évolution du vieillard "bien adapté"', in *La vieillesse, problème d'aujourd'hui*, Spes, Paris, 1961.

3. Jean-Louis Villa, 'L'hygiène mentale du vieillissement', in *Médecine et Hygiène*, Geneva, 1966.

4. G. Gaillard, ' "Les vieux" dans l'histoire et dans l'évolution sociale', in *La vieillesse, problème d'aujourd'hui*.

5. M. Aumont, 'Vieillissement et vieillesse dans leur signification et leurs implications', in *Vieillesse et longévité dans la société de demain*.

6. Paul Ricoeur, 'Vraie et fausse angoisse', in *L'angoisse du temps présent et les devoirs de l'esprit*, La Baconnière, Neuchâtel, 1954.

7. Herbert Marcuse, *One-Dimensional Man*, Routledge, London, 1964.

8. Louis Armand and Michael Drancourt, *Plaidoyer pour l'avenir*, Calmann-Lévy, Paris, 1961.

9. Paul Tournier, *Dynamique de la guérison*, Delachaux & Niestlé, Neuchâtel & Paris, 1967.

10. Alphonse Maeder, *De la psychanalyse à la psychothérapie appellative*, Payot, Paris, 1970.

11. Théo Bovet, 'Santé et vie spirituelle', in *4ᵉ Congrès médico-social protestant de langue française, Strasbourg, mai 1957*, Oberlin, Paris, 1958.

12. M. Schelsky, *Sociologie comparée de la famille contemporaine*, Colloques internationaux, Centre national de la recherche scientifique, Paris, 1955.

13. Paul Balvet, 'Problèmes de vie du psychiatre', in *Présences*, 2nd Term, No. 87, 1964, Draveil.

14. Paul Tournier, *A Place for You*.

15. *La vieillesse*, Gallimard, Paris, 1970.

16. M. Grégoire, 'L'amour de toute une vie', in *Esprit*, Paris, May 1963.

17. M. Philibert, 'Le rôle et l'image du vieillard dans notre société', in *Esprit*, Paris, May 1963.

18. A. Sauvy, *La montée des jeunes*, Calmann-Lévy, Paris, 1959.

19. Kurd Vogelsang, *Gedanken über die Zeit der Pensionierung* (unpublished).

20. Jacques Leclercq, *Joie de vieillir*, Editions Universitaires, Paris.

21. André Berge, 'Les grands-parents', in *La vieillesse, problème d'aujourd'hui*, Spes, Paris, 1961.

22. Paul Tournier, 'A Dialogue between Doctor and Patient', in *The III International Congress of Christian Physicians, Oslo, 1969*, Universitets forlaget, Oslo, 1969.

23. Eric Berne, *Games People Play*, Andre Deutsch, London, 1966.

24. Paul Morand, *Discours de Réception à l'Académie Française*, 20 March 1969.

25. Louis Tournier, *Les enfantines*, Jeheber, Geneva, 1895.

26. Louis Tournier, *Les chants de la jeunesse: le rouet*, Cherbuliez, Geneva, 1888.

PART THREE

1. Théo Bovet, *L'art de trouver du temps*, Oberlin, Strasbourg, 1955.

2. Karlfried von Dürckheim, *Pratique de la voie intérieure. Le quotidien comme exercice*, Le Courrier du Livre, Paris, 1968.

3. Eric Martin, 'Hygiène générale du vieillissement. Journées d'étude de Lausanne, Oct. 1970', in *Revue de Médecine preventive*, Special Issue, Vol. 16, No. 1, Zurich.

4. In *Vieillesse et longévité dans la société de demain*.

5. J.-M. Arnion, 'La société et les vieillards', in *La vieillesse, problème d'aujourd'hui*, Spes, Paris, 1971.

6. Suzanne G. Meyer, 'Trois millions de veuves', in *Esprit*, May 1963.

7. Roger Mehl, *Le vieillissement et la mort*, Presses Universitaires de France, Paris, 1962.

8. P. Magnin, 'Les Ressources et le logement du vieillard', in *La vieillesse, problème d'aujourd'hui*.

9. M. Philibert, 'Le Centre de Préparation à la retraite', in *Du Grenoble olympique au Grenoble social*, Office pour les personnes âgées, Grenoble.

10. Dorothy Cole Wedderburn, 'Les aspects économiques du vieillissement', in *Revue internationale des sciences sociales*, Unesco, Paris, Vol. XV, No. 3, 1963.

11. Hans Thomae, 'Vieillissement et problèmes d'adaptation', in *Revue internationale des sciences sociales*, No. 3, 1963.

12. Daric, 'Vieillissement de la population et prolongation de la vie active', in *Rapport du Haut-Comité Consultatif de la Population et de la Famille sur la Population française*, La Documentation française, Paris, 1955.

13. Hervé Conte, *Retraites pour tous*, Neret, Paris.

14. Caisse Nationale de Retraite des Ouvriers du Bâtiment et des Travaux Publics, *Réalités du 3e âge*, Dunod, Paris, 1968.

15. P. B. Schneider, *L'hygiène mentale de la vieillesse*, Cartel romand d'hygiène sociale et morale, Lausanne, 1959-60.

16. J.-P. Baujat, *Comment se préparer à la retraite*, Entreprise Moderne d'Editions, Paris, 1963.

17. Marcel Jouhandeau, *Réflexions sur la vieillesse et la mort*, Grasset, Paris, 1956.

18. See Dorothy C. Wedderburn, op. cit.

19. Cipra, op. cit.

20. Paul Balvet, 'Psychiatrie des vieillards', in *Esprit*, May 1963.

21. Caisse Nationale de Retraite, op. cit.

22. Cipra, op. cit.

23. Caisse Nationale de Retraite, op. cit.

24. F. Corvez, OP, 'Spiritualité de la vieillesse', in *La vieillesse, problème d'aujourd'hui*.

25. L. Rosenmayr and E. Köckeis, 'Essai d'une théorie sociologique de la vieillesse et de la famille', in *Revue des sciences sociales*, Unesco, Paris, Vol. XV, No. 3, 1963.

26. Caisse Nationale de Retraite, op. cit.

27. Jean Dublineau, 'Psychologie du vieillissement chez l'homme', in *La vieillesse, problème d'aujourd'hui*.

28. Louis-Henry Sebillote, 'Regards sur la mort', in *Présences*, No. 103, 2nd Term, 1968.

29. Paul Miraillet, op. cit.

30. G. Gusdorf, *La Parole*, Presses Universitaires de France, Paris, 1953.

31. P. Plattner, *Glücklichere Ehen*, Huber, Berne, 1971.

32. René Biot, 'Le vieillissement du couple', in *La vieillesse, problème d'aujourd'hui*.

33. Quoted in Jeanne Hersch, *L'angoisse du temps présent et les devoirs de l'esprit*, La Baconnière, Neuchâtel, 1954.

34. Paul and Jacqueline Chauchard, *Vieillir à deux*, Editions Universitaires, Paris, 1967.

35. Rosenmayr and Köckeis, op. cit.

36. Elaine Cumming, 'Nouvelles réflexions sur la théorie du désengagement', in *Revue internationale des sciences sociales*, Unesco, Paris, Vol. XV, No. 3, 1963.

37. P. Magnin, 'Le logement des personnes âgées', in *Esprit*, Paris, May 1963.

38. Paul Miraillet, op. cit.

39. M. Philibert, 'L'essor de la gérontologie sociale aux États-Unis', in *Esprit*, May 1963.

40. Caisse Nationale de Retraite, op. cit.

41. Robert Hugonot, 'L'Institut d'esthétique des personnes âgées', in *Du Grenoble olympique au Grenoble social*.

42. Robert Hugonot, 'Gériatrie et gérontologie grenobloises', in *Grenoble médico-chirurgical*, Vol. VI, 1968.

43. Paul Miraillet, op. cit.

44. Paul Miraillet, op. cit.

45. R. Gentis, 'Les travailleurs de 45 à 65 ans', in *La vieillesse, problème d'aujourd'hui*.

46. Cipra, op. cit.

47. W. Weideli, 'Ne déracinez pas les vieillards, c'est un crime!', in *Construire*, Zurich, 26 May 1971.

48. Suzanne Pacaud and M. O. Lahalle, 'Attitudes, comportements, opin-

ions des personnes âgées dans le cadre de la famille moderne', in *Monographies françaises de Psychologie*, No. 16, Centre National de la Recherche Scientifique, Paris.

49. Rosenmayr and Köckeis, op. cit.

50. P. Townsend, 'Faut-il renoncer aux maisons de retraite?', in *Revue internationale des sciences sociales*, Vol. XV, No. 3, 1963.

51. P. Miraillet, op. cit.

52. Jean-Louis Villa, op. cit.

53. C. Müller, *Manuel de gérontopsychiatrie*, Masson, Paris, 1969.

54. Paul Miraillet, op. cit.

55. Anne Denard-Toulet, 'Prévention gérontologique', in *Esprit*, May 1963.

56. G. Daniel, *Les vocations du 3ᵉ âge dans le monde moderne – un médecin vous parle*, Spes, Paris, 1969.

57. Inge Pabel, 'L'intégration des personnes âgées dans notre société', in *Frankfürter Rundschau*, 27 March 1971.

58. Le Seuil, Paris, 1971.

59. Editions du Mont Blanc, Geneva, 1970.

60. L'Epi, Paris, 1968.

PART FOUR

1. Beuve-Méry, 'Sur la retraite de M.', in *Le Monde*, Paris, 24 December 1969.

2. Paul Lafargue, *Le droit à la paresse*, Paris, 1883.

3. Maurice Roch, *Dialogues cliniques*, Payot, Lausanne, 1953.

4. Alessandro Pizzorno, 'Accumulation, loisirs et rapports de classe', in *Esprit*, June 1959.

5. D. Riesman, 'Work and Leisure in Post-industrial Society', in *Mass Leisure*, The Free Press, Glencoe, Ill., 1959.

6. See Joffre Dumazedier, op. cit.

7. C. G. Jung, *Structure and Dynamics of the Psyche*.

8. Raymond Cartier, 'En feuilletant ses vingt ans, *Paris-Match* raconte votre époque', in *Paris-Match*, No. 1036, Paris, 15 March 1969.

9. Daric, op. cit.

10. Pitkin, 'Life Begins at Forty', quoted by Vischer, *La vieillesse*, Flammarion, Paris.

11. Roger Mehl, op. cit.

12. Gilles Lambert, 'Ce n'est pas une question d'âge', in *Constellation*, No. 55, November 1952.

13. Pabel Inge, op. cit.

14. Pierre Arents, 'Loisirs et éducation permanente', in *Esprit*, Special Issue on Leisure, June 1959.

15. Georges Guéron, 'Vieillesse et société', in *Vieillesse et longévité dans la société de demain*.

16. Anne Denard-Toulet, op. cit.

17. Viktor E. Frankl, 'La logothérapie et son emploi clinique', in *Wiener Medizinische Wochenschrift*, No. 117, 1967. See also his *La psychothérapie et son image de l'homme*, Resma, Paris, 1970.

18. Arthur Jores, *Erfülltes und unerfülltes Leben*, Wege zum Menschen, Göttingen, 1968.

19. Walter Weideli, 'Table ronde sur les problèmes de la retraite', in *Construire*, Zurich, 9 June 1971.

20. 'Der Mensch und seine Krankheit', in *Grundlagen einer anthropologischen Medizin*, Klett, Stuttgart, 1956.

21. *Um eine Medizin von Morgen*, H. Huber, Berne, 1969.

22. Arthur Jores, *Vom Sinn der Krankheit*, University of Hamburg, 1950.

23. Viktor von Weizsäcker, *Grundfragen medizinischer Anthropologie*, Furche Verlag, Hamburg.

24. Alphonse Maeder, 'Zur geschichtlichen Entwicklung der prospektiv-finalen Konzeption', in *Dialog mit dem Menschen, eine Festschrift für Wilhelm Bitter*, Ernst Klett, Stuttgart.

25. Karlfried von Dürckheim, 'Religious Experience Beyond Religions', in *Modern Trends in World Religions*, The Open Court Publishing Co., LaSalle, Ill., 1959.

26. Heinrich Huebschmann, 'Psyche und Tuberkulose', in *Deutsche Medizinische Wochenschrift*, 4 May 1951.

PART FIVE

1. Nicolas Mikhailovitch Amossov, *J'opère à coeur ouvert*, Casterman, Paris, 1968.

2. Max Scheller, *Mort et survie*, Aubier, Paris, 1952.

3. H. van der Horst, *6ᵉ Congrès de gérontologie, Copenhagen, August 1963*, Documenta Geigy, Basle.

4. Quoted by Roger Mehl, op. cit.

5. René Schaerer, 'Le philosophe moderne en face de la mort', in *L'homme face à la mort*, Delachaux and Niestlé, Neuchâtel and Paris, 1952.

6. Caisse Nationale de Retraite, op. cit.

7. Paul Ricoeur, *De l'interprétation. Essai sur Freud*, Le Seuil, Paris, 1956.

8. Michel Crozier, 'Employés et petits fonctionnaires parisiens', in *Esprit*, June 1959.

9. André Gide, *Journals*, Penguin Books, London, 1967.

10. Karlfried von Dürckheim, *Le sens de la vieillesse*.

11. François Mauriac, 'La victoire sur l'angoisse', in *L'angoisse du temps présent et les devoirs de l'esprit*, Rencontre internationale de Genève, 1953, La Baconnière, Neuchâtel, 1954.

12. E. Minkowski, *Vers une cosmologie. Fragments philosophiques*, Aubier-Montaigne, Paris, 1936.

13. Hamish Hamilton, London, 1955.

14. Adolf Portmann, *Um eine basale Anthropologie*, Rentsch, Erlenbach-Zurich, 1955.

15. Vladimir Jankelevitch, *La mort*, Flammarion, Paris, 1966.

16. Quoted by François Mauriac, op. cit.

17. Jean Delay, 'Leçon inaugurale', in *La Semaine des Hôpitaux*, Paris, 14 October 1947.

18. Jean-Marie Domenach, 'Description d'un monde nouveau', in *Bulletin du Centre Protestant d'étude*, Geneva, June 1965.

19. Roger Schutz, *Violent for Peace*, Darton, Longman and Todd, London, 1970.

20. S. Pacaud and M. O. Lahalle, 'Attitudes, comportements, opinions des personnes âgées dans le cadre de la famile moderne', in *Monographes françaises de Psychologie*, No. 16, Centre national de la Recherche scientifique, Paris.

21. Eliane Lévy-Valensi and Claude Veil, 'Les loisirs et la fatigue', in *Esprit*, June 1959.

PART SIX

1. Georges Gusdorf, *Dialogue avec le médecin*, Labor et Fides, Geneva, 1962.
2. Rudolf Affemann, 'Aggressivität als tiefenpsychologisches, soziologisches und theologisches Phänomen', a lecture to the 22nd International Session of the Medicine of the Person, Stuttgart-Hohenheim, 1970. Published in Dutch in *Epoca*, 1971.
3. Le Seuil, Paris.
4. Paolo Rovasio, 'Le conflit religieux chez les mourants', in *Présences*, No. 76, 3rd Term, 1961, Draveil.
5. 'Réponse au Dr Rovasio', in *Présences*, No. 76.
6. Martin Heidegger, *Being and Time*, Harper & Row, New York, 1962. Republished by Blackwell, Oxford, 1967.
7. Jean-Paul Sartre, *Being and Nothingness*, Methuen, London, 1957.
8. Published by Mame, Tours, 1969.
9. D. Kurzen, *Das Alter in der Bibel*, unpublished, available from the author: 8635 Durnten – Zürich, Switzerland.
10. Paul Ricoeur, *Vraie et fausse angoisse*.
11. Marc Oraison, *La mort . . . et puis après?*, Le Signe-Fayard, Paris, 1967.
12. Marc Oraison, *Le célibat*, Editions du Centurion, Paris.
13. Paul Tournier, *The Adventure of Living*, Harper & Row, New York, 1965.
14. Paul-Louis Landsberg, *Essai sur l'expérience de la mort*, Le Seuil, Paris, 1951.
15. Jean Lescure, 'Intervention dans le débat sur l'angoisse', in *L'angoisse du temps présent et les devoirs de l'esprit*.
16. Philippe H. Menoud, 'La signification chrétienne de la mort', in *L'homme face à la mort*, Delachaux and Niestlé, Neuchâtel and Paris, 1952.
17. Bruno Lagrange and Marc Oraison, 'Ailleurs existe . . .', in *La Résurrection*, Fayard, Paris, 1969.
18. C. G. Jung, *Psychology and Religion*, Yale University Press, New Haven, 1938.